HINGE HOURS
for LENT and EASTER

Psalms, Canticles, and
Readings of the Seasons

a meditation rendering by
Stephen Joseph Wolf

www.idjc.org

THE MORNING BEGINNING: PSALM 51:17

✛ Lord, open my lips
and my mouth will declare your praise.

Glory to the Father and to the Son and to the Holy Spirit
As it was in the beginning, is now, and will be forever. Amen.

INVITATION ANTIPHONS

LENT

Ash Wednesday until the Fifth Week of Lent:
If today you hear the voice of the Lord,
harden not your heart.

OR, *through Holy Thursday:*
Come and worship Christ the Lord,
who for our sake endured temptation and suffering.

EASTER

Easter Sunday until Ascension:
The Lord is risen, alleluia!

Ascension through Pentecost:
Come and adore Christ the Lord who promised
to send the Holy Spirit on his people, alleluia!

THE EVENING BEGINNING: PSALM 70:2

✛ God, come to my assistance;
make haste, Adonai, to help me!

Glory to the Father and to the Son and to the Holy Spirit
As it was in the beginning, is now, and will be forever. Amen.

INVITATION PSALM to Adonai (*ah-duh-'nigh*)

PSALM 24

The earth and everything,
the world and all who are alive are to Adonai,
who founded the earth on the seas
and established the earth on the waters.

Who may ascend to the hill of Adonai?
And who may stand in the holy place?
The clean of hand and pure of heart
who do not lift the soul to an idol
and do not swear by falsehood
will receive the blessing from Adonai
and vindication from the God who saves.

Such is the generation of ones who seek,
who seek your faces, God of Jacob.

Lift up your heads, you gates;
be lifted up you ancient doors,
that the King of glory may come in.

Who is this King of glory?
Adonai, strong and mighty,
Adonai, mighty of battle.

Lift up your heads, you gates;
lift up, you ancient doors,
that the King of glory may come in.

Who is this King of glory?
Adonai Sabaoth is the King of glory.

Glory to the Father and to the Son and to the Holy Spirit
As it was in the beginning, is now, and will be forever. Amen.

The antiphon is traditionally repeated.

Hinge Hours for Lent and Easter
Copyright © 2015
Stephen Joseph Wolf
All rights reserved. No part of this book may be
copied or reproduced in any form or by any means,
except for the inclusion of brief quotations in a review,
without the written permission of the publisher.

For the holy name YHVH or Yahweh,
the Hebrew word for "my Lord" (*Adonai*) is used,
pronounced *ah-duh-'nigh.E123*
See page 514
for the other choices made in this meditation rendering.

ISBN 978-1-937081-30-0

printed and distributed by Ingram Books
published by idjc press
www.idjc.org

THE FOUR-WEEK REPEATING CYCLE FOR MORNING & EVENING

Hinge Hours for Ordinary Time	ISBN 978-1-937081-16-4
Hinge Hours for Advent	ISBN 978-1-937081-17-1
Hinge Hours for Christmas	ISBN 978-1-937081-31-7
Hinge Hours for Lent and Easter	ISBN 978-1-937081-30-0

Hinge Hour Singer, the songs used in the Hinge Hours prayer books

ONCE-A-DAY PRAYER THROUGH THE LITURGICAL YEAR
A Simple Family Breviary, updating the Psalms of Saint Francis of Assisi

ONE-WEEK REPEATING CYCLE FOR MORNING & EVENING
In Health & In Healing, encouraging passages for the ill & depressed
Work Hours, drawn from the daytime hours, for morning & afternoon
Best of the Psalter, drawn from commons of the saints, includes IHIH & WH

SPECIAL PURPOSE PRAYER
Gospel of Life Prayer Cycle, a prayer for peace and justice study groups
Gone Before Us, praying for the dead

Hinge Hours for Lent and Easter

Invitation Psalm   3

	LENT		EASTER	
	MORNING	EVENING	MORNING	EVENING
Sundays	10	14	60	63
Mondays	17	20	66	69
Tuesdays	23	26	72	75
Wednesdays	29	32	78	81
Thursdays	35	38	84	87
Fridays	41	44	90	93
Saturdays	47	7	96	99

Ash Wednesday	29	32
Triduum – Holy Thursday	35	50
Triduum – Good Friday	52	54
Triduum – Holy Saturday	56	

	VIGIL	MORNING	EVENING
Easter Sunday	58	60	63
Ascension of the Lord	101	104	106
Pentecost Sunday	108	110	112

Hinge Hours Psalter	115
Daily Gospel Readings	510
Acknowledgements	514
Index of Psalms	517
Index of Canticles and Readings	518
Index of Songs	520
Morning Prayer Canticle of Zechariah	521
Morning Prayer Petitions	522
Evening Prayer Canticle of Mary	523
Evening Prayer Intercessions	523

LENT

VIGILS OF SUNDAY (Saturday Evening)

Lord, who through-out these for-ty days
For us did fast and pray,
Teach us with you to mourn our sins
And close by you to stay.

As you with Sa-tan did con-tend,
And did the vic-t'ry win,
O give us strength in you to fight,
In you to con-quer sin.

As you did hun-ger bear, and thirst,
So teach us, gra-cious Lord,
To die to self, and so to live
In your most ho-ly Word.

And through these days of pen-i-tence,
And in your Pas-chal Way,
Yes, ev-er-more through life and death,
Lord Je-sus, with us stay.

A-bide with us, and when this life
With suf-fer-ing has passed
An East-er of un-end-ing joy
May we at-tain at last.

Text: Claudia F. Hernaman, *Child's Book of Praise: A Manuel of Devotion*, 1873, altered
Music: ST. FLAVIAN, CM, *Day's Psalter*, 1563

PSALMS &	WEEK I, go to page 116	WEEK IV, go to page 414
CANTICLES	WEEK II, go to page 214	WEEK V (Week I) page 116
	WEEK III, go to page 318	WEEK VI (Week II) page 214

READING, Weeks 1 to 4: **2 CORINTHIANS 6:1-4a**

Working together, we urge you
to not receive in vain the grace of God, who says,
In an acceptable time I heard you
and on a day of salvation I helped you.
Behold now an acceptable time;
behold now a day of salvation.
Nothing giving cause to stumble,
lest the ministry be blamed, in all things
we commend ourselves as servant-ministers of God.

RESPONSORY

Listen to us, O Lord, and have mercy…
…*for we have sinned against you.*
Christ Jesus, hear our humble petitions…

READING, Weeks 5 and 6: **1 PETER 1:17-21**

You who call on the one Father who judges without partiality the work of each, pass your time with the fear of one in exile, knowing that not with corruptible silver or gold were you redeemed from your vain conduct and delivered from that of your ancestors, but by the precious blood of Christ, as of a lamb unblemished and unspotted, chosen from the foundation of the world and shown

LENT - VIGILS OF SUNDAYS (Saturday Evenings)

forth in the last of times for you, believing through him in God who raised him from the dead and gave him glory, so that your faith and hope are in God.

RESPONSORY

We worship you, O Christ…
…and we praise you.
By your cross you have redeemed the world…

GOSPEL CANTICLE (**Canticle of Mary**) see page 523.

Antiphon, Week I
Human beings cannot live on bread alone but by every word that comes from the mouth of God.

Antiphon, Week II
A voice spoke from the cloud: This is my beloved Son in whom I am well pleased; listen to him.

Antiphon, Week III
Now that we have been justified by faith, let us be at peace with God through our Lord Jesus Christ.

Antiphon, Week IV
God loved the world so much that he gave his only Son to save all who have faith in him, and to give them eternal life.

Antiphon, Week V
Unless a grain of wheat falls into the ground and dies, it remains only a single grain; but if it dies, it produces a rich harvest.

Ant., Passion Sunday   Praise to our King, Son of David,
World Redeemer, and Savior
coming as foretold by the prophets.

EVENING PRAYER INTERCESSIONS AND CLOSING PRAYER, see page 523.

LENT
SUNDAY MORNINGS

LENT - SUNDAY MORNINGS (Weeks 1-5)

Praise\ to the Ho-liest in the height,
And/ from the depth\ come praise;
The\ words of God most won-der-ful,
Most/ sure are all\ God's ways.
O/ lov-ing wis\-dom of our God!
When/ all was\ sin and shame,
A\ sec-ond A-dam to the fight
And/ to the res\-cue came.

And\ in the gar-den se-cret-ly,
And/ from the Cross\ on high,
Should\ teach dis-cip-les, and in-spire
To/ suf-fer and\ to die.
And/ that a high\-er gift than grace
Should/ flesh and\ blood re-fine,
God's\ Pres-ence and God's ve-ry Self,
And/ Es-sence all\ di-vine.

Text: from Psalm 148:1, John Henry Newman, *The Dream of Gerontius,* 1865, altered
Music: KINGSFOLD, CMD, trad. English melody, adapt. by Ralph Vaughan Williams, 1906
Popular melody for: *I Heard the Voice of Jesus Say*

PALM SUNDAY MORNING (6th Sunday of Lent)

All glo-ry, laud, and hon-or,
    to you, re-deem-er, King,
To whom the lips of chil-dren
    make sweet ho-san-nas ring.
The King you are of Is-ra-el,
    and Da-vid's roy-al Son,
Be-lov-ed of the Fa\-ther,
    our Roy-al Bless-ed One.

The com-pa-ny of an-gels
    are prais-ing you on high,
With hu-man be-ings too all
    cre-a-tion makes re-ply.
The Cho-sen of the Cov-e-nant
    with psalms be-fore you went;
So too our praise and an\-thems
    be-fore you we pre-sent.

To you, be-fore your pass-ion,
    A-pos-tles sang your praise;
To you, now high ex-al-ted,
    our mel-o-dy we raise.
Ac-cep-ta-ble their voi\-ces;
    hear too the praise we bring:
De-light in your be-lov\-ed,
    our Sa-vior and our King.

Text: Saint Theodulph of Orleans, c. 821, for Palm Sunday;
translated by John M. Neal, 1854, altered
Music: 76 76 D, ST. THEODULPH, Melchior Teschner, 1613

PSALMS &	WEEK I, go to page 127	WEEK IV, go to page 424
CANTICLES	WEEK II, go to page 226	WEEK V (Week I) page 127
	WEEK III, go to page 326	WEEK VI (Week II) page 226

READING, Weeks 1 to 4: **NEHEMIAH 8:9,10**

Nehemiah the governor and Ezra the priest and scribe
and the Levites instructing the people said to all of them,
"This day is sacred to Adonai your God. Do not mourn
and do not weep," for all the people wept as they
listened to the words of the Law. And he said to them,
"Go! Eat choice foods! And drink sweet things!
And send portions to ones with nothing prepared,
for this day is sacred to our Lord, and do not grieve,
for the joy of Adonai is your strength."

RESPONSORY Luke 18:13

Lord Jesus Christ, Son of the living God...
...have mercy on us.
You were wounded for our offenses...

READING, Weeks 5 and 6: **LEVITICUS 23:4-7**

These are feasts of Adonai, sacred assemblies that
you will proclaim at their time: the Passover of Adonai
in the first month on the fourteenth day, the twilight,
and the Feast of the Unleavened Breads to Adonai
on the fifteenth day of that month,
seven days of unleavened breads you will eat.
On the first day there will be a sacred assembly
and none of you will do any regular work.

LENT - SUNDAY MORNINGS 13

RESPONSORY Rev. 5:9
> Lord, by your own blood…
>> …*you brought us back to God.*
> From every tribe and tongue and people and nation…

GOSPEL CANTICLE (**Canticle of Zechariah**) see page 521.

Antiphon, Week I	Jesus was led by the Spirit into the desert
A. Mt 4:1-11	to be tempted by the devil; and when he
B. Mk 1:12-15	had fasted for forty days and forty nights,
C. Lk 4:1-13	he was hungry.

Antiphon, Week II	Our Lord Jesus Christ
A. Matthew 17:1-9	abolished death
B. Mark 9:2-10	and through the Gospel
C. Luke 9:28b-36	revealed eternal life.

Antiphon, Week III	Destroy this temple, says the Lord,
A. John 4:5-42	and in three days I will rebuild it.
B. John 2:13-25	He was speaking
C. Luke 13:1-9	of the temple of his body.

Antiphon, Week IV	It was unheard of for anyone
A. John 9:1-41	to open the eyes of a man born blind
B. John 3:14-21	until the coming of Christ,
C. Lk 15:1-3,11-32	the Son of God.

Antiphon, Week V		Our friend Lazarus
A. John 11:1-45		has fallen asleep;
B. John 12:20-33	C. John 8:1-11	let us go and wake him.

Ant., Passion Sunday	With palms we run
A. Mt 26:14-27:66	to welcome the Lord who comes,
B. Mk 14:1-15:47	and meet him with songs and hymns
C. Lk 22:14-23:56	and our joy and worship and blessing.

MORNING PRAYER PETITIONS AND CLOSING PRAYER, see page 522.

LENT
SUNDAY EVENINGS

When/ I sur\-vey the/ won-drous cross
On which the Prince of glo-ry died,
My rich-est/ gain\ I count\ as loss,
And pour con-tempt on all my pride.

For/-bid it\, Lord, that/ I should boast,
Save in the death of Christ my God!
May all vain/ things\ that charm\ me most,
Be sac-ri-ficed as with his blood.

Were/ the whole\ realm of/ na-ture mine,
That trea-sure would be far too small;
Love so a/-ma\-zing, so\ div-ine,
De-mands my soul, my life, my all.

Text: Isaac Watts, *Hymns and Spiritual Songs*, 1707, altered
Music option: ERHALT UNS HERR, LM; Klug's *Geistliche Lieder*, 1543;
Popular melody for: *The Glory Of These Forty Days*

PSALMS &	WEEK I, go to page 136	WEEK IV, go to page 431
CANTICLES	WEEK II, go to page 236	WEEK V (Week I) page 136
	WEEK III, go to page 333	WEEK VI (Week II) page 236

READING, Weeks 1 to 4: **1 CORINTHIANS 9:24-27**

Do you not know that runners on a racecourse all run,
but one receives the prize? Run so that you may get it.
Every athlete exercises discipline in all things,
and they in order to receive a corruptible crown.
But we, one incorruptible. And so
I do not run without clarity nor fight beating the air.
But I train my body and lead it as a slave,
lest having proclaimed to others I myself be disqualified.

RESPONSORY

Listen to us, O Lord, and have mercy…
…for we have sinned against you.
Christ Jesus, hear our humble petitions…

READING, Weeks 5 and 6: **ACTS 13:26-30**

Men and women, brothers and sisters, daughters and
sons of Abraham, and those among you fearing God,
to us this word of salvation was sent forth. For the
dwellers of Jerusalem and their rulers, knowing neither
this man nor the voices of the prophets being read every
sabbath, fulfilled them in judging him. Finding no
cause for death, they asked Pilate that he be destroyed.
When they finished all the things written concerning him,
taking him down from the tree, they laid him in a tomb.
But God raised him out of the dead.

RESPONSORY

We worship you, O Christ…
…and we praise you.
By your cross you have redeemed the world…

GOSPEL CANTICLE (**Canticle of Mary**) see page 523.

Antiphon, Week I — Watch over us, eternal Savior
and let not the cunning tempter seize us.
All our trust in your unfailing help.

Antiphon, Week II — Tell no one about the vision you
have seen until the Son of humanity
has risen from the dead.

Antiphon, Week III — Whoever drinks the water that I shall give
will never be thirsty again, says the Lord.

Antiphon, Week IV — My son, you are with me all the days
and everything I have is yours.
But we rightly feast and rejoice,
because your brother was dead
and has come to life again;
he was lost to us and now has been found.

Antiphon, Week V — When I am lifted up from the earth,
I will draw all people to myself.

Ant., Passion Sunday — The shepherd will be struck
and his flock will be scattered.
But when I have risen,
I will go before you into Galilee.
There you shall see me, says the Lord.

EVENING PRAYER INTERCESSIONS AND CLOSING PRAYER, see page 523.

LENT
MONDAY MORNINGS

At break of day fill us with wis-dom and love;
Give fa-vor and pros-per the work of our hands.
A thou-sand years hu-man like one day to you,
Our ref-uge through each gen-er-a-tion, re-new.

Be-fore bring-ing forth world-ly moun-tains and earth,
You are God e-ter-nal with no end or birth.
There is some-where in us made sad when we learn
That we are dust and to this dust we return.

Though sev-en-ty years is the sum of our days,
Or eigh-ty if we are made strong in your ways.
Like grass that sprouts green in the new mor-ning air
Years end like a sigh, ebb a-way, this we share.

So hum-bled with trou-bles, we now com-pre-hend:
You want us to sing a glad song in the land.
At break of day fill us with wis-dom and love;
Give fa-vor and pros-per the work of our hands.

Text: Psalm 90, by Stephen J. Wolf, 2007, tribute to the priesthood of William J. Fleming
Music: 11 11 11 11, ST. DENIO, Welsh Melody, John Roberts, *Canaidau y Cyssagr,* 1839
Popular melody for: *Immortal, Invisible, God Only Wise*

PSALMS &	WEEK I, go to page 144	WEEK IV, go to page 437
CANTICLES	WEEK II, go to page 242	WEEK V (Week I) page 144
	WEEK III, go to page 340	WEEK VI (Week II) page 242

READING, Weeks 1 to 4: **EXODUS 19:4-6a**

You saw what I did in Egypt.
I carried you on wings of eagles
and brought you to myself. Now if to obey
you obey my voice and you keep my covenant,
you will be my possession from all the nations,
although all the earth is mine. You will be for me
a kingdom of priests, a holy nation.

RESPONSORY Luke 18:13

The Lord God will set me free...
...from the hunter's snare.
From all those who would trap me with lying words, and...

READING, Weeks 5 and 6: **JEREMIAH 11:19-20**

As a gentle lamb led to slaughter,
I did not realize that they plotted plots against me
to destroy the tree with his fruit
and to cut him off from the land of the living
so his name would be remembered no more.
But Adonai Sabaoth, judging justice,
testing minds and heart,
let me see your vengeance upon them,
for to you I have committed my cause.

RESPONSORY Rev. 5:9

Lord, by your own blood...
...you brought us back to God.
From every tribe and tongue and people and nation...

LENT - MONDAY MORNINGS

GOSPEL READING OF THE DAY (or use the **Canticle of Zechariah** from page 521)

Antiphon, Week I **Matthew 25:31-46**	You have been blessed by my Father; come and receive the kingdom prepared for you from the foundation of the world.
Antiphon, Week II **Luke 6:36-38**	Be compassionate and forgiving as your Father is, says the Lord.
Antiphon, Week III **Luke 4:24-30**	I tell you assuredly, no prophet is accepted in his own country.
Antiphon, Week IV **John 4:43-54**	A royal official, hearing that Jesus had come to Galilee, begged him to heal his son who lay ill in Capernaum.
Antiphon, Week V **John 8:1-11**	Whoever follows me does not walk in the dark but will have the light of life.
Antiphon, Holy Week **John 12:1-11**	Father, righteous One, the cosmos does not know you, but I know you for you are the One who sent me.

MORNING PRAYER PETITIONS AND CLOSING PRAYER, see page 522.

LENT
MONDAY EVENINGS

At the name of Je/-sus, ev-'ry knee shall bow,
Ev-'ry tongue con-fess/ him King of glo-ry now;
'Tis the Fa/-ther's plea\-sure that we call him Lord,
Who from the be-gin\-ning is the migh-ty Word.

At his voice cre-a/-tion sprang at once to sight,
All the an-gels' fa/-ces, all the hosts of light,
Thrones and dom/-in-a\-tions, stars up-on their way,
All the heav'n-ly or\-ders, in their great ar-ray.

Hum-bled for a sea/-son, to re-ceive a name
From the lips of sin/-ners un-to whom he came,
Faith-ful-ly/ he bore\ it, spot-less to the last,
Carr-ied it vic-tor\-ious when from death he passed.

Bro-thers, Sis-ters, name/ him, with love strong as death
But with awe and won/-der, and with ba-ted breath!
He is God/ our Sa\-vior, he is Christ the Lord,
Ev-er to be wor\-shipped, trust-ed and a-dored.

see Philippians 2:6-11
Text: Caroline M. Noel, *The Name of Jesus and Other Verses for the Sick and Lonely*, 1870, altered
Music: 11 11 11 11 ADORO TE DEVOTE, Benedictine Plainsong, Mode V, 13th Century

PSALMS &	WEEK I, go to page 150	WEEK IV, go to page 446
CANTICLES	WEEK II, go to page 250	WEEK V (Week I) page 150
	WEEK III, go to page 347	WEEK VI (Week II) page 250

READING, Weeks 1 to 4: **ROMANS 12:1-2**

I appeal to you, brothers and sisters, through the
compassion of God, to present your bodies as a living
sacrifice, holy and well-pleasing to God, your worship
and reasonable service. Be not conformed to this eon,
but be transformed by the renewal of your mind
that what you do may be proven to be the will of God,
the good and well-pleasing and perfect.

RESPONSORY Luke 18:13

To you, O Lord…
…I make my prayer for mercy.
Heal my soul, for I have sinned against you…

READING, Weeks 5 and 6: **ROMANS 5:6-10**

With us still weak, Christ died for the ungodly
at the right time. Hardly will anyone die for a just
person, though perhaps someone would dare die for a
good person. But God commends God's own love for
us in that while we were still sinners Christ died for us.
Justified now by his blood, by much more through him
shall we be saved from the anger. For if being enemies
we were reconciled to God through the death of the
Son of God, by much more having been reconciled
we will be saved by his life.

RESPONSORY Rev. 5:9

We worship you, O Christ…
…and we praise you.
By your cross you have redeemed the world…

GOSPEL CANTICLE (**Canticle of Mary**) see page 523.

Antiphon, Week I
Whatever you do for one of these
least of my brothers and sisters,
you do for me.

Antiphon, Week II
Do not judge others
and you will not be judged,
for as you have judged them
so God will judge you.

Antiphon, Week III
Jesus walked through the crowd
and went away.

Antiphon, Week IV
The father realized that it was
at the very hour when Jesus had told him:
your son will live;
he and all his household became believers.

Antiphon, Week V
I am my own testimony, says the Lord,
and my Father who sent me
also testifies on my behalf.

Antiphon, Holy Week
As Moses lifted up
the serpent in the desert,
so is the Son of Man to be raised up
so that all who believe in him
may have eternal life.

EVENING PRAYER INTERCESSIONS AND CLOSING PRAYER, see page 523.

LENT
TUESDAY MORNINGS

For-ty days and for-ty nights
You were fast-ing in the wild;
For-ty days and for-ty nights
Temp-ted, and yet un-de-filed.

Should not we your sor-row share
And from world-ly joys ab-stain,
Fast-ing with un-ceas-ing prayer,
Strong with you to suf-fer pain?

When temp-ta-tions on us press,
Je-sus, Sa-vior, hear our call!
Vic-tor in the wil-der-ness,
Grant we may not faint nor fall!

Keep, O keep us, Sa-vior dear,
Ev-er con-stant by your side;
That with you we may ap-pear
At th'e-ter-nal Eas-ter-tide.

Text: George H. Smyttan, *The Penny Post*, 1856, altered
Music: 7 7 7 7 HEINLEIN, Attributed to Martin Herbst, d. 1681

PSALMS &	WEEK I, go to page 155	WEEK IV, go to page 452
CANTICLES	WEEK II, go to page 257	WEEK V (Week I) page 155
	WEEK III, go to page 353	WEEK VI (Week II) page 257

READING, Weeks 1 to 4: **JOEL 2:12-13**

Even now, declares Adonai,
return to me with all your heart
and with fasting and weeping and mourning!
Rend now your heart, not your garments,
and return to your God Adonai,
gracious and compassionate,
slow of angers
and abundant of love
and relenting from the calamity.

RESPONSORY — Luke 18:13

The Lord God will set me free...
...from the hunter's snare.
From all those who would trap me with lying words, and...

READING, Weeks 5 and 6: **ZECHARIAH 12:10-11a**

I will pour out on the house of David
and on the ones living in Jerusalem
a spirit of grace and supplications
and they will look on him whom they pierced
and they will mourn as one mourns for an only child
and grieve bitterly as one grieves for a firstborn.
On that day the weeping in Jerusalem will be great.

RESPONSORY — Rev. 5:9

Lord, by your own blood...
...you brought us back to God.
From every tribe and tongue and people and nation...

GOSPEL READING OF THE DAY (or use the **Canticle of Zechariah** from page 521)

Antiphon, Week I	Lord, teach us to pray
Matthew 6:7-15	as John taught his disciples.

Antiphon, Week II	You have one teacher,
Matt. 23:1-12	and he is in heaven:
	Christ your Lord.

Antiphon, Week III	The Lord said to Peter,
Matt. 18:21-35	I do not tell you to forgive
	only seven times,
	but seventy times seven.

Antiphon, Week IV	The man who cured me told me
John 5:1-16	to pick up my sleeping mat
	and go in peace.

Antiphon, Week V	When you have lifted up the Son of Man,
John 8:21-30	says the Lord,
	you will know that I am he.

Antiphon, Holy Week	Father, give me the glory
Jn 13:21-33,36-38	that I had with you
	before the world was made.

MORNING PRAYER PETITIONS AND CLOSING PRAYER, see page 522.

LENT
TUESDAY EVENINGS

The word of God, pro-ceed-ed forth
Yet leav-ing not his Fa-ther's side,
And go-ing to his work on earth
Had reached at length life's eve-ning tide.

Soon by his own false friend be-trayed,
Giv-en to foes, to death he went;
His ve-ry self, in form of bread,
Gi-ven to them, his friends he sent.

The man-ger, Christ their e-qual made;
That up-per room, their soul's re-past;
The cross, their ran-som dear-ly paid,
Heav-en, their high re-ward at last.

All praise and thanks to you as-cend
For ev-er-more, blest one in three.
O grant us life that shall not end
In our true na-tive land to be.

Text: Thomas Aquinas, d. 1274; translated, st. 1 & 4 by John M. Neale, d. 1866,
st. 2 & 3 by Gerard Manley Hopkins, d. 1889, altered
Music: OLD HUNDREDTH, LM, Louis Bourgeois, first published in Genevan Psalter, 1551
Popular Melody: *Praise God From Whom All Blessings Flow*
Alternate Melody: *From All That Dwells Below The Skies*

PSALMS &	WEEK I, go to page 163	WEEK IV, go to page 459
CANTICLES	WEEK II, go to page 266	WEEK V (Week I) page 163
	WEEK III, go to page 361	WEEK VI (Week II) page 266

HINGE HOURS for LENT and EASTER 27

READING, Weeks 1 to 4: **JAMES 2:14-18**

What is the profit, my brothers and sisters,
if anyone claims to have faith but has not works?
Can the faith save that one? If a brother or sister is
naked and lacks the daily food, and anyone of you says,
"Go in peace, be warm and filled," and not give
the necessaries of the body, what is the profit?
So indeed faith if it has not works is dead by itself.
But someone will say, "You have faith and I have works."
Show me your faith without the works,
and I will show you by my works the faith.

RESPONSORY Luke 18:13

To you, O Lord…
…I make my prayer for mercy.
Heal my soul, for I have sinned against you…

READING, Weeks 5 and 6: **1 CORINTHIANS 1:27b-30**

God chose the weak things of the world to shame the
strong things. God chose the base things of the world
and the despised things, the things of no account,
so that God might abolish the things of account, so that
no flesh might boast before God, of whom you are
in Christ Jesus, who became to us wisdom from God,
and justice and holiness and redemption.

RESPONSORY Rev. 5:9

We worship you, O Christ…
…and we praise you.
By your cross you have redeemed the world…

GOSPEL CANTICLE (**Canticle of Mary**) see page 523.

Antiphon, Week I
When you wish to pray,
go to your room, shut the door,
and pray to your Father in secret.

Antiphon, Week II
You are all brothers and sisters,
sons and daughters of one Father
who is in heaven.
Do not call anyone on earth your father.
Nor must any of you be called teacher,
for your only teacher is Christ.

Antiphon, Week III
This is how my heavenly Father
will treat each one of you, unless
you forgive your brothers and sisters
from the heart.

Antiphon, Week IV
Do you want to be well?

Antiphon, Week V
The One who sent me is with me;
he has not left me alone,
because I always do what pleases him.

Antiphon, Holy Week
I have power to lay down my life
and I have power to take it up again.

EVENING PRAYER INTERCESSIONS AND CLOSING PRAYER, see page 523.

LENT
WEDNESDAY MORNINGS

The/ glo-ry\ of these/ for-ty days
We cel-e-brate with songs of praise;
For Christ, by/ whom\ all things\ were made,
Him-self has fast-ed and has prayed.

A/-lone and\ fast-ing/ Mo-ses saw
The lov-ing God who gave the law;
And to E/-li\-jah, fast\-ing, came
The steeds and char-i-ots of flame.

So/ Dan-iel\ trained his/ mys-tic sight,
De-liv-ered from the li-on's might;
And John, the/ Bride\-groom's friend\, be-came
The her-ald of Mes-si-ah's Name.

Then/ grant us\, Lord, like/ them to be
In faith-ful fast and prayer with thee;
Our spir-its/ strength\-en with\ your grace,
And give us joy to see your face.

Text: Gregory the Great, 6th Century, translated by Maurice F. Bell,
The English Hymnal, 1906, altered
Music: ERHALT UNS HERR, LM; Klug's *Geistliche Lieder,* 1543

PSALMS &		ON ASH WEDNESDAY, go to page **464**
CANTICLES	WEEK I, go to page **168**	WEEK IV, go to page **464**
	WEEK II, go to page **271**	WEEK V (Week I) page **168**
	WEEK III, go to page **367**	WEEK VI (Week II) page **271**

READING, Weeks 1 to 4: **DEUTERONOMY 7:6b,8-9**

Your God Adonai chose you to be the people treasured
from all the peoples on the faces of the earth. Because
of Adonai's love for you and to keep the oath sworn to
your ancestors, Adonai brought you out with a mighty
hand and redeemed you from the house of slaveries at
the hand of Pharaoh, king of Egypt, so you know that
your God Adonai is the God, the faithful God keeping
the covenant and the love to a thousand generations
of those loving God and keeping God's commands.

RESPONSORY Luke 18:13

The Lord God will set me free…
…from the hunter's snare.
From all those who would trap me with lying words, and…

READING, Weeks 5 and 6: **ISAIAH 50:4b-7**

Sovereign Adonai wakens my ear to hear as a disciple
and opens my ear, and I did not rebel nor draw back.
I offered my back to beaters
and my cheeks to beard pullers
and did not hide my faces from mockings and spittings
because Sovereign Adonai helps me.
For this I will not be disgraced.
For this I set my faces like the flint
and I know that I will not be shamed.

RESPONSORY Rev. 5:9

Lord, by your own blood…
…you brought us back to God.
From every tribe and tongue and people and nation…

LENT - WEDNESDAY MORNINGS

GOSPEL READING OF THE DAY (or use the **Canticle of Zechariah** from page 521)

Ant., Ash Wednesday
Matt. 6:1-6,16-18

When you fast, do not put on
a gloomy face, like the hypocrites.

Antiphon, Week I
Luke 11:29-32

This faithless generation asks for a sign,
but no sign will be given it
except the sign of the prophet Jonah.

Antiphon, Week II
Matt. 20:17-28

The Son of Man did not come
to be served but to serve,
to give his life as a ransom for the many.

Antiphon, Week III
Matt. 5:17-19

The Lord said: Do not think that I have
come to abolish the law and the prophets;
I have come not to abolish
but to fulfill them.

Antiphon, Week IV
John 5:17-30

Whoever hears my words, says the Lord,
and believes in him who sent me
has eternal life.

Antiphon, Week V
John 8:31-42

If you are faithful to my teaching, says the
Lord, you will indeed be my disciples.
You will know the truth
and the truth will make you free.

Antiphon, Holy Week
Matt. 26:14-25

Through the eternal Spirit, Christ offered
himself to God as the perfect sacrifice.
His blood purifies us from sin
making us fit servants of the living God.

MORNING PRAYER PETITIONS AND CLOSING PRAYER, see page 522.

LENT
WEDNESDAY EVENINGS

There's a wide/-ness in God's mer\-cy
Like the wide-ness of\ the sea;
There's a kind/-ness in God's jus\-tice
Which is more than lib\-er-ty.
There is plen\-ti-ful re-demp\-tion
In the blood/ that has\ been shed;
There\ is joy\ for all\ the mem//\-bers
In the sor\-rows of the Head.

For the love/ of God is broad\-er
Than the meas-ures of\ our mind,
And the heart/ of the E-ter\-nal
Be-yond won-der-ful\ and kind.
If our love\ were but more simp\-le
We might take/ him at\ his word,
And\ our lives\ would be\ thanks-giv//\-ing
For the good\-ness of the Lord.

Troub-led souls/, why will you scat\-ter
Like a crowd of fright\-ened sheep?
Fool-ish hearts/, why will you wan\-der
From a love so true\ and deep?
There is wel\-come for the sin\-ner
And more gra/-ces for\ the good;
There\ is mer\-cy with\ the Sa//\-vior,
There is heal\-ing in his food.

Text: Frederick W. Fabor, 1814, 1863, altered
Music: 87 87 D, HYFRYDOL; Rowland Prichard, 1811-1887
Popular melody for: *Love Divine, All Love Excelling*

PSALMS &		ON ASH WEDNESDAY, go to page 471
CANTICLES	WEEK I, go to page 174	WEEK IV, go to page 471
	WEEK II, go to page 278	WEEK V (Week I) page 174
	WEEK III, go to page 375	WEEK VI (Week II) page 278

READING, Weeks 1 to 4: **PHILIPPIANS** 2:12b-16

My beloved, with fear and trembling you work out your salvation, for God is the one working in you both to will and to work on behalf of God's good will. Do what you do without murmurings or disputes, blameless and harmless, children of God faultless in the midst of a crooked generation. Among those having been corrupted you shine as luminaries in the world holding up a word of life, a boast to me in the day of Christ that not in vain did I run nor in vain labor.

RESPONSORY — Luke 18:13

To you, O Lord…
…I make my prayer for mercy.
Heal my soul, for I have sinned against you…

READING, Weeks 5 and 6: **EPHESIANS** 4:32 - 5:2

Be kind to one another, tenderhearted, and forgive yourselves as also God in Christ has forgiven you. Be therefore imitators of God, as beloved children, and walk in love. Christ has loved you and gave up himself on our behalf, an offering and a sacrifice to God for an odor of sweetness.

RESPONSORY — Rev. 5:9

We worship you, O Christ…
…and we praise you.
By your cross you have redeemed the world…

GOSPEL CANTICLE (**Canticle of Mary**) see page 523.

Ant., Ash Wednesday When you give alms, do not let your left hand know what your right is doing.

Antiphon, Week I As Jonah was three days and three nights in the belly of the big fish, so will the Son of humanity spend three days and three nights in the earth.

Antiphon, Week II The Son of humanity will be handed over to the gentiles to be mocked, scourged and crucified; and on the third day he will rise again.

Antiphon, Week III The one who obeys God's law and teaches others to do so will be great in the kingdom of heaven.

Antiphon, Week IV By myself, says the Lord, I can do nothing. I judge as I am told and my sentence is just.

Antiphon, Week V Why are you set on killing me when I have told you the truth?

Antiphon, Holy Week The Master says: My hour is close at hand; I and my disciples shall celebrate the Passover in your house.

EVENING PRAYER INTERCESSIONS AND CLOSING PRAYER, see page 523.

35

LENT
THURSDAY MORNINGS

Some-bod-y's knock-in' at your door,
Some-bod-y's knock-in' at your door,
O/ sin-ner, why don't you an-swer?
Some-bod-y's knockin' at your door.

Knocks like Je-sus,
Some-bod-y's knock-in' at your door,
Knocks like\ Je-sus,

Refrain   **S**ome-bod-y's knock-in' at your door.
O/ sin-ner, why don't you an-swer?
Some-bod-y's knock-in' at your door.

Can't you hear him?
Some-bod-y's knock-in' at your door,
Can't you\ hear him?   *Refrain*

An-swer Je-sus,
Some-bod-y's knock-in' at your door,
An-swer\ Je-sus,   *Refrain*

Text & Music: Traditional spiritual

PSALMS &		WEEK OF ASH WEDNESDAY, go to page	**478**
CANTICLES	WEEK I, go to page **181**	WEEK IV, go to page	**478**
	WEEK II, go to page **283**	WEEK V (Week I) page	**181**
	WEEK III, go to page **379**	WEEK VI (Week II) page	**283**

READING, Weeks 1 to 4:   **1 KINGS 8:51-53a**

For your people and your inheritance
whom you brought from Egypt,
from the midst of the iron furnace,
let your eyes be open to the plea of your servant
and to the plea of your people Israel,
to listen to them in all their calls to you,
for you singled them out from all nations of the earth
as an inheritance for you.

RESPONSORY   Luke 18:13

The Lord God will set me free…
                         …from the hunter's snare.
From all those who would trap me with lying words, and…

READING, Weeks 5 and 6:   **HEBREWS 2:9-10**

Having been made a little less than the angels,
we see Jesus by the suffering of death
crowned with glory and honor, that by the grace of
God he might taste of death on behalf of every human.
Because of whom all things are
and through whom all things are,
it was fitting for the author of their salvation
to lead the many children to glory
through sufferings to the perfection.

RESPONSORY   Rev. 5:9

Lord, by your own blood…
                         …you brought us back to God.
From every tribe and tongue and people and nation…

LENT - THURSDAY MORNINGS

GOSPEL READING OF THE DAY (or use the **Canticle of Zechariah** from page 521)

Antiphon, Thursday
after Ash Wednesday
Luke 9:22-25

Anyone who wishes to be my disciple,
let that one deny the self, take up his or
her cross, and follow me, says the Lord.

Antiphon, Week I
Matthew 7:7-12

If you, bad as you are, know how to give
your children what is good, how much
more will your Father in heaven
pour out his gifts on all who pray to him.

Antiphon, Week II
Luke 16:19-31

Son, remember the good things
you received in your lifetime and
the bad things Lazarus received in his.

Antiphon, Week III
Luke 11:14-23

It is by the power of God
that I throw out demons, says the Lord;
the kingdom of God has come already.

Antiphon, Week IV
John 5:31-47

John gave witness to the truth,
and though I need no human witness,
says the Lord, I remind you of this
for your own salvation.

Antiphon, Week V
John 8:51-59

Jesus said to the authorities:
Whoever comes from God
hears the word of God. You will not listen
because you do not come from God.

Antiphon, Holy Week
Luke 4:16-21

I have longed to eat this meal with you
before I suffer.

MORNING PRAYER PETITIONS AND CLOSING PRAYER, see page 522.

LENT
THURSDAY EVENINGS
(In Holy Week, go to page 50)

O Sa-cred Head, now wound-ed
With grief and shame\ weighed down,
Now scorn-ful-ly sur-round-ed
With thorns, your on\-ly crown.
They mock\ and taunt and jeer you,
Your no-ble coun-ten-ance,
Though migh/-ty worlds shall fear you
And flee be-fore your glance.

My bur-den in your pas-sion,
Lord, you have borne\ for me.
For it was my trans-gres-sion
Which brought this woe\ on thee.
I cast\ me down be-fore you,
Wrath were my right-ful lot;
Have mer/-cy, I im-plore you;
Re-deem-er, spurn me not!

What lang-uage shall I bor-row
To thank you, dear\-est friend,
For this your dy-ing sor-row,
Your pit-y with\-out end?
O make\ me yours for-ev-er,
And should I faint-ing be,
Lord, let/ me nev-er, nev-er
Out-live my love to thee.

Text: possibly Bernard of Clairvaux, 1153;
translated to English by James W. Alexander, 1830, altered
Music: 76 76 D PASSION CHORALE, Hans L. Hassler, 1601

HINGE HOURS for LENT and EASTER

PSALMS & CANTICLES

WEEK OF ASH WEDNESDAY, go to page **484**	
WEEK I, go to page **187**	WEEK IV, go to page **484**
WEEK II, go to page **291**	WEEK V (Week I) page **187**
WEEK III, go to page **385**	WEEK VI (Week II) page **291**

READING, Weeks 1 to 4: **JAMES 4:7-10**

Be subject to God, but oppose the diabolo
who will flee from you. Draw near to God
who will draw near to you. Cleanse your hands, sinners;
and purify your hearts, you two-souled.
Be distressed and mourn and weep; let your laughter
be turned to mourning and your joy to dejection.
Be humbled before the Lord, who will exalt you.

RESPONSORY — Luke 18:13

To you, O Lord…
…*I make my prayer for mercy.*
Heal my soul, for I have sinned against you…

READING, Weeks 5 and 6: **HEBREWS 13:11-15**

The bodies of animals brought by the high priest
into the holies for the sin offerings
are burned outside the camp.
Indeed that he might sanctify the people through
his own blood, Jesus suffered outside the gate.
So let us go forth to him outside the camp
bearing his reproach, for we have here no lasting city
but seek the one coming.
Through him let us offer up always a sacrifice of praise
to God. This is the fruit of lips confessing his name.

RESPONSORY   Rev. 5:9
> We worship you, O Christ...
>> ...*and we praise you.*
> By your cross you have redeemed the world...

GOSPEL CANTICLE (**Canticle of Mary**) see page 523.

Antiphon, Thursday after Ash Wednesday
> Whoever gives up his or her life for my sake in this world will find it again forever in the next, says the Lord.

Antiphon, Week I
> Ask and you will receive,
> seek and you will find,
> knock and the door will be opened to you.

Antiphon, Week II
> The rich man, who had refused Lazarus a crust of bread, pleaded for a drop of water

Antiphon, Week III
> A woman in the crowd called out:
> How happy your mother must be;
> she bore you and fed you at her breast.
> Jesus answered: Happier still are those
> who hear the word of God and live by it.

Antiphon, Week IV
> The works that I do
> witness on my behalf, says the Lord.
> They prove that the Father has sent me.

Antiphon, Week V
> You are not yet fifty years old; how can you have seen Abraham? Amen amen I tell you, before Abraham was, I am.

EVENING PRAYER INTERCESSIONS AND CLOSING PRAYER, see page 523.

LENT
FRIDAY MORNINGS

(On Good Friday in Holy Week, go to page 52)

"**Take**/ **up your**\ **cross**," the/ Sa-vior said,
"If you would my dis-ci-ple be;
De-ny your/-self\, the world\ for-sake,
And hum-bly fol-low af-ter me."

Take/ up your\ cross, let/ not its weight
Fill your weak spir-it with a-larm;
His strength shall/ bear\ your spir\-it up,
And brace your heart and nerve your arm.

Take/ up your\ cross and/ fol-low Christ,
Nor think til death to lay it down;
In faith-ful/ bear\-ing of\ our cross
We hope to wear his glo-rious crown.

To/ you, great\ Lord, the/ One in Three,
All praise for-ev-er-more as-cend:
O grant us/ in\ our home\ to see
The heav'n-ly life that knows no end.

Text: Charles W. Everest, *Visions of Death and Other Poems*, 1833, altered
Music option: ERHALT UNS HERR, LM; Klug's *Geistliche Lieder, 1543;*
Popular melody for: *The Glory Of These Forty Days*

PSALMS &	WEEK OF ASH WEDNESDAY, go to page **489**
CANTICLES	WEEK I, go to page **194** — WEEK IV, go to page **489**
	WEEK II, go to page **297** — WEEK V (Week I) page **194**
	WEEK III, go to page **391**

READING, Weeks 1 to 4: **ISAIAH 53:11b-12**

After the suffering of the soul
my servant will justify the many and bear their iniquity.
And so I will give him a portion among the many
and a division of the spoil among the numerous
because he poured out his life to the death
and was numbered with the transgressors
for he bore the sins of the many
and interceded for the transgressors.

RESPONSORY Luke 18:13

The Lord God will set me free...
...*from the hunter's snare.*
From all those who would trap me with lying words, and...

READING, Week 5: **ISAIAH 52:13-15**

See, my servant will act wisely
and be raised and lifted up and exalted highly!
Just as many were appalled at him,
so disfigured beyond human appearance
and his form beyond that of human sons,
so will he startle many nations.
Kings will shut their mouth,
for what was not told to them they will see
and what they did not hear they will understand.

RESPONSORY Rev. 5:9

Lord, by your own blood...
...*you brought us back to God.*
From every tribe and tongue and people and nation...

LENT - FRIDAY MORNINGS

GOSPEL READING OF THE DAY (or use the **Canticle of Zechariah** from page 521)

Antiphon, Friday after Ash Wednesday
Matthew 9:14-15

When you meet whose who are in need of clothing, do not turn away from them, for they are your brothers and sisters. Then your light shall break forth like the dawn, and your good deeds shall go before you. *Isaiah 58*

Antiphon, Week I
Matt 5:20-26

If your virtue does not surpass that of the scribes and pharisees, you will not enter the kingdom of heaven.

Antiphon, Week II
Mt 21:33-43,45-46

He will bring those evil men to an evil end and entrust his vineyard to other tenants who will give him the harvest at the proper season.

Antiphon, Week III
Mark 12:28-34

Teacher, what is the greatest command in the law? Jesus said to him: You shall love the Lord your God with your whole heart.

Antiphon, Week IV
Jn 7:1-2,10,25-30

Indeed you know me, says the Lord, and you know from where I come. Yet I have not come of my own accord; it was my Father who sent me.

Antiphon, Week V
John 10:31-42

The Lord said: I have done you many acts of kindness; for which of them do you want to kill me?

MORNING PRAYER PETITIONS AND CLOSING PRAYER, see page 522.

LENT
FRIDAY EVENINGS

(for Lent)

Crown him with ma-ny crowns
The Lamb up-on his throne;
Hark how the heav'n-ly an-them\ drowns
All mu-sic but its own.
A-wake, my soul, and sing
Of him who died for thee
And hail him as your King of kings
Through all e-ter-ni-ty.

Crown him the Lord of Love.
Be-hold his hands and side,
Rich wounds, yet vis-ib-le a\-bove,
In beau-ty glo-ri-fied.
No an-gel in the sky
Can ful-ly bear that sight,
But down-ward bends his wond'-ring\ eye
At mys-te-ry so bright!

Crown him the Lord of Life
Who tri-umphed o'er the grave
And rose vic-to-rious in the\ strife
For those he came to save.
His glo-ries now we sing
Who died and rose on high,
Who died e-ter-nal life to bring
And lives that death may die.

Text: From Revelation 19:12; verses for Lent by Matthew Bridges, 1851, altered
Music: DIADEMATA, George J. Elvey, 1868

HINGE HOURS for LENT and EASTER   45

PSALMS &   WEEK OF ASH WEDNESDAY, go to page 497
CANTICLES   WEEK I, go to page 201   WEEK IV, go to page 497
                   WEEK II, go to page 305   WEEK V (Week I) page 201
                   WEEK III, go to page 399

READING, Weeks 1 to 4:   **JAMES 5:16,19-20**

And so confess your sins to one another, and pray
on behalf of one another, that you may be healed.
A prayer of a just person made effective is very strong.
Brothers and sisters, if one among you
wanders from the truth and is turned by someone,
know the one turning a sinner from a wandering way
will save that soul out of death
and will cover a multitude of sins.

RESPONSORY   Luke 18:13
To you, O Lord…
…I make my prayer for mercy.
Heal my soul, for I have sinned against you…

READING, Weeks 5 and 6:   **1 PETER 2:21-24**

To this you were called, because indeed Christ suffered on your behalf, leaving you an example to follow in the steps of him who was found neither in sin nor with guile in his mouth, who being reviled reviled not in return, who in suffering threatened not, but delivered himself to the one judging justly and carried up our sins in his body onto the tree, that dying to sins we might live to righteousness, by whose wounds you are healed.

RESPONSORY   Rev. 5:9

> We worship you, O Christ…
> *…and we praise you.*
> By your cross you have redeemed the world…

GOSPEL CANTICLE (**Canticle of Mary**) see page 523.

Antiphon, Friday after Ash Wednesday	When the bridegroom is taken away from them, then will be the time for the wedding guests to fast.
Antiphon, Week I	If you are bringing your gift to the altar, and there you remember that your brother or sister has something against you, leave your gift in front of the altar; go at once and make peace, and then come back and offer your gift.
Antiphon, Week II	They would have arrested Jesus but they feared the people who regarded him as a prophet.
Antiphon, Week III	It is far more important to love your neighbor as yourself than to offer sacrifice.
Antiphon, Week IV	No one could lay a hand on Jesus, because his time had not yet come.
Antiphon, Week V	Even if you have no faith in my words, at least believe the evidence of the works I do in God's name.

EVENING PRAYER INTERCESSIONS AND CLOSING PRAYER, see page 523.

LENT
SATURDAY MORNINGS

Ho-ly Ma-ry, grace-ful Mo-ther,
hear your sons and daugh-ters say,
Mo-ther, Bless-ed a-mong wo-men,
for your sons and daugh-ters, pray.

> **May the grace of Christ our Sa-vior**
> And the Fa-ther's bound-less love
> With the Ho-ly Spir-it's fa-vor
> Rest up-on us from a-bove.

Thus may we a-bide in u-nion
With each oth-er and the Lord,
And pos-sess, in sweet com-mu-nion,
Joys which earth can-not af-ford.

> **May the grace . . .**

Text: Verses 2 & 3 by John Newton, *Olney Hymns*, 1779
Music: 87 87 D, STUTTGART, Christian F. Witt, 1715;
adapted by Henry J. Gauntlett, 1805-1876
Popular melody for: *Come Thou Long Expected Jesus*
[Alternate melody: *Sing of Mary Pure and Lowly:*
1st Verse: Holy Mary... + May the Grace...
2nd Verse: Thus May... + May the Grace...]

PSALMS &	WEEK OF ASH WEDNESDAY, go to page	503
CANTICLES	WEEK I, go to page 206	WEEK IV, go to page 503
	WEEK II, go to page 309	WEEK V (Week I) page 206
	WEEK III, go to page 407	

READING, Weeks 1 to 4: **ISAIAH 1:16-18**

Wash! Make yourselves clean!
Take your evil deeds from before my eyes!
Stop doing wrong! Learn to do right!
Seek justice! Encourage the oppressed!
Defend orphans! Plead the case for the widow!
Come! Let us come to an understanding!, says Adonai.
Though your sins are like scarlet
they shall be white as snow;
though they are red as crimson
they shall be like wool.

RESPONSORY   Luke 18:13

The Lord God will set me free...
...*from the hunter's snare.*
From all those who would trap me with lying words, and...

READING, Week 5: **ISAIAH 65:1-3a**

I revealed myself to those who did not ask,
to be found by those who did not seek me.
To a nation not called by my name I said,
"Here am I! Here am I!"
I held out my hands all the day to people obstinate,
walkers after their imaginings of a way not good,
the people provoking me continually to my faces.

RESPONSORY   Rev. 5:9

Lord, by your own blood...
...*you brought us back to God.*
From every tribe and tongue and people and nation...

LENT - SATURDAY MORNINGS

GOSPEL READING OF THE DAY (or use the **Canticle of Zechariah** from page 521)

Antiphon, Saturday
after Ash Wednesday
Luke 5:27-32

Store up for yourselves
treasures in heaven
where neither rust nor moth can destroy.

Antiphon, Week I
Matt 5:43-48

Be a true child of your heavenly Father:
pray for those who persecute you
and speak all the bad against you,
says the Lord.

Antiphon, Week II
Lk 15:1-3,11-32

Father, I have sinned
against heaven and against you;
I no longer deserve to be called your son;
treat me as one of your servants.

Antiphon, Week III
Luke 18:9-14

The tax collector stood far away and
would not even raise his eyes to heaven.
He struck his breast and prayed:
God, have mercy on me, a sinner.

Antiphon, Week IV
John 7:40-53

Store up for yourselves treasures in heaven
where neither rust nor moth can destroy.

Antiphon, Week V
John 11:45-56

Jesus died to gather into one family
all the scattered children of God.

MORNING PRAYER PETITIONS AND CLOSING PRAYER, see page 522.

WEEKS OF LENT BEGIN ON PAGE 7

EASTER TRIDUUM
of the Passion & Resurrection
HOLY THURSDAY EVENING

(said only by those who do not participate in the evening Mass of the Lord's Supper)

Sing, my tongue, the Sa-vior's glo-ry,
Of his flesh the mys-t'ry sing,
Of the blood, all price ex-ceed-ing,
Shed by our im-mort-al King,
Des-tined, for the world's re-demp-tion,
From a no-ble womb to spring.

On the night of that Last Sup-per,
Seat-ed with his cho-sen band,
He, the pas-chal vic-tim eat-ing,
First ful-fills the law's com-mand;
Then as food to all his sib-lings
Gives him-self with his own hand.

To the ev-er-last-ing Fa-ther,
And the Son who made us free,
And the Spir-it, God pro-ceed-ing,
From them each e-ter-nal-ly,
Be sal-va-tion, hon-or, bles-sing,
Might and end-less maj-es-ty.

Text: Thomas Aquinas, *Pange lingua gloriosi*, d. 1274,
translated by Edward Caswell, 1849, altered
Music: 87 87 87 ST. THOMAS, Samuel Webbe, 1792
Popular melody for: *Down In Adoration Falling*

HINGE HOURS for LENT and EASTER

Antiphon	Jesus Christ, the firstborn from the dead and ruler of the kings of the earth, has made us a royal people to serve his God and Father.	***Psalm 60*** page 292
Antiphon	The Lord will be the champion of the helpless; he will free the poor from the grip of the powerful.	**Psalm 72** page 294
Antiphon	The saints won their victory over death through the blood of the Lamb and the truth to which they bore witness.	**Rev. 11&12** page 296

READING **HEBREWS 13:11-15**

See Lent Thursday Evening, bottom of page 39

RESPONSORY

> For our sake Christ was obedient,
> accepting even death.

GOSPEL CANTICLE (**Canticle of Mary**) see page 523.

Antiphon While they were at supper,
Jesus took bread, said the blessing,
broke the bread, and gave it to his disciples.

EVENING PRAYER INTERCESSIONS AND CLOSING PRAYER, see page 523.

EASTER TRIDUUM
GOOD FRIDAY MORNING

O my God, my God, why have you a-ban-doned me?
Why so far from cries for help, rest-less an-guish call?
God, my God/, I call by day, no re-ply to hear.
God, my God, I call by night, no re-lief, I fear.

Yet en-throned, our Ho-ly One God of Is-ra-el,
Trust-ed by an-ces-tors you gave a place to dwell.
They cried out/ to you in need, beg-ging to be free,
Call-ing on their source of hope, free you let them be.

They say I am like a worm, hard-ly hu-man, scorned,
Mocked, de-spised by ev-'ry-one, tar-get of their fun.
All who see/ me mock and scorn, curl their lips and jeer:
"Let your Lord de-liv-er you, save you from your fear."

From the womb you drew me forth, safe-ty at the breast;
From the womb on you I fell, from my birth your guest.
Do not stay/ a-way from me, God, my God since birth;
Near are fear and trou-ble now, help-less I go forth.

Wild/ bulls sur-round a-round, brag-ging on their horns.
Li-ons fierce en-cir-cle me, rend a-bout and roar.
Drain-ing life/ like wa-ter soft, I can bare-ly speak.
Melt-ed is my heart, like wax, all my bones grow weak.

Dry as bro-ken bits of pots are my mouth and throat;
Dry tongue stuck in-side my mouth, ta-sting dust and dirt.
I can count/ each of my bones, wa-sted hands and feet;
Pack of dogs close in on me, dogs a-foot com-pete.

Text: Psalm 22, Part I, by Stephen J. Wolf, 2006, tribute to the priesthood of Bill Nolan
Music: 11 11 11 11 ADORO TE DEVOTE, Benedictine Plainsong, Mode V, 13th Century

Antiphon   Earthly kings rise up, in revolt;   ***Psalm 22***
            princes conspire together   page 399
            against the Lord and the Anointed.

Psalm 51, Habakkuk 3, & Psalm 147,
*go to **Friday Morning Week II**, page* 196

READING   **ISAIAH 52:13-15**

See, my servant will act wisely
and be raised and lifted up and highly exalted!
Just as many were appalled at him,
so disfigured beyond human appearance
and his form beyond that of human sons,
so will he startle many nations.
Kings will shut their mouth,
for what was not told to them they will see
and what they did not hear they will understand.

RESPONSORY

For our sake Christ was obedient,
accepting even death, death on a cross.

GOSPEL CANTICLE (**Canticle of Zechariah**) see page 521.

Antiphon   Over his head they hung their accusation:
            Jesus of Nazareth, King of the Jews.

MORNING PRAYER PETITIONS AND CLOSING PRAYER, see page 522.

EASTER TRIDUUM
GOOD FRIDAY EVENING

(said only by those who do not participate in the celebration of the Lord's passion)

At my life they stare and gloat, at my life torn up,
For my clo-thing cast-ing lots, gar-ments rip-ping up.
Save me from/ the li-on mouth, dogs & bulls & sword.
Quick-ly, help, de-liv-er me from this gath-ered hoard.

Then will I pro-claim your name in com-mu-nit-y!
In as-sem-bly, praise your name, this vow I will keep;
"Ja-cob now/ called Is-ra-el, all de-scen-dants call:
All who fear the Lord, give praise! Hal-le-lu-jah all!

"God did not spurn this one poor soul of mis-er-y,
Did not hide the face from mine, heard my cry in need.
All God's poor/ will eat their fill, all the an-a-wim,
Off-er praise and seek the Lord, hearts a-live in him."

From the edg-es of the earth all will wor-ship God,
Fam-il-ies and na-tions all turn-ing to the Lord.
All king-ship/ be-longs to God, ru-ler of us all.
All the liv-ing and the dead low in hom-age fall.

All who sleep in earth and dust bow in hom-age, kneel.
All de-scen-dants, serve the Lord, live for God, live well.
Tell each gen/-er-a-tion next of the Lord you've known,
Teach de-liv-er-ance to all peo-ple to be born.

Text: Psalm 22, Part II, by Stephen J. Wolf, 2006, tribute to the priesthood of Bill Nolan
Music: 11 11 11 11 ADORO TE DEVOTE, Benedictine Plainsong, Mode V, 13th Century

HINGE HOURS for LENT and EASTER

Antiphon — Look well, all you peoples, **Psalm 116:10-19**
and see my suffering. page 320

Antiphon — My soul is in anguish, **Psalm 143:1-11**
my heart is in torment. page 480

Antiphon — When Jesus had taken **Phil. 2:6-11**
the vinegar, he said: page 321
"It is accomplished."
Then he bowed his head and died.

READING **1 PETER 2:21-24**

see page 45

RESPONSORY

For our sake Christ was obedient, accepting even death.

GOSPEL CANTICLE (**Canticle of Mary**) see page 523.

Antiphon — When we were still God's enemies,
God reconciled us to God's self
by the death of God's Son.

GOOD FRIDAY INTERCESSIONS

Give unity to your Church.
Protect N. our Pope and all our Bishops.
Sanctify your faithful people by your Spirit.
Increase the faith and understanding of catechumens.
Gather all Christians in unity.
Be faithful to the Jewish people of the covenant.
Hear the praise of all who worship the One God.
Show the marks of your love in creation to those
    who do not yet see them.
Guide the minds and hearts of those who govern us.
Console all who are troubled.
Have mercy on those who have died.

OUR FATHER

EASTER TRIDUUM
of the Passion & Resurrection
HOLY SATURDAY MORNING

At the cross, **her sta-tion keep-ing**,
Stood the mourn-ful moth-er weep-ing,
Where he hung, the dy-ing Lord.

Saw him then from judge-ment ta-ken,
And in death by all for-sa-ken,
Till his Spir-it he re-signed.

Sit with her this Sab-bath Ho-ly
Let our time with her be whole-ly
Bless-ed in our grief to share.

Je-sus, may her deep de-vo-tion
Stir in me the same e-mo-tion,
Heart to heart ac-cep-tance find.

Text: Jacopone da Todi, *Stabat Mater dolorosa*, d. 1306,
translated by Edward Caswell, altered
Verse 3 by Stephen J. Wolf, 2011
Music: 88 7 STABAT MATER, *Mainz Gesanbbuch,* 1661

Antiphon	Lift high the ancient portals.	*Psalm* **24**
	The King of glory enters.	page 157

Antiphon	Though sinless, the Lord has been put to death; the world is in mourning as for an only son.	**Psalm 64** page 333
Antiphon	From the jaws of hell, Lord, rescue my soul.	**Isaiah 38:10-20** page 262
Antiphon	I was dead, but now I live forever, and I hold the keys of the nether world.	**Psalm 150** page 235

READING **HOSEA 6:1-6**

see page 322

RESPONSORY

For our sake Christ was obedient,
accepting even death, death on a cross.
Therefore God raised him on high and
gave him the name above all other names.

GOSPEL CANTICLE (**Canticle of Zechariah**) see page 521.

Antiphon Save us, Savior of the world.
On the cross you redeemed us
by the shedding of your blood;
we cry out for your help, O God.

MORNING PRAYER PETITIONS AND CLOSING PRAYER, see page 522.

from an ancient homily on Holy Saturday

*Something strange is happening - there is a
great silence on earth today, a great silence and stillness.
The whole earth keeps silence because the King is asleep.
The earth trembled and is still because God has fallen
asleep in the flesh and has raised up all who have slept
ever since the world began.
God has died in the flesh and hell trembles with fear.
He has gone in search for our first parents,
as for lost sheep...
The Lord approached Adam and Eve bearing the cross,
the weapon that had won him the victory...*

EASTER TRIDUUM
of the Passion & Resurrection
HOLY SATURDAY EVENING

At The Lamb's High Feast

see page 99

Antiphon	I know that I shall see the goodness of the Lord in the land of the living.	***Psalm 27*** page 176

Antiphon	Death,	**Psalm** 116:10-19
	you shall die in me;	page 320
	hell, you shall be destroyed by me.	

Antiphon	As Jonah was	**Psalm** 143:1-11
	three days and three nights	page 480
	in the belly of the big fish,	
	so will the Son of Man spend three days	
	and three nights in the heart of the earth.	

Antiphon	Destroy this temple,	**Phil.** 2:6-11
	says the Lord,	page 121
	and in three days I will rebuild it.	
	He was speaking of the temple of his body.	

READING **1 PETER** 1:17-21

see page 8

RESPONSORY

For our sake Christ was obedient,
accepting even death, death on a cross.
Therefore God raised him on high and
gave him the name above all names.

GOSPEL CANTICLE (**Canticle of Mary**) see page 523.

Antiphon Now the Son of Humanity has been glorified
and God has been glorified in him.

EVENING PRAYER INTERCESSIONS AND CLOSING PRAYER, see page 523.

EASTER DAY & SEASON
SUNDAY MORNINGS

The day of Res-ur-rec-tion!
Earth, tell it out a-broad
The Pass-o-ver of glad-ness,
The Pass-o-ver of God.
From death to life e-ter-nal,
From earth un-to the sky,
Our Christ has brought us o-ver,
The vic-t'ry song on high.

Our hearts be free of e-vil,
That we may see a-right
The Lord in rays e-ter-nal
Of res-ur-rec-tion light;
To lis-ten for his ac-cent,
May we be calm and plain;
May his own greet-ing hear-ing
We raise the vic-tor strain.

Now let the heav'ns be joy-ful!
Let earth the song be-gin!
A-round the world keep tri-umph,
And all that is there-in!
Let all things seen and un-seen
their notes in glad-ness blend
For Christ the Lord has ris-en,
Our joy that has no end.

HINGE HOURS for LENT and EASTER

Text: John of Damascus, d. 749, translated from Greek by John M. Neale, 1862, altered
Music: 76 76 D, AURELIA, Samuel S. Wesley, 1864
Popular melody for: *The Church's One Foundation*

PSALMS & CANTICLES	WEEK I, go to page 127	WEEK V (Week I) pg. 127
	WEEK II, go to page 226	WEEK VI (Week II) pg. 226
	WEEK III, go to page 326	
	WEEK IV, go to page 424	

READING   **ACTS 10:40-43**

God raised this one on the third day
and gave him to be visible not to all the people,
but to witnesses chosen by God,
to us who ate and drank with him
after his rising out of the dead.
And he commanded us to proclaim to the people
and witness solemnly that he is the one
designated by God as judge of the living and the dead.
To him all the prophets witness:
forgiveness of sins received through his name
by everyone believing in him.

RESPONSORY, Easter Sunday and Second Sunday of Easter: Ps 118:24
This is the day the Lord has made;
let us rejoice and be glad.

RESPONSORY, Easter Weeks 3 to 6:   Luke 18:13
Lord Jesus Christ, Son of the living God...
...have mercy on us.
You were wounded for our offenses...

GOSPEL CANTICLE (**Canticle of Zechariah**) see page 521.

Ant., Easter Sunday	Very early when the sun had just risen
A. Matthew 28:1-10	on the morning after the Sabbath
B. Mark 16:1-7	they came to the tomb,
C. Luke 24:1-12	alleluia.
Antiphon, Week II	With your hand,
ABC:	touch the mark of the nails;
John 20:19-31	doubt no longer, but believe,
	alleluia.
Antiphon, Week III	It was fitting for Christ to suffer
A. Luke 24:13-35	so on the third day
B. Luke 24:35-48	to rise from the dead,
C. John 21:1-19	alleluia.
Antiphon, Week IV	I am the shepherd of the sheep;
A. John 10:1-10	I know my sheep,
B. John 10:11-18	and my sheep know me,
C. John 10:27-30	alleluia.
Antiphon, Week V	One who lives in me
A. John 14:1-12	and I in that one
B. John 15:1-8	will yield much fruit,
C. Jn 13:31-33a,34-35	says the Lord, alleluia.
Antiphon, Week VI	As the Father has loved me
A. John 14:15-21	so I have loved you;
B. John 15:9-17	live on in my love,
C. John 14:23-29	alleluia.

MORNING PRAYER PETITIONS AND CLOSING PRAYER, see page 522.

EASTER DAY & SEASON
SUNDAY EVENINGS

Je-sus Christ is ris'n to-day\, A//\/-le/-lu\-ia!
Our tri-umph-ant ho-ly day\, A//\/-le/-lu\-ia!
Who did once up-on the cross, A//\/-le/-lu\-ia!
Suf/-fer\ to re-deem our loss\, A\/\//-le/-lu\-ia!

Hymns of praise, then, let us sing\, A//\/-le/-lu\-ia!
Un-to Christ, our heav'n-ly King\, A//\/-le/-lu\-ia!
Who en-dured the cross and grave, A//\/-le/-lu\-ia!
Sin/-ners\ to re-deem and save\, A\/\//-le/-lu\-ia!

But the pain which he en-dured\, A//\/-le/-lu\-ia!
Our sal-va-tion has pro-cured\, A//\/-le/-lu\-ia!
Now a-bove the sky he's King, A//\/-le/-lu\-ia!
Where/ the\ an-gels ev-er sing\, A\/\//-le/-lu\-ia!

Sing we to our God a-bove\, A//\/-le/-lu\-ia!
Praise e-ter-nal as God's love\, A//\/-le/-lu\-ia!
Praise God, all you heav'n-ly host, A//\/-le/-lu\-ia!
Fa/-ther\, Son, and Ho-ly Ghost\, A\/\//-le/-lu\-ia!

Text: Bohemian Carol, *Surrexit Christus hodie*, 1372, translated by John Walsh, 1708,
stanzas 1-3 by John Arnold, 1749, stanza 4 by Charles Wesley, 1740, altered
Music: 77 77 EASTER HYMN with alleluias, *Lyra Davidica*, 1708

PSALMS &	WEEK I, go to page 136	WEEK V (Week I) pg. 136
CANTICLES	WEEK II, go to page 236	WEEK VI (Week II) pg. 236
	WEEK III, go to page 333	
	WEEK IV, go to page 431	

READING, Before Ascension: **HEBREWS 10:**12-14

Having offered the single sacrifice for all time,
this Christ has sat at the right hand of God,
waiting since until his enemies
are put as a footstool of his feet,
for by one offering
he has made perfect for all time
the ones being made holy.

RESPONSORY, Easter Sunday and Second Sunday of Easter:
This is the day the Lord has made;
let us rejoice and be glad.

RESPONSORY, Easter Weeks 3 to 6:
The Lord is risen...
...alleluia, alleluia.
He has appeared to Simon...

GOSPEL CANTICLE (**Canticle of Mary**) see page 523.

Ant., Easter Sunday On the evening
of the first day of the week,
the disciples were gathered together
behind locked doors;
suddenly Jesus stood among them
and said: Peace be with you,
alleluia.

EASTER - SUNDAY EVENINGS

Antiphon, Week II
Because you have seen me, Thomas,
you have believed;
blessed are they who have not seen me
and yet believe,
alleluia.

Antiphon, Week III
Jesus said to his disciples: Bring me
some of the fish you have just caught.
Simon Peter went aboard
pulled to shore the net, full of big fish,
alleluia.

Antiphon, Week IV
My sheep will hear my voice.
I, their Lord, know them,
alleluia.

Antiphon, Week V
I give you a new commandment:
love one another as I have loved you,
says the Lord,
alleluia.

Antiphon, Week VI
One who loves me will keep my word
and my Father will love that one.
We will come
and make our home with that one,
alleluia.

EVENING PRAYER INTERCESSIONS AND CLOSING PRAYER, see page 523.

EASTER
MONDAY MORNINGS

The strife is o'er, the bat\-tle done;
Now is the vic-tor's tri\-umph won;
Now is the song of praise\ be-gun. Al-le-lu-ia!
Al-le-lu-ia!   Al-le-lu-ia!   Al-le-lu-ia!

Death's might-iest pow'rs have done\ their worst,
And Je-sus has his foes\ dis-persed;
Let shouts of praise and joy\ out-burst. Al-le-lu-ia!
Al-le-lu-ia!   Al-le-lu-ia!   Al-le-lu-ia!

On the third morn he rose\ a-gain
Glo-rious in ma-jes-ty\ to reign;
Oh, let us swell the joy\-ful strain! Al-le-lu-ia!
Al-le-lu-ia!   Al-le-lu-ia!   Al-le-lu-ia!

Text: from Psalm 98:1 by an unknown author, 1695, trans. by Francis Pott, 1859, altered
Music: 888 VICTORY with alleluias, Giovanni P. Da Palestrina, 1591,
adapted by William Monk, d.1889

PSALMS &	* WEEK I, go to page 127	WEEK V (Week I) pg. 144
CANTICLES	WEEK II, go to page 242	WEEK VI (Week II) pg. 242
	WEEK III, go to page 340	WEEK VII (Week III) pg. 340
	WEEK IV, go to page 437	

* **NOTE:**
  Through the first week of Easter (the *Octave of Easter*)
  the Psalms & Canticles are from SUNDAY of WEEK I.

READING   **ROMANS 10:8b-10**

The word is near you, in your mouth and in your heart;
>this is the word of faith we proclaim.
If you confess with your mouth the Lord Jesus,
>and believe in your heart
>that God raised him from the dead,
>you will be saved,
for with the heart one believes to righteousness,
and with the mouth one confesses to salvation.

RESPONSORY, in the Octave of Easter:
>This is the day the Lord has made;
>let us rejoice and be glad.

RESPONSORY, Easter Weeks 2 through 7:
>The Lord is risen from the tomb…
>>…*alleluia, alleluia.*
>He hung upon the cross for us…

GOSPEL READING OF THE DAY (or use the **Canticle of Zechariah** from page 521)

Ant., Easter Week I — Go quickly and tell his disciples:
Matthew 28:8-15 — The Lord is risen,
alleluia.

Antiphon, Week II — Truly I tell you,
John 3:1-8 — unless you are born again,
you cannot see the kingdom of God,
alleluia.

Antiphon, Week III **John 6:22-29**	Work not for food that perishes, but for food that remains to eternal life, alleluia.
Antiphon, Week IV **John 10:1-18**	I am the Good Shepherd; I pasture my sheep and I lay down my life for them, alleluia.
Antiphon, Week V **John 14:21-26**	Whoever loves me is loved by my Father, and I will love and show myself to them, alleluia.
Antiphon, Week VI **John 15:26-16:4a**	Raising Jesus Christ from the dead God has given us a new birth to a living hope in the promise of an inheritance that will last forever, alleluia.
Antiphon, Week VII **John 16:29-33**	The world will persecute you but have courage; I have overcome the world, alleluia.

MORNING PRAYER PETITIONS AND CLOSING PRAYER, see page 522.

EASTER
MONDAY EVENINGS

Full East-er joy the day was bright,
Sun shin-ing out/ with fair-er light,
When to their long-ing eyes re-stored,
His glad a-pos-tles saw their Lord.

He bade them see his hands, his side,
Where yet the glo/-rious wounds a-bide;
The to-kens true which made it plain
Their Lord in-deed was ris'n a-gain.

The Christ, the King of gen-tle-ness,
Now you, your-self/, our hearts pos-sess
That we may give you all our days
The trib-ute of our grate-ful praise.

Text: *Claro paschali gaudio*, 5th cent. unknown author,
translated by John M. Neale, 1851, 1861, altered
Music: PUER NOBIS NASCITUR, LM, Trier manuscript 15th Century,
Michael Praetorius, 1609
Alternate Music: CONDITOR, LM; *Conditor Alme Siderum*, Sarum plainsong, Mode IV
Popular melody for: *Creator of the Stars of Night*

PSALMS &	WEEK I, go to page 136	WEEK V (Week I) pg. 150
CANTICLES	WEEK II, go to page 250	WEEK VI (Week II) pg. 250
	WEEK III, go to page 347	WEEK VII (Week III) pg. 347
	WEEK IV, go to page 446	

READING, Before Ascension: **HEBREWS** 8:1b-3a

We have a high priest, who sat at the right of the throne
of the greatness in the heavens, a minister of the holy
things and of the true tabernacle, erected by the Lord,
not by human beings. Every high priest is appointed
to offer both gifts and sacrifices.

RESPONSORY, in the Octave of Easter:
This is the day the Lord has made;
let us rejoice and be glad.

RESPONSORY, Easter Weeks 2 to 6:
The disciples rejoiced…
…alleluia, alleluia.
When they saw the risen Lord…

READING, After Ascension: **ROMANS** 8:14-17

As many as are led by the Spirit of God, these are sons
and daughters of God. For you did not receive a spirit
of slavery, for fear again, but you received a spirit of
adoption, by which we cry, "Abba, Father." That very
Spirit gives witness to our spirit that we are children of
God. And if children, then also heirs, heirs on one hand
of God, joint heirs on the other of Christ, since we suffer
with him in order that we may also be glorified with him.

RESPONSORY, After Ascension:
The Holy Spirit is the Paraclete…
…alleluia, alleluia.
Who will teach you all things…

GOSPEL CANTICLE (**Canticle of Mary**) see page 523.

Ant., Easter Week I
Jesus met the women and greeted them.
They came up to him and knelt at his feet,
alleluia.

Antiphon, Week II
What is born of the flesh is flesh;
what is born of the spirit is spirit; alleluia.

Antiphon, Week III
This is what God asks of you: trust
in the one whom God has sent, alleluia.

Antiphon, Week IV
I have other sheep that are
not of this flock; these also I must lead.
They will hear my voice, and there will be
one fold and one shepherd, alleluia.

Antiphon, Week V
The Holy Spirit, the Paraclete,
whom the Father will send in my name,
will teach you, and remind you
of all that I told you, alleluia.

Antiphon, Week VI
The Spirit of truth
who proceeds from the Father
will be my witness,
and you will bear witness to me, alleluia.

Antiphon, Week VII
The Spirit, the Advocate, will remain
with you and live in you, alleluia.

EVENING PRAYER INTERCESSIONS AND CLOSING PRAYER, see page 523.

EASTER
TUESDAY MORNINGS

Ye sons and daugh\-ters of\ the King,
With heav'n-ly hosts\ in glo\-ry sing,
To-day the grave\ has lost\ its sting: Al-le-lu-ia!

On that first morn\-ing of\ the week,
Be-fore the day\ be-gan\ to break,
The Ma-rys went\ their Lord\ to seek: Al-le-lu-ia!

An an-gel bade\ their sor\-row flee,
By speak-ing thus\ un-to\ the three:
"Your Lord is gone\ to Gal\-i-lee": Al-le-lu-ia!

That night th'A-pos\-tles met\ in fear,
A-midst them came\ their Lord\ most dear
And said, "Peace be\ un-to\ you here": Al-le-lu-ia!

Bless-ed are they\ that have\ not seen
And yet whose faith\ has con\-stant been,
In life e-ter\-nal they\ shall reign: Al-le-lu-ia!

And we with ho\-ly Church\ u-nite,
As ev-er-more\ is just\ and right,
In glo-ry to\ the King\ of light: Al-le-lu-ia!

Al-le-lu-ia\! Al-le\-lu-ia! Al-le-lu-ia!

Text: see John 20; attrib. to Jean Tisserand, d. 1494; trans. by John M. Neal, 1851, altered
Music: 888, O FILII ET FILIAE; Chant Mode II, *Airs sur les hymnes sacrez, odes et noels,* 1623

HINGE HOURS for LENT and EASTER

PSALMS & CANTICLES

WEEK I, go to page 127	WEEK V (Week I) pg. 155
WEEK II, go to page 257	WEEK VI (Week II) pg. 257
WEEK III, go to page 353	WEEK VII (Week III) pg. 353
WEEK IV, go to page 452	

READING **ACTS 13:30-33**

God raised out of the dead Jesus, who appeared
over many days to the ones who came up with him
from Galilee to Jerusalem, who are now his witnesses
to the people. And we evangelize to you the promise
to our ancestors that God has fulfilled to their children,
raising up Jesus, as also it is written in the second psalm,
You are my Son; today I have begotten you.

RESPONSORY, in the Octave of Easter:

This is the day the Lord has made;
let us rejoice and be glad.

RESPONSORY, Easter Weeks 2 through 7:

The Lord is risen from the tomb...
...*alleluia, alleluia.*
He hung upon the cross for us...

GOSPEL READING OF THE DAY (or use the **Canticle of Zechariah** from page 521)

Ant., Easter Week I
John 20:11-18

Jesus called her by name: Mary.
She turned to him and said: Rabboni.
Then he said to her: Do not grab me;
I have not yet ascended to my Father,
alleluia.

Antiphon, Week II
John 3:7b-15

I am the Alpha and the Omega,
the first and the last,
the beginning and the end;
I am the root and offspring of David's race;
I am the splendor of the morning star,
alleluia.

Antiphon, Week III
John 6:30-35

Truly I say to you: Moses did not give you the bread of heaven; my Father gives you the true bread from heaven, alleluia.

Antiphon, Week IV
John 10:22-30

The works that I do
in the name of the Father
speak on my behalf, alleluia.

Antiphon, Week V
John 14:27-31a

Peace I leave with you, alleluia;
my peace is my gift to you, alleluia.

Antiphon, Week VI
John 16:5-11

In a little while
the world will no longer see me
but you will see me
for I live and you will live, alleluia.   Jn 16:16

Antiphon, Week VII
John 17:1-11a

The Lord is risen from the dead
as he promised;
let all the earth rejoice and be glad
for he shall reign forever, alleluia.

MORNING PRAYER PETITIONS AND CLOSING PRAYER, see page 522.

EASTER
TUESDAY EVENINGS

Sing with all the saints in glo-ry,
Sing the res-ur-rec-tion song!
Death and sor-row, earth's dark sto-ry,
To the for-mer days be-long.
All a-round the clouds are/ break-ing,
Soon the/ storms of time shall cease;
In God's im-age we, a-wa-king,
Know the ev-er-last-ing peace.

O what glo-ry, far ex-ceed-ing
All that eye has yet per-ceived!
Ho-liest hearts, for a-ges plead-ing,
Nev-er that full joy con-ceived.
God has prom-ised, Christ pre/-pares it,
There on/ high our wel-come waits.
Ev-'ry hum-ble spir-it shares it;
Christ has passed th'e-ter-nal gates.

Text: William J. Irons, 1873
Music: 8787D, HYMN TO JOY, Ludwig van Beethoven, 1770,
adapted by Edward Hodges, 1827
Popular melody for: *Joyful Joyful We Adore You*

PSALMS &	WEEK I, go to page 136	WEEK V (Week I) pg. 163
CANTICLES	WEEK II, go to page 266	WEEK VI (Week II) pg. 266
	WEEK III, go to page 361	WEEK VII (Week III) pg. 361
	WEEK IV, go to page 459	

READING, Before Ascension: **1 PETER 2:4-5**

Approach the Lord, a living stone, rejected by humans,
chosen precious by God. And as living stones you are
being built, a spiritual house for a holy priesthood,
to offer spiritual sacrifices acceptable to God
through Jesus Christ.

RESPONSORY, in the Octave of Easter:
> This is the day the Lord has made;
> let us rejoice and be glad.

RESPONSORY, Easter Weeks 2 to 6:
> The disciples rejoiced...
>> ...*alleluia, alleluia.*
> When they saw the risen Lord...

READING, After Ascension: **ROMANS 8:26-27**

The Spirit shares in our weakness. For we do not know
how to pray as is fitting, but the Spirit intercedes on
our behalf with inexpressible groanings. And the one
searching our heart knows what is the mind of the Spirit,
because the Spirit intercedes on behalf of the saints
according to the will of God.

RESPONSORY, After Ascension:
> The Holy Spirit is the Paraclete...
>> ...*alleluia, alleluia.*
> Who will teach you all things...

GOSPEL CANTICLE (**Canticle of Mary**) see page 523.

Ant., Easter Week I
While I was weeping at the tomb
I saw my Lord, alleluia.

Antiphon, Week II
Did not our hearts burn within us
as Jesus talked to us on the road?
Alleluia.

Antiphon, Week III
The bread of God
that comes down from heaven
gives life to the world, alleluia.

Antiphon, Week IV
I know my sheep and they follow me;
I give them eternal life, alleluia.

Antiphon, Week V
If you loved me, you would surely be glad
that I am going to the Father, alleluia.

Antiphon, Week VI
Believe me,
it is for your own good that I go
for if I do not go
the Paraclete will not come, alleluia.

Antiphon, Week VII
You will receive
the power of the Holy Spirit
and you will be my witnesses
to the ends of the earth, alleluia.

EVENING PRAYER INTERCESSIONS AND CLOSING PRAYER, see page 523.

EASTER
WEDNESDAY MORNINGS

Christ the Lord is ris'n to\-day, Al\\-le\-lu-ia!
Daugh-ters, sons and an-gels\ say, Al\\-le\-lu\-ia!
Raise your joys and tri\-umphs\ high, Al\/-le-lu-ia!
Sing, ye heav'ns, and earth, re\-ply, Al\\-le\-lu-ia!

Lives a-gain our glo-rious\ King, Al\\-le\-lu-ia!
Where, O Death, is now your\ sting, Al\\-le\-lu-ia!
Once he died our souls\ to\ save, Al\/-le-lu-ia!
Where your vic-to-ry, O\ Grave, Al\\-le\-lu-ia!

Hail the Lord of earth and\ heav'n, Al\\-le\-lu-ia!
Praise to God by both be\ giv'n! Al\\-le\-lu-ia!
Chil-dren of the Res-ur-rec\-tion, Al\/-le-lu-ia!
Our e-lec-tion has been\ won! Al\\-le\-lu-ia!

Text: Charles Wesley, 1739, altered
Music marked: 77 77 LLANFAIR with alleluias, Robert Williams, d. 1821
Alternate Music: 77 77 EASTER HYMN with alleluias, Lyra Davidica, 1708

PSALMS &	WEEK I, go to page 127	WEEK V (Week I) pg. 168
CANTICLES	WEEK II, go to page 271	WEEK VI (Week II) pg. 271
	WEEK III, go to page 367	WEEK VII (Week III) pg. 367
	WEEK IV, go to page 464	

READING **ROMANS** 6:8-11

If we died with Christ,
we believe that we shall also live with him,
knowing that Christ raised from the dead dies no more.
Death lords it over him no more,
for in that he died to sin he died once.
But in that he is alive, he is alive to God.
So also you reckon yourselves dead indeed to sin,
but alive to God in Christ Jesus.

RESPONSORY, in the Octave of Easter:
>This is the day the Lord has made;
>let us rejoice and be glad.

RESPONSORY, Easter Weeks 2 through 7:
>The Lord is risen from the tomb...
>>...*alleluia, alleluia.*
>He hung upon the cross for us...

GOSPEL READING OF THE DAY (or use the **Canticle of Zechariah** from page 521)

Ant., Easter Week I **Luke 24:13-35**	Beginning with Moses and the prophets, Jesus broke open for them all that had been written of him in the Scriptures, alleluia.
Antiphon, Week II **John 3:16-21**	God so loved the cosmos that he gave his only Son to save all who believe in him and give eternal life, alleluia.

Antiphon, Week III **John 6:35-40**	Who sees the Son and believes in him will live forever, and I will raise up on the last day, alleluia.
Antiphon, Week IV **John 12:44-50**	I am the light come into the cosmos that those who believe in me may not remain in the dark, alleluia.
Antiphon, Week V **John 15:1-8**	I am the true vine, alleluia; you are the branches, alleluia.
Antiphon, Week VI **John 16:12-15**	I have many more things to tell you but you cannot bear it now; when the Spirit of truth comes that One will guide you to all truth, alleluia.
Antiphon, Week VII **John 17:11b-19**	Thanks be to God who has given us the victory through our Lord Jesus Christ, alleluia.

MORNING PRAYER PETITIONS AND CLOSING PRAYER, see page 522.

EASTER
WEDNESDAY EVENINGS

(for Easter)

Ho-ly Feast, you ho-ly day!
To be hal-lowed ev-er-more,
Day when Christ our Lord was raised,
Break-ing down the reign of death.
Praise the Giv/-er of all good!
Con-cord Auth-er of all love,
Pour your balm on all our days;
To your peace guide all our ways.

Lo, fair beau-ty of the earth,
From the death of win-ter, rise!
With its Mas-ter now re-turns
Ev'-ry good gift of the year.
Ris-en from/ the grave, now Lord,
Au-thor of cre-a-ted life,
Tread-ing through the path of death,
New life to us all you give.

Text: Venantius Fortunatus, d. 609;
translated by Maurice F. Bell, *Hail Thee Festival Day*, 1906, altered
Music: 77 77 D, SALZBURG; Jakob Hintze, 1678
Popular melody for: *Songs of Thankfulness and Praise*

PSALMS &	WEEK I, go to page 136	WEEK V (Week I) pg. 174
CANTICLES	WEEK II, go to page 278	WEEK VI (Week II) pg. 278
	WEEK III, go to page 375	WEEK VII (Week III) pg. 375
	WEEK IV, go to page 471	

READING, Before Ascension: **HEBREWS 7:24-27**

Jesus, because he remains unto the eons, has the priestly office without end. And so he is able to save entirely those approaching to God through him, always alive to intercede for them. To us indeed was suitable such a high priest, holy, harmless, undefiled, set apart from sinners, becoming higher than the heavens. He does not have the daily need of the high priests to offer up sacrifices first for their own sins and then for the sins of the people. For he did this once for all, offering up his very self.

RESPONSORY, in the Octave of Easter:
This is the day the Lord has made;
let us rejoice and be glad.

RESPONSORY, Easter Weeks 2 to 6:
The disciples rejoiced...
...*alleluia, alleluia.*
When they saw the risen Lord...

READING, After Ascension: **1 CORINTHIANS 2:9b-10**

Things which eye has not seen and ear has not heard
and have not come upon the human heart,
how many are prepared for those loving God.
This has been revealed to us by God through the Spirit.
For the Spirit searches all things,
even the deep things of God.

EASTER - WEDNESDAY EVENINGS

RESPONSORY, After Ascension:
> The Holy Spirit is the Paraclete…
> > …*alleluia, alleluia.*
> Who will teach you all things…

GOSPEL CANTICLE (**Canticle of Mary**) see page 523.

Ant., Easter Week I
> Jesus went in with them,
> and while they were at table he took bread
> and said the blessing; he broke the bread
> and gave it to them, alleluia.

Antiphon, Week II
> The child of God welcomes the light
> that searches deeds done
> and finds them true, alleluia.

Antiphon, Week III
> All that the Father gives me will
> come to me, and whoever comes to me
> I shall not turn away, alleluia.

Antiphon, Week IV
> God sent the Son into the world
> not as judge but as savior, alleluia.

Antiphon, Week V
> If you live in me and my words live in you,
> all you ask for will be yours, alleluia.

Antiphon, Week VI
> The Spirit will glorify me
> and proclaim to you
> all that he has received from me, alleluia.

Antiphon, Week VII
> The Christ will baptize you
> with fire and the Holy Spirit, alleluia.

EVENING PRAYER INTERCESSIONS AND CLOSING PRAYER, see page 523.

EASTER
THURSDAY MORNINGS

Al-le-lu/-ia! sing to Je-\sus!
his the scep-ter, his\ the throne!
Al-le-lu/-ia! his the tri\-umph,
his the vic-to-ry\ a-lone.
Hark! the songs\ of peace-ful Zi\-on
thun-der like/ a migh\-ty flood.
Je\-sus out\ of ev\-'ry na//\-tion
has re-deemed\ us by his blood.

Al-le-lu/-ia! not as or\-phans
are we left in sor\-row now;
Al-le-lu/-ia! he is near\ us,
faith be-lieves, nor ques\-tions how;
Though the cloud\ from sight re-ceived\ him
when the for/-ty days\ were o'er.
Shall\ our hearts\ for-get\ his pro//\-mise:
"I am with\ you ev-er-more?"

Al-le-lu/-ia! King e-ter\-nal,
you the Lord we know as our own;
Al-le-lu/-ia! Son of Ma\-ry,
earth your foot-stool, heav'n\ your throne:
In-ter-ces\-sor, Friend of sin\-ners,
robed in flesh/ our great\ High Priest;
You\ on earth\ both priest\ and vic//\-tim
in the Eu\-cha-ris-tic feast.

Text: William C. Dix; *Altar Songs, Verses on the Holy Eucharist*, 1867, altered
Music: 87 87 D, HYFRYDOL, Rowland H. Prichard, 1811-1887

PSALMS &	WEEK I, go to page 127	WEEK V (Week I) pg. 181
CANTICLES	WEEK II, go to page 283	WEEK VI (Week II) pg. 283
	WEEK III, go to page 379	WEEK VII (Week III) pg. 379
	WEEK IV, go to page 478	

READING   **ROMANS 8:9-11**

You are not in flesh but in Spirit,
since the Spirit of God dwells in you.
If anyone does not have the Spirit of Christ,
this one is not of him. But if Christ is in you,
the body is dead because of sin
and the spirit is life because of righteousness.
If the Spirit of the one who raised Jesus from the dead
dwells in you,
the one who raised Christ from the dead
will also give life to your mortal bodies
through the indwelling of the Spirit in you.

RESPONSORY, in the Octave of Easter:

> This is the day the Lord has made;
> let us rejoice and be glad.

RESPONSORY, Easter Weeks 2 through 7:

> The Lord is risen from the tomb...
>   ...*alleluia, alleluia.*
> He hung upon the cross for us...

GOSPEL READING OF THE DAY (or use the **Canticle of Zechariah** from page 521)

Ant., Easter Week I **Luke 24:35-48**	Jesus stood in the midst of his disciples, showed them his wounds, and said: Peace be with you, alleluia.
Antiphon, Week II **John 3:31-36**	God does not ration the gift of the Spirit, alleluia.
Antiphon, Week III **John 6:44-51**	Amen, amen, I say to you: Whoever believes in me will live forever, alleluia.
Antiphon, Week IV **John 13:16-20**	No disciple is greater than the teacher; be glad to become like your master, alleluia.
Antiphon, Week V **John 15:9-11**	If you keep my commandments, you will live in my love, alleluia.
Antiphon, Week VI **John 16:16-20**	In a little while you will no longer see me, says the Lord; then a little later you will see me again since I am going to the Father, alleluia.
Antiphon, Week VII **John 17:20-26**	Go into the world and teach all nations. Baptize them in the name of the Father and of the Son and of the Holy Spirit, alleluia.

MORNING PRAYER PETITIONS AND CLOSING PRAYER, see page 522.

EASTER
THURSDAY EVENINGS

Lord, when at your Last Supper you did pray
That all your Church might be forever one.
Grant us at ev'ry Eucharist to say
With longing heart and soul, "Your will be done."
O may we all one bread, one body be,
Through this blest Sacrament of Unity.

For all your Church, O Lord, we intercede;
Make all our sad divisions soon to cease;
Draw us the nearer each, to each we plead,
By drawing all to you, O Prince of Peace;
Thus may we all one bread, one body be,
Through this blest Sacrament of Unity.

We pray for all who wander from your fold;
O bring them home, Good Shepherd of the sheep,
Back to the faith which saints believed of old,
Back to the Church which still the faith does keep;
Soon may we all one bread, one body be,
Through this blest Sacrament of Unity.

So, Lord, at length when sacraments shall cease,
May we be one with all your Church above,
One with your saints in one unbroken peace,
One with your saints in one unbounded love;
More blessed still in peace and love to be
One with the Trinity in Unity.

Text: William H. Turton, 1859-1938, altered
Music: 10 10 10 10 10 10 UNDE ET MEMORES, William H. Monk, 1823-1899

PSALMS &	WEEK I, go to page 136	WEEK V (Week I) pg. 187
CANTICLES	WEEK II, go to page 291	WEEK VI (Week II) pg. 291
	WEEK III, go to page 385	WEEK VII (Week III) pg. 385
	WEEK IV, go to page 484	

READING, Before Ascension: **1 PETER** 3:18,21b-22

Christ died once for sins, a just man for the unjust,
put to death in the flesh and made alive in the spirit,
that he might bring you to God. Jesus Christ,
at the right hand of God, having gone into heaven,
subject to him are angels and authorities and powers.

RESPONSORY, in the Octave of Easter:
> This is the day the Lord has made;
> let us rejoice and be glad.

RESPONSORY, Easter Weeks 2 to 6:
> The disciples rejoiced…
> *…alleluia, alleluia.*
> When they saw the risen Lord…

READING, After Ascension: **1 CORINTHIANS** 6:19-20

Do you not know that your body is a temple of the
Holy Spirit in you, whom you have from God, and that
you are not of yourself? For you were bought at a price.
So, glorify God in your body.

RESPONSORY, After Ascension: Jn 17:20 or 26??
> The Holy Spirit is the Paraclete…
> *…alleluia, alleluia.*
> Who will teach you all things…

EASTER - THURSDAY EVENINGS

GOSPEL CANTICLE (**Canticle of Mary**) see page 523.

Ant., Easter Week I See my hands and my feet
and know I am here among you, alleluia.

Antiphon, Week II Whoever believes in the Son
possesses eternal life, alleluia.

Antiphon, Week III I am the living bread come down from
heaven; anyone who eats this bread will
live forever; the bread that I will give is
my flesh, for the life of the world, alleluia.

Antiphon, Week IV I am the shepherd of my sheep;
I have come that they may have life
and have it more abundantly, alleluia.

Antiphon, Week V I have said these things to you
so that my joy may be in you
and your joy may be complete, alleluia.

Antiphon, Week VI Your sorrow will be turned into joy
that no one will take from you, alleluia.

Antiphon, Week VII When the Spirit of truth comes
he will teach you all truth
and proclaim to you the things to come,
alleluia.

EVENING PRAYER INTERCESSIONS AND CLOSING PRAYER, see page 523.

EASTER
FRIDAY MORNINGS

I know that my Re/-deem-er\ lives;
What com-fort this sweet sen-tence gives!
Liv-ing\ Proph/-et/, Priest\, and\ King:
Liv-ing and as he lives I'll sing.

He lives/ hun-gry/ souls to\ feed,
Liv-ing to help in time of need.
Liv-ing to grant/ us/ rich\ sup\-ply,
Liv-ing to guide us with his eye.

He lives/ qui-et/-ing our\ fears,
Liv-ing to wipe a-way our tears,
Liv-ing to calm/ our/ troubl\-ed hearts,
Liv-ing all bless-ings to im-part.

He lives/; glo-ry/ to his\ Name!
Liv-ing, my Je-sus, still the same.
Oh, sweet the joy/ this/ sen\-tence\ gives:
"I know that my Re-deem-er lives!"

Text: from Job 19:25-27, Samuel Medley, 1775, altered
Music: DUKE STREET, LM, John Hatton, 1793

PSALMS &	WEEK I, go to page 127	WEEK V (Week I) pg. 194
CANTICLES	WEEK II, go to page 297	WEEK VI (Week II) pg. 297
	WEEK III, go to page 391	WEEK VII (Week III) pg. 391
	WEEK IV, go to page 489	

READING   **ACTS 5:30-32**

The God of our ancestors raised Jesus,
whom you killed by hanging on a tree. This one
is exalted to the right hand of God as ruler and savior
to give conversion to Israel and forgiveness of sins.
Of these things we are witnesses with the Holy Spirit
given by God to the obedient.

RESPONSORY, in the Octave of Easter:

> This is the day the Lord has made;
> let us rejoice and be glad.

RESPONSORY, Easter Weeks 2 through 7:

> The Lord is risen from the tomb…
>   …*alleluia, alleluia.*
> He hung upon the cross for us…

GOSPEL READING OF THE DAY (or use the **Canticle of Zechariah** from page 521)

Ant., Easter Week I
John 21:1-14

> This was the third time
> Jesus showed himself to his disciples
> after he had risen from the dead,
> alleluia.

Antiphon, Week II
John 6:1-15

> Jesus took bread,
> and when he had given thanks,
> he gave it to those at table with him,
> alleluia.

Antiphon, Week III **John 6:52-59**	Whoever eats my flesh and drinks my blood shall live in me and I in him, alleluia.
Antiphon, Week IV **John 14:1-6**	I go now to prepare a place for you but I shall return to take you with me so that where I am you also may be, alleluia.
Antiphon, Week V **John 15:12-17**	My command is this: love one another as I have loved you, alleluia.
Antiphon, Week VI **John 16:20-23**	Because he suffered death, we see Jesus crowned with glory and honor, alleluia.
Antiphon, Week VII **John 21:15-19**	Jesus Christ died and is risen from the dead. Now he lives forever at the right hand of the Father where he intercedes for us, alleluia.

MORNING PRAYER PETITIONS AND CLOSING PRAYER, see page 522.

EASTER
FRIDAY EVENINGS

The/ Head that once was/ crowned with thorns
Is crowned in glo\-ry/ now;
A/ roy-al di-a-dem a-dorns
The/ migh/-ty vic\-tor's brow.

    The/ high-est place that/ heav'n af-fords
    Be-longs to him\ by/ right;
    The/ King of kings and Lord of lords
    and/ heav'ns/ e-ter\-nal Light.

        The/ joy of all who/ dwell a-bove,
        The joy of all\ be/-low,
        To/ whom he man-i-fests his love
        And/ grants/ his Name\ to know.

To/ them the cross with/ all its shame,
With all its grace\, is/ giv'n;
Their/ name an ev-er-last-ing name,
Their/ joy/ the joy\ of heav'n.

Text: Thomas Kelly, *Hymns on Various Passages of Scripture*, 1820, altered
Music: MCKEE, CM; African American Spiritual,
arranged by Harry T. Burleigh, 1866-1949
Popular melody for: *In Christ There Is No East Or West*
Alternate melody: *Shepherd of Souls*

PSALMS &	WEEK I, go to page 136	WEEK V (Week I) pg. 201
CANTICLES	WEEK II, go to page 305	WEEK VI (Week II) pg. 305
	WEEK III, go to page 399	WEEK VII (Week III) pg. 399
	WEEK IV, go to page 497	

READING, Before Ascension: **HEBREWS** 5:8-10

Though being a Son, he learned obedience from things he suffered, and being perfected he became the source of eternal salvation to all those obeying him, designated by God a high priest in the order of Melchizedek.

RESPONSORY, in the Octave of Easter:
This is the day the Lord has made;
let us rejoice and be glad.

RESPONSORY, Easter Weeks 2 to 6:
The disciples rejoiced...
...*alleluia, alleluia.*
When they saw the risen Lord...

READING, After Ascension: **GALATIANS** 5:16,22-23,25

Walk in the spirit and you will not act on the desires of the flesh. The fruit of the spirit is love, joy, peace, patience, kindness, goodness, faith, meekness, and self-control. Against such things there is no law. We live in the Spirit; in the Spirit also let us walk.

RESPONSORY, After Ascension: Jn 17:20 or 26??
The Holy Spirit is the Paraclete...
...*alleluia, alleluia.*
Who will teach you all things...

GOSPEL CANTICLE (**Canticle of Mary**) see page 523.

Ant., Easter Week I — The disciple whom Jesus loved said:
It is the Lord, alleluia.

Antiphon, Week II — To destroy the power of hell
Christ died upon the cross;
clothed in strength and glory,
on the third day he triumphed over death;
alleluia.

Antiphon, Week III — Our crucified and risen Lord
has redeemed us,
alleluia.

Antiphon, Week IV — The Good Shepherd
laid down his life for his sheep,
alleluia.

Antiphon, Week V — To lay down your life for your friends,
there is no greater love;
alleluia.

Antiphon, Week VI — To those who ask him,
the Father will send the Holy Spirit,
alleluia.

Antiphon, Week VII — Together they persevered in prayer
with Mary, the mother of Jesus, alleluia.

EVENING PRAYER INTERCESSIONS AND CLOSING PRAYER, see page 523.

EASTER
SATURDAY MORNINGS

Je-sus, my Lord\, my God/, my all\;
How late, my Je-sus, have I sought.
You pour down rich\-es of/ your grace\;
How can I love you as I ought?
Je-sus, our Lord, we you a-dore!
Call us to love you more/ and more\.
Call us to love you more and more.

Je-sus, what could you have found/ in me\
That you have dealt so pa-tient-ly?
How great the joy\ that you/ have brought\,
So far ex-ceed-ing hope or thought!
Je-sus, our Lord, we you a-dore!
Call us to love you more/ and more\.
Call us to love you more and more.

Had I but Ma\-ry's sin/-less heart\
With which to love you, dear-est King;
O! with what bursts\ of fer/-vent praise\
Your good-ness, Je-sus, would I sing.
Sweet Sac-ra-ment, we you a-dore!
Call us to love you more/ and more\.
Call us to love you more and more.

Text: Henry A. Collins, 1854, altered; vs. 3 Frederick W. Faber, d. 1863, altered
Music: SWEET SACRAMENT, LM with refrain, *Romischkatholisches Gesanguchlein*, 1826

HINGE HOURS for LENT and EASTER

PSALMS &	WEEK I, go to page 127	WEEK V (Week I) pg. 206
CANTICLES	WEEK II, go to page 309	WEEK VI (Week II) pg. 309
	WEEK III, go to page 407	WEEK VII (Week III) pg. 407
	WEEK IV, go to page 503	

READING **ROMANS 14:7-9**

None of us lives to the self,
and no one dies for the self.
While alive, we live for the Lord;
if we die, we die for the Lord.
And so whether we live or we die, we are of the Lord.
For this Christ died and lived again,
that of both the dead and of the living
he might be Lord.

RESPONSORY, in the Octave of Easter:

This is the day the Lord has made;
let us rejoice and be glad.

RESPONSORY, Easter Weeks 2 through 7:

The Lord is risen from the tomb…
…*alleluia, alleluia.*
He hung upon the cross for us…

GOSPEL READING OF THE DAY (or use the **Canticle of Zechariah** from page 521)

Ant., Easter Week I
Mark 16:9-15

When Jesus had risen from the dead
on the morning after the sabbath,
he appeared first to Mary Magdalene,
from whom he had thrown seven demons,
alleluia.

Antiphon, Week II	Peace be with you; it is I, alleluia.
John 6:16-21	Do not be afraid, alleluia.

Antiphon, Week III	Simon Peter said:
John 6:60-69	Lord, to whom shall we go?
	You have the words of eternal life;
	and we believe and are convinced
	that you are the Christ, the Son of God,
	alleluia.

Antiphon, Week IV	And you will do greater things than these
John 14:7-14	for I am going to the Father,
	alleluia.

Antiphon, Week V	Christ died and rose from the dead
John 15:18-21	that he might be the Lord
	of the living and the dead,
	alleluia.

Antiphon, Week VI	I promise that the Father will give you
John 16:23b-28	anything you ask for in my name,
	alleluia.

Antiphon, Week VII	Know that I am with you always,
John 21:20-25	even to the end of the cosmos,
	alleluia.

MORNING PRAYER PETITIONS AND CLOSING PRAYER, see page 522.

EASTER
VIGILS OF SUNDAYS (Saturday Evenings)

At the Lamb's high feast we sing,
Praise to our vic-tor-ious King,
Who has washed us in the tide
Flow-ing from his pier-ced side;
Praise we him/, whose love div-ine
Gives his sa-cred blood for wine,
Gives his bod-y for the feast,
Christ the Vic-tim, Christ the Priest.

Where the Pas-chal blood is poured,
Death's dark an-gel sheathes his sword;
Is-rael's hosts tri-um-phant go
Through the wave that drowns the foe.
Praise we Christ/, whose blood was shed,
Pas-chal Vic-tim, Pas-chal Bread;
With sin-cer-i-ty and love
Eat we Man-na from a-bove.

Migh-ty Vic-tim from the sky,
Hell's fierce pow'rs be-neath you lie;
You have o-pened Par-a-dise,
That in you your saints may rise.
Hymns of glo/-ry and of praise,
Fa-ther now to you we raise;
Ris-en Lord, all praise to thee,
Ev-er with the Spir-it be.

Text: Author unknown, 6th Century?, translated by Robert Campbell, 1849, altered
Music: 77 77 D, SALZBURG; Jakob Hintze, 1678
Popular melody for: *Songs of Thankfulness and Praise*

EASTER - VIGILS OF SUNDAYS (Saturday Evenings)

PSALMS & CANTICLES	WEEK II, go to page 136	WEEK V (Week I) pg. 116
	WEEK III, go to page 318	WEEK VI (Week II) pg. 214
	WEEK IV, go to page 414	

READING, Before Ascension: **1 PETER 2:9-10**

You are a chosen race, a royal priesthood, a holy nation, a people belonging so you may tell out your having been called out of darkness into the marvellous light of God. Then you were not a people but now are people of God; then you saw no mercy, but now are shown mercy.

RESPONSORY, in the Octave of Easter:
> This is the day the Lord has made;
> let us rejoice and be glad.

RESPONSORY, Easter Weeks 3 to 6:
> The disciples rejoiced...
> ...*alleluia, alleluia.*
> When they saw the risen Lord...

GOSPEL CANTICLE (**Canticle of Mary**) see page 523.

Ant., Easter Week II After eight days, the doors being locked, the Lord came into their midst and said: Peace be with you, alleluia.

Antiphon, Week III Stay with us, Lord, for evening draws near and daylight is fading, alleluia.

HINGE HOURS for LENT and EASTER

Antiphon, Week IV I am the gate, says the Lord;
whoever enters through me will be saved
and find pasture, alleluia.

Antiphon, Week V I am the way, the truth, and the life;
all who come to the Father
come through me, alleluia.

Antiphon, Week VI I will ask the Father
and he will give you another Paraclete
to remain with you forever, alleluia.

EVENING PRAYER INTERCESSIONS AND CLOSING PRAYER, see page 523.

For Easter Sunday Mornings, Return to Page 60

VIGIL OF ASCENSION
Saturday Evening
Vigil of the Seventh Sunday of Easter

(for Easter Season)

Crown him with ma-ny crowns
The Lamb up-on his throne;
Hark how the heav'n-ly an-them\ drowns
All mu-sic but its own.
A-wake, my soul, and sing
Of him who died for thee
And hail him as your King of kings
Through all e-ter-ni-ty.

Crown him the Lord of Love.
Be-hold his hands and side,
Rich wounds, yet vis-ib-le a\-bove,
In beau-ty glo-ri-fied.
No an-gel in the sky
Can ful-ly bear that sight,
But down-ward bends his wond'-ring eye
At mys-te-ry so bright!

Crown him the Lord of Heav'n,
En-throned in worlds a-bove,
Crown him the King to whom is\ giv'n
The won-drous name of Love.
Crown him with ma-ny crowns
As thrones be-fore him fall;
Crown him, you kings, with ma-ny crowns
For he is King of all.

Text: From Revelation 19:12; Verses by Matthew Bridges, 1851, altered
Music: DIADEMATA, George J. Elvey, 1868

Antiphon	Alleluia, alleluia, alleluia.	***Psalm 61***
		page 318
Antiphon	When he came to us	**Psalm 113**
	Christ did not leave heaven;	page 319
	nor did he withdraw from us	
	when he went again into heaven.	*-St. Augustine*

EASTER - VIGIL OF ASCENSION

Antiphon — After he spoke to his disciples, the Lord Jesus ascended into heaven where he is seated at the right hand of the Father, alleluia. **Psalm 117** page 213

Antiphon — No one has ascended into heaven except the one who descended from heaven, the Son of Man, who is in heaven, alleluia. **Rev. 11&12** page 193

READING, Vigil of the Ascension: **EPHESIANS 2:4-6**

Being rich in mercy and because of loving us with much love even when we were dead in transgressions, God made us alive in Christ (by grace you are and have been saved) and raised us and seated us in the heavens with and in Christ Jesus.

RESPONSORY, Vigil of the Ascension: Ps. 47:6

God ascends to shouts of joy…
…*alleluia, alleluia.*
The Lord to the blast of trumpets…

GOSPEL CANTICLE (**Canticle of Mary**) see page 523.

Antiphon — Father, I have shown your name to the ones you have given me, and now I pray for them rather than for the cosmos, for I am coming to you, alleluia.

EVENING PRAYER INTERCESSIONS AND CLOSING PRAYER, see page 523.

ASCENSION MORNING
Seventh Sunday of Easter

(for Ascension)

Ho-ly Feast, you ho-ly day!
To be hal-lowed ev-er-more,
Day when Christ our Ris-en Lord,
Rose to hea-ven then to reign.
He who to/ a cross was nailed,
Now is ru-ler, Lord of all.
All you crea-tures of the earth
Sing the glo-ry of your God.

Dai-ly grows the love-li-ness
Blos-somed glo-ry so a-dorned.
Gates of hea-ven o-pen wide
Fling-ing her in-crease of light.
Je-sus, heal/-er of the world,
Light our minds, Re-deem-er great,
One be-got-ten Son of God,
Pray for us from God's right hand.

Text: Venantius Fortunatus, d. 609;
translated by Maurice F. Bell, *Hail Thee Festival Day*, 1906, altered
Music: 77 77 D, SALZBURG; Jakob Hintze, 1678
Popular melody for: *Songs of Thankfulness and Praise*

Antiphon The Lord God *Psalm 68*
ascended on high, page 353
leading captivity into captivity,
alleluia.

*Psalm 63, Daniel 3, & Psalm 149,
go to **Sunday Morning Week I**, page 128*

READING **HEBREWS 10:11-14**

Every other priest stands daily ministering and offering
often the same sacrifices, which can never take away sins.
Having offered the single sacrifice for all time,
this Christ has sat at the right hand of God, waiting
since until his enemies are put as a footstool of his feet,
for by one offering he has made perfect for all time
the ones being made holy.

RESPONSORY
Christ ascended into heaven…
…*alleluia, alleluia.*
He led captivity captive…

GOSPEL CANTICLE (**Canticle of Zechariah**) see page 521.

Antiphon I am ascending to my Father and your
Father, to my God and your God, alleluia.

MORNING PRAYER PETITIONS AND CLOSING PRAYER, see page 522.

ASCENSION EVENING

Seventh Sunday of Easter

O-pen the por-tals an-cient of the Lord;
The King of glo-ry en-ters by the Word.
Earth is the Lord's, and all that she con-tains;
Built by the Lord o'er seas and riv-er rains.
Who is the king of glo-ry, migh-ty One?
The Lord of hosts the king of glo-ry is.

Who may go up the moun-tain of the Lord?
The clean of hand with pu-ri-ty of heart.
They are the ones who seek the face of God
Who saves by jus-tice ev-'ry ho-ly place.
Who is the king of glo-ry, migh-ty One?
The Migh-ty Lord the king of glo-ry is.

O-pen the por-tals an-cient of the Lord;
The King of glo-ry en-ters by the Word.
Lift high, you gates, rise up you an-cient doors;
Wel-come your king and lov-ers of the Lord.
Who is the king of glo-ry, migh-ty One?
Lord Sab-a-oth the king of glo-ry is.

Text: Psalm 24, by Stephen J. Wolf, 2007, tribute to the priesthood of Alan Cunningham
Music: 10 10 10 10 10 10 UNDE ET MEMORES, William H. Monk, 1823-1899
Popular melody for: *Lord Who At The First Eucharist Did Pray*

Antiphon	Alleluia, alleluia, alleluia.	**Psalm 8**
		page 317

HINGE HOURS for LENT and EASTER

Antiphon	He ascended into heaven and is seated at the right hand of the Father, alleluia.	**Psalm 110** page 139
Antiphon	God ascends with shouts of joy, the Lord amid trumpets blasting, alleluia.	**Psalm 47** page 173
Antiphon	Now the Son of humanity has been glorified and God has been glorified in him, alleluia.	**Rev. 11&12** page 193

READING **1 PETER 3:18,21-22**

See Easter Thursday Evenings, page 88

RESPONSORY

I am ascending to my Father and your Father…
…*alleluia alleluia.*
To my God and your God…

GOSPEL CANTICLE (**Canticle of Mary**) see page 523.

Antiphon O Victor King, Lord of power and might,
you ascended in glory above the heavens.
Do not leave us orphans
but send us the Father's promised gift,
the Spirit of truth, alleluia.

EVENING PRAYER INTERCESSIONS AND CLOSING PRAYER, see page 523.

FOR WEEKDAYS AFTER THE ASCENSION, go to page 66

VIGIL OF PENTECOST
Saturday Evening

For all the saints who from their la-bors rest,
Who you by faith be-fore the world con-fess
Your name, O Je-sus, be for-ev\-er\ blest,
Al/-le\-lu-ia! Al//-le-lu-ia!

You were their rock, their for-tress and their might;
You, Lord, their cap-tain in the well-fought fight;
You, in the dark of night, their one\ true\ light.
Al/-le\-lu-ia! Al//-le-lu-ia!

O blest com-mu-nion, ho-ly and div-ine,
While yet we strug-gle, they in glo-ry shine;
Yet all are one in you, for all\ are\ thine.
Al/-le\-lu-ia! Al//-le-lu-ia!

So when there breaks a yet more glo-rious day;
The saints tri-umph-ant rise in bright a-rray;
The King of Glo-ry pass-es on the Way.
Al/-le\-lu-ia! Al//-le-lu-ia!

From earth's wide bounds, from o-cean's farth-est coast,
Through gates of pearl stream in the count-less host,
Sing-ing to Fa-ther, Son, and Ho\-ly\ Ghost:
Al/-le\-lu-ia! Al//-le-lu-ia!

Text: William H. How, 1864, altered
Music: 10 10 10 SINE NOMINE with alleluias, by Ralph Vaughan Williams, 1906

HINGE HOURS for LENT and EASTER

Antiphon	Alleluia, alleluia, alleluia.	***Psalm 34***
		page 214
Antiphon	On the day of Pentecost they had all gathered together in one place, alleluia.	**Psalm 113**
		page 319
Antiphon	Tongues as of fire appeared before the apostles and the Holy Spirit came upon each of them, alleluia.	**Psalm 147**
		page 303
Antiphon	The Spirit who comes from the Father will glorify me, alleluia.	**Rev. 15:3b-4**
		page 205

READING **ROMANS 8:9-11**

See Easter - Thursday Mornings, page 85

RESPONSORY

The Holy Spirit is the Paraclete…
…*alleluia, alleluia.*
Who will teach you all things…

GOSPEL CANTICLE (**Canticle of Mary**) see page 523.

Antiphon Come, Holy Spirit, fill up believing hearts
and set them on fire with your love.
Though speaking many different languages,
you united the nations
in professing the same faith, alleluia.

EVENING PRAYER INTERCESSIONS AND CLOSING PRAYER, see page 523.

PENTECOST
SUNDAY MORNING

(for Pentecost)

Ho-ly Feast, you ho-ly day!
To be hal-lowed ev-er-more,
Day the Ho-ly Spir-it came
Full of grace in-to the world.
Bright and shi/-ning like the fire
On those wait-ing for the Lord,
Sud-den swift, the Spir-it fell,
Whom Christ Je-sus did fore-tell.

From the Son and Fa-ther come
Sev'n-fold gifts of mys-ter-y
Pour-ing on all hu-man souls
Rich-es in-fin-ite di-vine.
Ho-ly Spir-it of life and pow'r,
Flow in us, O sac-red font,
Light that light-ens up us all,
Breath of God's vo-ca-tion call.

Text: Venantius Fortunatus, d. 609; translated by Maurice F. Bell,
Hail Thee Festival Day, 1906, altered
Music: 77 77 D, SALZBURG; Jakob Hintze, 1678
Popular melody for: *Songs of Thankfulness and Praise*

Antiphon	Send forth your Spirit	***Psalm 104***
	and they shall be created;	page 226
	and you will renew	
	the face of the earth, alleluia.	

Psalm 63, Daniel 3, and Psalm 149, go to Sunday Morning Week I, page 128

READING **ACTS 5:30-32**

The God of our ancestors raised Jesus,
whom you killed by hanging on a tree. This one
is exalted to the right hand of God as ruler and savior
to give conversion to Israel and forgiveness of sins.
Of these things we are witnesses with the Holy Spirit
given by God to the obedient.

RESPONSORY

> All were filled with the Holy Spirit…
> …*alleluia, alleluia.*
> They began to speak…

GOSPEL CANTICLE (**Canticle of Zechariah**) see page 521.

Antiphon Receive the Holy Spirit;
 whose sins you forgive are forgiven them,
 alleluia.

MORNING PRAYER PETITIONS AND CLOSING PRAYER, see page 522.

PENTECOST
SUNDAY EVENING

Come/, **Cre**\-**a-tor**\ **Spir**/-**it**,
Souls\ of yours, now\ vis/-it:
Fill/ with grace\ be\-yond/ na/-ture
All/ these hearts\ that you have cre-a\-ted.

You/ have the name Com-fort-Par-a-clete,
The high-est gift of our giv-ing God,
Font/ of life and fire and lov-ing char-i-ty,
Font/ of spir-it-u-al a\-noin\-ting.

You/ sev\-en-fold\ ho-ly gift,
Fing-er of the right\ hand of God,
You who were prom-ised du-ly by the Fa/-ther,
En-rich our throats\ to speak words\ you want heard.

Kin-dle light in our minds, your ho-ly light,
Send and in-fuse in-to hearts your love.
Hu-man weak-ness dwell-ing in hu-man bod/-ies
Your pow-er streng-thens in-to per-pet-u-i-ty.

Spir-it, drive a-way ev-'ry en-mit-y
Bring-ing now peace ev-er-last/-ing.
With you, our faith-ful lead-er pro/-ceed/-ing
May we a-void\ all harm/ and e\-vil.

Spir-it, come and fill all your faith-ful hearts,
Set fire in us your con-firm-ing love,
Send forth your Spir-it Breath to all cre-a/-tion
And/ the face of the earth you\ will re-new.

Give us Wis-dom to seek the face of God,
Un-der-stand-ing of bap-tis-mal grace,
Right Judg-ment to dis-cern Christ's call in free/-dom,
Give/ us grace\ to know/ the Fa-ther's will.

Give us Cour-age for the vo-ca-tion "yes!",
Know-ledge of what Je-sus teach/-es,
Rev-er-ence for the ways of our good Fa/-ther;
Give/ us Strength\ to do/ the will of God.

In your pres-ence, won-der and awe give us;
Our wit-ness giv'n to the Ris-en Son,
May it be pleas\-ing\ to the Fa/-ther
And help you, Spir-it, re-new all the face of earth.

Through you may we know our\ Fa/-ther,
And bet-ter know our Lord Je-sus Christ.
You are the Spir-it of the Fa-ther and the Son;
May/ our trust be in you for all time to come.

Glo-ry be to God/ the Fa/-ther,
To the Son Res-u\-rec/-ted,
And to the Ho-ly Spir-it, Com-fort-Par-a-clete,
For gen-er-a-tions and gen-er\-a\-tion.
A/\-men/.

Text: verses 1-5,10-11 from the Latin by Rabanus Mauras, d. 856, Veni Creator Spiritus,
with assistance from the literal translation © 2008 by Bard Suverkrop-IPA Source, LLC
verses 6-9 from an Easter Prayer for Vocations by Stephen J. Wolf, 2011
Music: VENI CREATOR SPIRITUS, LM; Mode VIII

Antiphon	Alleluia, alleluia, alleluia.	***Psalm 76***
		page 432

Antiphon	Seek the things that are above where Christ is seated at God's right hand, alleluia.	**Psalm 110** page 139
Antiphon	In the darkness he dawns; a light for upright hearts, alleluia.	**Psalm 112** page 433
Antiphon	Alleluia, salvation, glory and power to our God, alleluia.	**Rev. 19:**1-7 page 436

READING   **EPHESIANS 4:3-6**

Be eager to keep the unity of the Spirit in the bond of peace. There is one body and one Spirit, as also you were called in one hope of your calling, one Lord, one faith, one baptism, one God and Father of all, over all and through all and in all.

RESPONSORY

The Spirit of the Lord has filled the whole world...
...*alleluia alleluia.*
Sustaining all creation and knowing every word spoken...

GOSPEL CANTICLE (**Canticle of Mary**) see page 523.

Antiphon	The Holy Spirit appeared before the apostles in tongues of fire, gave them spiritual gifts, and sent them to preach to the whole world, alleluia.

EVENING PRAYER INTERCESSIONS AND CLOSING PRAYER, see page 523.

HINGE HOURS Psalter

*Lent begins on Ash Wednesday,
forty-six days prior to Easter Sunday.*

*Easter Day is the Sunday
after the first full moon after the vernal equinox.*

*Evening Prayer On Pentecost Sunday concludes the Season of Easter.
Ordinary Time resumes on the following day.*

WEEK I
VIGIL OF SUNDAY
(Saturday Evening)

PSALM 4

Antiphon for Lent   My God, be merciful to me
and hear my prayer.

Easter   Alleluia, alleluia, alleluia.

When I call, answer me, righteous God.
From distress you give me relief.
Be merciful to me and hear my prayer.

Until when, human, will you shame the glory?
Until when will you love delusion and seek the lie?
Know that Adonai set apart the faithful for Adonai
and will hear when I call.

When you are angry, do not sin.
Search in your heart and on your bed, and be silent.
Offer sacrifices of goodness, and trust Adonai.

Many are asking,
"Who can show us good?
  Adonai, let the light of your faces shine upon us."

HINGE HOURS for LENT and EASTER   117

You put joy in my heart, more joy
than when their grain and new wine abound.
In the peace of God's face I will lie down and sleep,
for you alone, Adonai, make me dwell in safety.

Traditional Doxology   *Glory to the Father and to the Son*
                              and to the Holy Spirit,
                          As it was in the beginning, is now,
                              and will be forever. Amen.

The antiphon is traditionally repeated: My God, be merciful to me
                                             and hear my prayer.

        Easter   Alleluia, alleluia, alleluia.

PSALM 141

Lent, 1st Sunday

Lord God,
we ask you to receive us and be pleased
with the sacrifice we offer you this day
with humble and contrite hearts.

Lent, 5th Sunday

I will place my law in their hearts;
I will be their God,
and they will be my people.

Easter, 5th Sunday

Like the evening offering
my hands rise up in prayer
to you, O Lord, alleluia.

WEEK I - VIGIL OF SUNDAY (Saturday Evening)

PSALM 141

Adonai, I call to you; be quick to come to me.
Hear my voice when I call to you.
May my prayer of incense be set before you,
lifting my hands in evening sacrifice.

Set guard, Adonai, over my mouth.
Keep watch over the door of my lips.
Let my heart not be drawn to evil matter,
to join in wicked deeds with their doers
or to eat of their delicacies.

Let the just person strike me with kindness
and rebuke me with oil on my head;
my head will not refuse this,
my prayer is ever against evil deeds.

Their rulers will drop over cliff edge;
they will learn that my words were well spoken:
"As a plower breaks up the earth
  our bones were scattered at the mouth of Sheol."

But on you, Lord Adonai, are my eyes,
and in you I take refuge;
my self you do not give over to death.

Keep me from the hands of the snares
and from the traps of those doing evil.
When they fall together into their nets,
keep me in safety.

Glory…

Repeat antiphon.

PSALM 142

Lent, 1st Sunday
Call upon the Lord who will hear you
and to your cries will answer: Here I am.

Lent, 5th Sunday
I count as loss everything but the surpassing
worth of knowing Christ Jesus my Lord.

Easter, 5th Sunday
You have led me forth from my prison,
that I may give praise to your name, alleluia.

My voice cries to Adonai;
my voice asks for mercy from Adonai,
before whom I pour out my complaint,
before whom I tell my trouble.
When my spirit grows faint within me
then you know my way.

In the path where I walk they hid a snare for me.
Look right and see: the one with concern for me
has fled away from me for refuge;
there is no one who cares for my life.

I cry to you, Adonai, and say you are my refuge,
my portion in the land of the living.
Listen, El, to my cry, for I am in desperate need.

Rescue me from the strong ones pursuing me;
set my self free from prison to praise your name.
The righteous ones will gather about me
because you will be good to me.

Glory…

Repeat antiphon.

PHILIPPIANS 2:6-11

Lent, 1st Sunday
Christ died for our sins, the innocent
for the guilty to bring us back to God.
In the body he was put to death,
but in the spirit he was raised to life.

Lent, 5th Sunday
Although he was the Son of God,
Christ learned obedience through suffering.

Easter, 5th Sunday
The Son of God learned obedience through
suffering and became for all who obey him
the source of eternal salvation, alleluia.

Christ Jesus, subsisting in the form of God,
did not deem equality with God something to grab,
but emptied himself, taking the form of a slave,
becoming in human likeness.

And being found in human fashion,
he humbled himself,
becoming obedient until death,
and death on a cross.

And so God highly exalted him,
and gave to him the name above every name,
that in the name of Jesus every knee should bend,
of heavenly beings and earthly beings,
and beings under the earth;

And every tongue acknowledge
to the glory of God the Father
that Jesus Christ is Lord.

Glory...   Repeat antiphon.

WEEK I
RESURRECTION VIGIL

ISAIAH 33:2-10

Antiphon   In Christ who rose from the dead
　　　　　　our hope of resurrection dawned.

Adonai, be gracious to us; for you we long;
be our strength in the mornings
and our salvation in times of distress.

At the voice of thunder peoples flee,
at your rising the nations scatter
and your plunder is harvested
as a harvesting by the young locust,
like a swarm of locusts pouncing.

Dwelling on the height, exalted is Adonai,
who will fill Zion with justice and righteousness,
who will be the sure foundation for your times,
the rich store of salvation, wisdom and knowledge;
fear of Adonai is the treasure.

Look! Their brave ones cry in the street,
envoys of peace in bitter weeping.
Highways are deserted, road travel ceases,
treaties are broken, cities are despised,
and no one is respected.

The land mourns and wastes away,
Lebanon withers in shame.
The Sharon is like the Arabah;
dropping are Bashan and Carmel.
"Now I will arise," says Adonai,
"Now I will be exalted,
 now I will be lifted up."

Glory…

Repeat antiphon.

FOR SUNDAYS OF WEEK 1

MATTHEW 28:1-11,16-20

After the Sabbath,
the first day of the week drawing on,
Mary the Magdalene and the other Mary
came to view the grave.
And behold a great earthquake occurred,
for an angel of the Lord
descended out of heaven
and approaching
rolled away the stone and sat upon it.
His appearance was as lightning,
and his dress white as snow.
The guards, shaken from fear of him, became as dead.
The angel answered the women, saying,
"Fear you not;
for I know that you seek Jesus,
the one crucified.

He is not here,
for he was raised as he said.
Come see the place where he lay.
Go quickly and tell his disciples
that he was raised from the dead,
and behold he goes before you to Galilee.
There you will see him.
Behold, I have told you."
Going away from the tomb quickly,
with fear and great joy,
they ran to announce to his disciples.
Behold, Jesus met them saying, "Rejoice."
Approaching they held of his feet and worshipped him.
Jesus said to them,
"Fear you not;
go announce to my brothers
that they may go away into Galilee,
and there they will see me."
As they were going,
behold some of the guard coming into the city
announced to the chief priests
all the things that happened...
So the eleven disciples went to Galilee,
to the mountain where Jesus appointed them,
and seeing him they worshipped,
but some doubted.
And approaching, Jesus talked with them saying,
"All authority in heaven and on earth
has been given to me.

WEEK 1 - SUNDAY RESURRECTION VIGIL 125

Go therefore, you disciples, to all the nations,
baptizing them in the name of the Father
and of the Son and of the Holy Spirit,
teaching them to observe all things
whatever I gave command to you.
And behold I am with you all the days
until the completion of the eon."

•

FOR SUNDAYS OF WEEK 5

LUKE 24:35-53

They related the things on the way
and how he was known by them
in the breaking of the bread.
These things being said by them,
he stood in their midst.
But becoming scared and terrified,
they thought they beheld a spirit.
He said to them,
"Why have you been and are being troubled?
And why do thoughts come up in your heart?
See my hands and my feet, that I am myself.
Feel me and see,
because a spirit has no flesh or bones
as you behold me having."
And yet disbelieving from their joy and marvelling,
he said to them,
"Have you any food here?"

LUKE 24:35-53, continued

They handed to him part of a broiled fish,
and taking he ate before them.
He said to them,
"These my words I spoke to you while yet with you,
of the need to be fulfilled
of all the things written concerning me
in the law of Moses and the prophets and the psalms."
Then he opened up their mind
to understand the scriptures,
and said to them,
"Thus it has been written:
the Christ to suffer
and to rise again out of the dead on the third day,
and in his name a proclamation
of repentance unto forgiveness of sin,
to all the nations beginning from Jerusalem.
You are witnesses of these things.
And behold I send forth on you
the promise of my Father,
but sit in the city until you are
clothed out of the height with power."
He led them out to Bethany,
and lifting up his hands he blessed them.
And it came to pass
that while he blessed them
he withdrew from them.
They returned to Jerusalem with great joy,
and were constantly in the temple blessing God.

•

WEEK I
SUNDAY MORNING

PSALM 1

Antiphon for Lent See how the cross of the Lord
stands revealed as the tree of life.

Easter The Lord is risen, alleluia.

Blessings are on the human being
who stands not in wicked counsel,
who walks not on the path of sinners,
who sits not in the seat of mockers,
but rather delights in the law of Adonai
and meditates on it by day and by night.

This blessed one is like a tree
being planted by streams of water
which yields fruit in the season
and its leaf withers not
and prosperity finds what this one does.

Not so those who do wicked,
but rather like the chaff blown in the wind
those who do wicked
will be unable to stand in the judgment
nor sinners in the assembly of the righteous.

Adonai watches over the way of righteous ones
and wicked ways will perish.

Glory... Repeat antiphon.

PSALM 63:1-8

Lent, 1st Sunday

I will praise you all my life, O Lord;
in your name I will lift up my hands.

Lent, 5th Sunday

My God, you have become my help.

Easter Sunday
thru 2nd Sunday

The splendor of Christ
risen from the dead
has shone on the people
redeemed by his blood, alleluia.

Easter, 5th Sunday

Whoever thirsts will drink freely
of life-giving water, alleluia.

Ascension

Men of Galilee,
why are you looking up into the sky?
Jesus who has been taken up into heaven
will return in the same way, alleluia.

Pentecost Sunday

O Lord, how good and gentle
is your Spirit in us, alleluia.

PSALM 63:1-8

God, you are my God; you I earnestly seek.
My soul, she thirsts for you,
my body, he longs for you,
as in a land with no water, dry and weary.

So in the sanctuary I saw you,
beheld you in your power and glory.
Your love is better than life itself;
my lips will glorify you.

So I will praise you in all the ways I am alive;
in your name I will lift up my hands.
As with fatness and richness,
my soul will be satisfied;
with singing lips my mouth will sing praise.

When I remember you on my bed,
through night watches I think of you,
you who are my help;
then in the shadow of your wings I sing.
My very self stays close to you;
your right hand upholds me.

Glory…

Repeat antiphon.

DANIEL 3:57-90

Lent, 1st Sunday

Sing a hymn of praise to our God;
praise God above all forever.

Lent, 5th Sunday

Free us by your wonderful works;
deliver us from the power of death.

Easter Sunday
thru 2nd Sunday

Our Redeemer has risen from the tomb;
let us sing a hymn of praise
to the Lord our God, alleluia.

Easter, 5th Sunday

Worship the Lord
who made the heavens and the earth,
springs of water and the mighty sea, alleluia.

Ascension

Give glory to the King of kings,
sing praise to God, alleluia.

Pentecost Sunday

Let streams and rivers
and all creatures that live in the waters
sing praise to God, alleluia.

DANIEL 3:57-90

Bless the Lord, all you works of the Lord,
exalt and sing praise to forever.
Angels of the Lord, bless the Lord,
You heavens, bless the Lord,
All you waters above the heavens, bless the Lord,
All you powers, bless the Lord,
Sun and moon, bless the Lord,
Stars of heaven, bless the Lord.

All you rain and dew, bless the Lord,
All you winds, bless the Lord,
You fire and heat, bless the Lord,
You ice and cold, bless the Lord,
You dews and falling snows, bless the Lord,
You snows and frosts, bless the Lord,
You nights and days, bless the Lord,
You light and darkness, bless the Lord,
You lightning and clouds, bless the Lord.

Let the earth bless the Lord,
exalt and sing praise to forever.
You mountains and hills, bless the Lord,
All things growing in the ground, bless the Lord,
You seas and rivers, bless the Lord,
You springs and rain, bless the Lord,
You sea monsters and all swimmers, bless the Lord,
All you birds of the air, bless the Lord,
All you wild beasts and cattle, bless the Lord,
You sons and daughters, bless the Lord.

DANIEL 3:57-90, continued

O Israel, bless the Lord,
exalt and sing praise to forever.
You priests of the Lord, bless the Lord,
You servants of the Lord, bless the Lord,
You spirits and souls of the just, bless the Lord,
You holy and humble in heart, bless the Lord,
Hananiah, Azariah, and Mishael, bless the Lord,
exalt and sing praise to forever...

Give thanks to the Lord, who is good,
whose mercy endures to forever.
Bless the God of "gods"
all you who worship the Lord;
sing praise and give thanks to the One God
whose mercy endures to forever.

(*No doxology*)

Lent, 1st Sunday	Sing a hymn of praise to our God; praise God above all forever.
Lent, 5th Sunday	Free us by your wonderful works; deliver us from the power of death.

WEEK I - SUNDAY MORNING 133

Easter Sunday
thru 2nd Sunday

Our Redeemer has risen from the tomb;
let us sing a hymn of praise
to the Lord our God, alleluia.

Easter, 5th Sunday

Worship the Lord
who made the heavens and the earth,
springs of water and the mighty sea, alleluia.

Ascension

Give glory to the King of kings,
sing praise to God, alleluia.

Pentecost Sunday

Let streams and rivers
and all creatures that live in the waters
sing praise to God, alleluia.

PSALM 149:1-6,9c

Lent, 1st Sunday
The Lord takes delight in his people,
crowning the humble with salvation.

Lent, 5th Sunday
The hour has come
for the Son of Man to be glorified.

Easter Sunday
thru 2nd Sunday
Alleluia,
the Lord is risen as he promised,
alleluia.

Easter, 5th Sunday
The saints will rejoice in glory, alleluia.

Ascension
As they watched, he was lifted up, and
a cloud took him from their sight, alleluia.

Pentecost Sunday
The apostles preached in different tongues
and proclaimed the great works of God,
alleluia.

PSALM 149:1-6,9c

Praise Adonai!

Sing to Adonai a new song,
praise in the assembly of saints.
Let Israel rejoice in their Maker,
let the people of Zion be glad in their King.

Let them praise the name
with dance, tambourine and harp.
Let them make music for Adonai
who delights in Adonai's people.

Adonai crowns humble ones with salvation.
Let the saints rejoice in honor,
Let them sing for joy on their beds...

Praise Adonai!

Glory...

Repeat antiphon.

WEEK I
SUNDAY EVENING

PSALM 91

Antiphon for Lent Have no fear of terror at night;
in the shadow of the Almighty, find rest.

Easter Alleluia, alleluia, alleluia.

One who dwells in the shelter of Elyon,
in the shadow of Shaddai, will find rest.
I will say of Adonai, my refuge, my fortress:
in my God do I trust.

Surely the Lord will save you
from fowler snare, from deadly pestilence.
With the feather of the Lord you will be covered,
and under those wings you will find refuge,
shield and rampart, the faithfulness of the Lord.

You will have no fear of terror at night
nor of arrows flying by day,
of pestilence stalking in the darkness,
nor of plague that destroys at midday.

A thousand may fall at your side,
and ten thousand at your right hand;
near to you they will not come.

Observe with your eyes, simply watch;
punishment of wicked ones you will see.
Make Adonai, who is my refuge,
make Elyon your dwelling.

Harm will not befall you,
nor will disaster come near your tent.
God's own Angels, the Lord will command
to guard you in all of your ways.

In their hands they will lift you up;
your foot will not strike against the stone.
Upon lion and cobra you will tread,
you will trample the great lion and serpent.

"Because you love me, I will rescue you,
 I will protect all who acknowledge my Name.
 You will call upon me and I will answer.
 I am with you in trouble;
 I will deliver you and honor you.

 In length of days I will satisfy you,
 and show you my salvation."

Glory…

Antiphon for Lent   Have no fear of terror at night;
in the shadow of the Almighty, find rest.

Easter   Alleluia, alleluia, alleluia.

PSALM 110:1-6a,7

Lent, 1st Sunday
Worship your Lord;
serve your God alone.

Lent, 5th Sunday
As the serpent was lifted up in the desert,
so the Son of Man must be lifted up.

Easter Sunday
thru 2nd Sunday
Mary Magdalene and the other Mary
came to see the Lord's tomb,
alleluia.

Easter, 5th Sunday
The Lord is risen
and is seated at the right hand of God,
alleluia.

PSALM 110:1-6a,7

Adonai said to my Lord:
"Sit at my right hand
 until I make enmity as a footstool for your feet."

A scepter of your might
Adonai will extend from Zion,
and rule in the midst of enmity!

Your troops are willing on the day of your battle.
In majesties of holiness from the womb of the dawn
to you is the dew of your youth.
Adonai swore and this mind will not change,
"You are a priest to forever
 in the order of Melchizedek."

The Lord is at your right hand
and will crush kings on the day of wrath,
will judge the nations...,
and will drink from a brook on the way
with head lifted up because of all this.

Glory...

Repeat antiphon.

PSALM 114

Lent, 1st Sunday
This is the time to win God's favor,
a good and acceptable day to be saved.

Lent, 5th Sunday
The Lord Sabaoth protects us,
sets us free,
and guides us,
saving his people.

Easter Sunday
thru 2nd Sunday
Come and see the place
where the Lord was buried,
alleluia.

Easter, 5th Sunday
He has rescued us
from the power of darkness
and has brought us
into the kingdom of his Son,
alleluia.

PSALM 114

When Israel came out from Egypt,
the house of Jacob
free from people of another tongue,
Judah became as God's sanctuary,
and Israel God's dominion.

The sea looked and fled, the Jordan turned back.
The mountains skipped like rams
and hills like a flock of lambs.

What to you, sea, that you fled?
Jordan, that you turned back?
Mountains, that you skipped like rams?
You hills, like a flock of lambs?

Tremble, earth, at the presences of the Lord!
Tremble at the presences of the God of Jacob,
the one turning the rock into pools of waters,
hard rock into springs of waters.

Glory...

Repeat antiphon.

(Easter) REVELATION 19:1b,2a,5b,6b,7

Easter Sunday Jesus said: Be not afraid.
thru 2nd Sunday Go and tell my brothers and sisters
to set out for Galilee;
there they will see me, alleluia.

Easter, 5th Sunday Alleluia, our God is king;
glory and praise to our God, alleluia.

Alleluia! Praise the Lord!
Salvation and glory and power are to our God,
whose judgments are true and just.

Alleluia! Praise the Lord!
Praise our God, all you slaves of the Lord,
you small and you great, who hold God in awe.

Alleluia! Praise the Lord!
The Lord is reigning, our God, the Almighty.
Let us rejoice and let us exult,
and we will give the glory to the Lord.

Alleluia! Praise the Lord!
The day has come
for the marriage of the Lamb,
and the bride has prepared herself.

Glory...

Repeat antiphon.

(Lent) 1 **PETER** 2:21-24

Lent, 1st Sunday
Now we must go up to Jerusalem,
where all that has been written
about the Son of humanity will be fulfilled.

Lent, 5th Sunday
He was pierced for our offenses
and burdened with our sins;
by his wounds we are healed.

To this you were called,
for indeed Christ suffered on behalf of you,
leaving to you an example to follow in his steps:

He did not sin, nor was guile found in his mouth;
he was reviled and did not revile in return;
suffering he did not threaten,
but delivered himself to the one judging justly.

Our sins he carried in his body up onto the tree,
that dying to sins, we might live for justice.
By his bruises, you are cured.

Glory…

Repeat antiphon.

***During the Octave of Easter**,*
through the 2nd Sunday of Easter,
Morning Prayer and Evening Prayer Psalms and Canticles
are from Sunday, Week I; page 127

WEEK I
MONDAY MORNING

PSALM 9

Antiphon
The Lord is a refuge for the oppressed,
a stronghold in times of trouble.
(alleluia)

I will praise Adonai with all my heart;
I will tell of all the wonderful things.
I will be glad and rejoice in you,
I will sing praise to your name, Most High.

When enmity turns back
it stumbles before you
for you upheld my right and my cause;
you sat on the throne judging justly.

You rebuked nations, you destroyed wicked ways;
their name you blotted out to forever and ever.
Enmity is overtaken by endless ruin;
cities are uprooted and their memories perish.

Adonai reigns to forever,
set up on the throne for judgment
to judge the world in righteousness
and to govern peoples with justice.

Adonai is the refuge for the oppressed,
the stronghold in times of trouble.
Those who know your name will trust in you,
for you have never forsaken seekers of Adonai.

Sing praise to Adonai, enthroned in Zion.
Proclaim the deeds among the nations
for the One who can avenge bloodshed remembers
and does not ignore the cry of the afflicted.

Have mercy on me, Adonai,
and see the persecution by enmity.
Lift me up from the gates of death
that I may declare all of your praises
in the gates of your daughter Zion.
I will rejoice in your salvation.

Nations fell into the pit they dug;
in the net that they hid are their own feet caught.
Adonai is known in justice;
wicked ways are ensnared in their handiwork.

The nations forgetting God return to Sheol,
but the needy will not be forgotten
nor will the hope of the afflicted ever perish.

Arise Adonai; let not the human triumph.
Let the nations be judged in your presences.
Strike the nations, Adonai,
and let them know their humanity.

Glory...

Antiphon   The Lord is a refuge for the oppressed,
a stronghold in times of trouble. (alleluia)

PSALM 5

Antiphon for Lent   Lord, you hear my morning voice;
with my morning request before you, I wait.

Easter   All those who love your name
will rejoice in you, alleluia.

Give ear to my words, Adonai;
consider my sighing.
Listen to the sound of my cry for help,
for to you I pray, my King and my God.

Hear, Adonai, my morning voice;
with my morning request before you, I wait.

You are not pleased with evil,
nor can the doer of evil dwell with you.
The arrogant cannot stand before your eyes.
You hate when wrong is done, you destroy lies,
you abhor bloodshed and deceit.

By the greatness of your mercy, Adonai,
I will come into your house,
I will bow toward your holy temple in reverence.

Lead me in your justice, Adonai;
because of enmity
make straight before me your way.

Their mouth is not to be trusted,
their heart is destruction,
their throat an open grave,
and their tongue speaks deceit.

If you, God, declare them guilty
let their fall be by their intrigue;
let them be banished if they have sinned,
if they have rebelled against you.

But let all who take refuge in you be glad;
let them sing for joy forever.
You spread protection over them
that they may rejoice in you and love your name.

You bless the righteous, Adonai,
surrounding them with favor as a shield.

<small>Glory…</small>

<small>Antiphon for Lent</small> Lord, you hear my morning voice;
with my morning request before you, I wait.

<small>Easter</small> All those who love your name
will rejoice in you, alleluia.

1 CHRONICLES 29:10b-13

<small>Antiphon for Lent</small> Now, our God,
we praise your name and your glory.

<small>Easter</small> Yours is the kingdom, Lord;
you rule over all the rulers, alleluia.

Praise be to you, Adonai, God of Israel,
our Father from everlasting to everlasting.

1 CHRONICLES 29:10b-13, continued

To you, Adonai, are the greatness and power
and glory and majesty and splendor
for all in the heavens and on the earth.

To you, Adonai, are the kingdom
and exaltation as head over all,
and wealth and honor from before you.

And you rule over all in your hand,
strength and power in your hand,
to exalt and give strength to all.

Now, our God, we give thanks to you
and praise your name and your glory.

Glory…

Antiphon for Lent　Now, our God,
we praise your name and your glory.

Easter　Yours is the kingdom, Lord;
you rule over all the rulers, alleluia.

PSALM 29

Antiphon for Lent　Worship the Lord in the holy splendor.

Easter　The Lord is enthroned as king forever, alleluia.

Ascribe to Adonai, mighty ones.
Ascribe to Adonai glory and strength.
Ascribe to Adonai the glory of the name.
Worship Adonai in holy splendor.

The voice of Adonai over the waters,
the God of glory thunders.
Adonai over mighty waters,
the voice of Adonai in power,
the voice of Adonai in majesty,
the voice of Adonai breaking cedars,

Adonai breaks the cedars of Lebanon
and makes Lebanon skip like a calf
and Sirion like the son of a wild ox.

The voice of Adonai strikes flashes of lightning,
the voice of Adonai shakes the desert,
Adonai shakes the desert of Kadesh.

The voice of Adonai makes the deer give birth
and strips the forests bare,
and all in the temple cry, "glory."
Adonai sits over the flood
and King Adonai is enthroned to forever.

Adonai gives strength to the people;
Adonai blesses the people with peace.

Glory…

Antiphon for Lent   Worship the Lord in the holy splendor.

Easter   The Lord is enthroned as king forever, alleluia.

WEEK I
MONDAY EVENING

PSALM 7

Antiphon for Lent   Lord, my God, save me;
I take refuge in you.

Easter   Alleluia, alleluia, alleluia.

My God, Adonai, in you I take refuge;
save me and deliver me from all who pursue me.
Like lions they want to tear me up,
rip my self to pieces with no one to rescue me.

My God, Adonai, if I deserve this,
if there is guilt on my hands,
if I did wrong to one at peace with me
or if I robbed without cause from an enemy,
then let that one pursue my self
and overtake my life
and trample my honor to the ground;
let that one put me to sleep in the dust.

Arise, Adonai, rise up in your anger
against the rages of enmity.
Awake, my God, and decree your justice
and let the assembly of peoples surround you;
rule over us from the height.
Let Adonai be the judge of the peoples.

Judge me, Adonai, as you judge me in justice,
as you judge my integrity, Most High.
May violence end now and the righteous be secure;
search our minds and hearts, righteous God.
My shield, God Most High, saves the upright heart,
and judges each day with justice, threatening wrath.

If none repent, they will sharpen their sword
and bend their bow with string and make ready
with weapons of death and flaming arrows.
See, trouble is conceived and evil is pregnant,
then comes to birth disillusionment.

They dig holes and scoop them out
but fall into the pits they made.
Their trouble recoils on their heads;
on their heads their violence makes landing.

I give thanks for Adonai's righteousness
and sing praise to the name of Most High Adonai.

Glory...

Antiphon for Lent	Lord, my God, save me; I take refuge in you.
Easter	Alleluia, alleluia, alleluia.

PSALM 11

Antiphon for Lent   Blessed are you poor,
for yours is the kingdom of God.   Luke 6:20b

Easter   Have courage;
I have overcome the world,
alleluia.

In Adonai I take refuge.
How can you say to my self,
"Flee, bird, to your mountain

for look, doers of bad now bend their bow,
they set their arrow on the string
to shoot from the shadow at the upright of heart.
When the foundations are destroyed,
what can the righteous do?"

Adonai is in the holy temple,
on Adonai's throne in the heavens
with eyes observing, examining
the sons and daughters of humanity.

Adonai examines the righteous,
hating in the soul the love of violence,
will rain onto wicked ways coal and sulphur on fire
and scorching wind, the lot of their cup,

for righteous is Adonai, loving justice;
we will see the faces of the upright One.

Glory…

Repeat antiphon.

PSALM 15

Antiphon for Lent   Blessed are the clean of heart,
for they shall see God.   Matthew 5:8

Easter   This one will abide in your tent
and live on your holy mountain,
alleluia.

Adonai, who may dwell in your sanctuary?
Who may live on your holy hill?
One walking without blame, one doing the right,
speaking truth in that one's heart,

whose tongue does not slander,
who does no wrong to a neighbor,
who casts no slur on a mutual human,
in whose eyes vile acts are despised

while those who fear Adonai are honored,
whose sworn oath is not changed even to pain,
who lends money without usury,
and accepts no bribe against the innocent.

One faithful in these
will be unshaken to forever.

Glory...

Antiphon for Lent   Blessed are the clean of heart,
for they shall see God.   Matthew 5:8

Easter   This one will abide in your tent
and live on your holy mountain, alleluia.

EPHESIANS 1:3-10

Antiphon for Lent
God gives us a destiny
as adopted sons and daughters
through Jesus Christ himself.

Easter
When I am lifted up from the earth
I will draw all people to myself, alleluia.

Blessed be the God and Father
of our Lord Jesus Christ,
who has blessed us in Christ
with every spiritual blessing in the heavens.

God chose us in Christ
before the foundation of the world,
to be holy and free of blemish before him.

In love, God gave us a destiny:
as sons are adopted, through Jesus Christ himself,
in accord with the good pleasure of God's will
to the praise of the glory of grace
by which we are favored as God's beloved.

In Christ we have the redemption
through his blood, the forgiveness of sins,
in accord with the riches of his grace
which he made abound to us.

In all wisdom and intelligence
the mystery of God's will is made known to us
in accord with God's good pleasure and purpose:

A stewardship of the fullness of time,
heading up all things in Christ,
the things in the heavens and the things on earth.

<small>Glory…</small>

<small>Repeat antiphon.</small>

WEEK I
TUESDAY MORNING

PSALM 10

<small>Antiphon</small>   The Lord hears the desire of the afflicted,
defends the fatherless, and frees the oppressed.
(alleluia)

Why, Adonai, do you stand at far off
and hide in times of the trouble?
In arrogance doers of bad hunt the weak;
they are caught in schemes they devise.

Doers of badness boast of what their hearts crave,
blessing the greedy and reviling Adonai.
In pride they point their nose away
and seek God in none of their thoughts.

Their haughty ways prosper at all times,
your laws are kept at a distance,
and they sneer at all their enemies.

PSALM 10, continued

They say to themselves
"I will not be shaken, but happy,
  untroubled for generations to come."
Their mouths are full of curses and lies and threats,
trouble and bad things kept under their tongue.

They lie in wait to ambush villages and murder,
their secret eyes on the innocent victim.
They lie in wait to ambush like a lion,
undercover lying in wait to catch the helpless,
they catch and drag the helpless off in their nets.

The victims are crushed and collapse,
falling under their strength.
They say to themselves "El has forgotten,
  with faces covered, and sees nothing anymore."

Arise, Adonai! God, lift up your hand!
Do not forget the helpless ones.
For why do those doing bad revile God and say,
to themselves, "God will not call an accounting"?

But you do see trouble and grief,
and consider taking the matter in hand;
to you the victims commit themselves,
to you, the One helping the fatherless.

Stop the arm of the doer of badness;
call to account lest bad things be kept secret.
Adonai is King forever and ever;
the nations will perish from Adonai's land.

You hear, Adonai, the desire of the afflicted;
you encourage their heart and open your ear
to defend the fatherless and the oppressed.
May humanity repeat no terror on the earth.

Glory…

Antiphon   The Lord hears the desire of the afflicted,
defends the fatherless, and frees the oppressed.
(alleluia)

PSALM 24

Antiphon for Lent   The pure of heart with clean hands
ascend the hill of the Lord.

Easter   The one who came down from heaven
has ascended above all the heavens, alleluia.

The earth and everything,
the world and all who are alive are to Adonai,
who founded the earth on the seas
and established the earth on the waters.

Who may ascend to the hill of Adonai?
And who may stand in the holy place?
The clean of hand and pure of heart
who do not lift the soul to an idol
and do not swear by falsehood
will receive the blessing from Adonai
and vindication from the God who saves.

PSALM 24, continued

Such is the generation of ones who seek,
who seek your faces, God of Jacob.

Lift up your heads, you gates;
be lifted up you ancient doors,
that the King of glory may come in.

Who is this King of glory?
Adonai, strong and mighty,
Adonai, mighty of battle.

Lift up your heads, you gates;
lift up, you ancient doors,
that the King of glory may come in.

Who is this King of glory?
Adonai Sabaoth is the King of glory.

Glory…

Antiphon for Lent	The pure of heart with clean hands ascend the hill of the Lord.
Easter	The one who came down from heaven has ascended above all the heavens, alleluia.

TOBIT 13:1b-8

Antiphon for Lent	Blessed be God and the kingdom forever.
Easter	Keep this day as a festival day and give praise to the Lord, alleluia.

Blessed be God who lives forever
and the kingdom of our God,
who scourges but then has mercy,
casts down to the deepest grave
and brings up from the great abyss.
No one can escape this hand.

Israelites, acknowledge before the nations
God who has scattered you among them
and even there shown you great mercy.

Let God be exalted by every living being
because our Lord is our God,
our Father and God forever.

Though scourged for your iniquities,
mercy will be on you all;
you will be gathered from all the nations
among whom you have been scattered.

With all your heart and soul
turn with honesty to the Lord
who will turn the face to you and no longer hide.

See now what has been done for you,
and with full voice praise Adonai.
Bless the Lord of justice
and exalt the King of the ages.

In the land of my exile I acknowledge the Lord
and make known to a sinful nation
this power and majesty:
"Turn, you sinners, and do right before the Lord,
  who may look upon you with favor and mercy."

TOBIT 13:1b-8, continued

My God, I will exalt you
and rejoice in the King of Heaven.
Let all speak of this majesty
in Jerusalem with exaltation.

Glory...

Antiphon for Lent   Blessed be God and the kingdom forever.

Easter   Keep this day as a festival day
and give praise to the Lord, alleluia.

PSALM 33

Antiphon for Lent   The loyal heart will praise the Lord.

Easter   The mercy of the Lord fills the earth, alleluia.

Sing joyfully to Adonai, righteous ones,
for praise is fitting for the upright.

Praise Adonai with a harp,
make music on the lyre of ten.
Sing a new song with skill
and play with a shout of joy.

For right is the word of Adonai
and all the faithful deeds done.
Loving righteousness and justice,
the earth is full of Adonai's unfailing love.

The heavens were made by the word of Adonai
and all their hosts by the breath of this mouth,
as one gathers in a heap the waters of the sea,
as one puts into the deep of the storehouses.

Let all the earth, let them fear,
let all alive in the world revere Adonai
who spoke and it came to be,
who commanded and it stood firm.

Adonai foils the plans of the nations
and thwarts the purposes of peoples.
The plan of Adonai stands firm to forever,
heartfelt purpose to generation and generation.

PSALM 33, continued

Blessed is the nation for whom Adonai is God,
the people chosen for this inheritance.
From the heavens Adonai looks down and sees
all sons and daughters of Adam and Eve,

and from the place of dwelling watches
all those alive on the earth.
The one who formed our heart
considers all our deeds.

No king is saved by the size of an army;
no warrior escapes by greatness of strength.
The horse is a vain hope for deliverance;
despite greatness of strength it cannot save.

See the eye of Adonai on those who place
their fear and hope in the unfailing love
that delivers them from death
and keeps them alive in the famine.

Our being waits for Adonai,
who is our help and our shield,
in whom our heart rejoices,
the holy name in whom we trust.

Adonai, may you rest on us your unfailing love
even as we hope in you.

Glory…

Antiphon for Lent	The loyal heart will praise the Lord.
Easter	The mercy of the Lord fills the earth, alleluia.

WEEK I
TUESDAY EVENING

PSALM 14

Antiphon for Lent   If we say we have no sin,
we deceive ourselves;
if we confess our sins,
God is faithful and forgiving.   1 John 1:8,9

Easter   Alleluia, alleluia, alleluia.

The fool says in the heart, "There is no God."
They are corrupt, vile are their deeds;
no one is doing good.

Adonai looks down from the heavens
on sons and daughters of Adam and Eve
to see if one understands, if one is seeking God.

All turned aside together to corruption;
no one is doing good, not even one.

Will the doers of bad things never learn?
Devouring my people as they eat bread,
they do not call on Adonai.

There they are, in dread of dread,
for God is in the company of the righteous.
They frustrate the plans of the poor,
but in Adonai the poor find their refuge.

164 HINGE HOURS for LENT and EASTER

PSALM 14, continued

Who from Zion could bring the salvation of Israel?
When Adonai restores the fortune to the people,
let Jacob rejoice, let Israel be glad.

Glory...

Antiphon for Lent   If we say we have no sin,
we deceive ourselves;
if we confess our sins,
God is faithful and forgiving.   1 John 1:8,9

Easter   Alleluia, alleluia, alleluia.

PSALM 20

Antiphon for Lent — Now I know that the Lord saves
the Lord's own anointed.

Easter — Now the reign of our God has begun and
power is given to Christ, the anointed, alleluia.

May Adonai answer you on the day of distress.
May the name of the God of Jacob protect you,
send you help from the sanctuary,

support you from Zion,
remember all of your sacrifices,
accept your burnt offerings,
give to you as your heart desires,
and make all of your plans succeed.

We will shout for joy at your victory
and lift a banner in the name of our God;
may Adonai grant all your requests.

Now I know that Adonai saves the chosen anointed
and answers from the holy heavens
with a right hand of saving powers.

Some trust in the chariot
and others in the horses,
but we in the name of our God Adonai.
They kneel and they fall,
but we rise up and stand firm.

Adonai, save the king;
answer us on the day of our call.

Glory...   Repeat antiphon.

PSALM 21:2-8,14

Antiphon for Lent   Be exalted, Lord, in your strength;
we sing praise of your might.

Easter   You have assumed the authority that is yours;
you have established your kingdom,
alleluia.

In your strength, Adonai, the king rejoices,
and in your victory; how great is the joy!
You granted to him the desire of his heart
and did not withhold the request of his lips.

Indeed, you welcomed him with rich blessings
and placed on his head a crown of pure gold.
He asked from you life
and you gave length of days forever and ever.

Great is the glory through your victory;
on him you bestowed splendor and majesty.
Surely you granted him blessings for eternity
making him glad with joy in your presences,

for the king trusts in Adonai and will be unshaken
through the unfailing love of the Most High…
Be exalted, Adonai, in your strength!
We will sing and we will praise your might.

Glory…

Repeat antiphon.

REVELATION 4:8b,11; 5:9,10,12,13b

Antiphon for Lent
 Lord, out of every tribe and tongue
and people and nation,
you made to our God a kingdom and priests.

Easter
 Let all creation serve you,
for all things came into being at your word,
alleluia.

Worthy are you, our Lord and our God,
to receive the glory and honor and power,
because you have created all things,
and by your will all things were created and are.

Worthy are you to receive the scroll
and to open its seals,
because you were slain
and purchased for God by your blood
from every tribe and tongue and people and nation.

You made of them to our God
a kingdom and priests,
and they will reign over the earth.

Worthy is the Lamb, slain to receive
the power and riches and wisdom and strength
and honor and glory and blessing.

Glory...

               Repeat antiphon.

WEEK I
WEDNESDAY MORNING

PSALM 18:2-30

Antiphon I love you, Lord, my deliverer.
(alleluia)

I love you, Adonai, my strength,
my rock Adonai, my fortress and deliverer;
in my God and Rock I take refuge,
my shield and horn, my salvation and stronghold.

I call out praise to Adonai
and am saved from enmity.

They tangled me in cords of death
and overwhelmed me in torrents of destruction.
Cords of Sheol coiled around me
and snares of death confronted me.

In my distress I called "Adonai,"
I cried for help from my God,
who heard from the temple my voice;
my cry went into those ears.

The earth trembled and quaked
and foundations of mountains shook
and trembled because of anger.
Smoke rose from the nostrils
and fire from the mouth consumed blazing coals.

The heavens parted
and dark clouds came down under the feet.
Mounted on the cherub,
flying and soaring on wings of wind,
a canopy of darkness covered all around,
dark waters in the clouds of the skies.

From the brightness of the presence
the clouds advanced hailstone and lightning bolts.
Adonai thundered from the heavens,
the voice of the Most High resounding
as hailstone and lightning bolts.

Arrows shot, scattering them all;
with great lightning bolts they are routed.
Valleys of waters were exposed and laid bare,
foundations of earth at your rebuke.

At the blast of the breath of your nostril, Adonai,
you reached from on high and took hold of me
and drew me out from the deep waters;
you rescued me from enmity
and from powerful foes,
for they were too strong for me.

They confronted me in the day of my disaster
but Adonai was my support,
brought me out to the spacious place,
and rescued me because of delight in me.

PSALM 18:2-30, continued

Adonai dealt with me as my ways are righteous,
rewarded me as my hands are clean,
for I kept to the ways of Adonai.
Indeed all of God's laws are before me
and I did not turn from those decrees.

Blameless before God, I kept myself from sin
and seen by the eyes of Adonai I am rewarded
as my ways are right and my hands are clean.

You show yourself faithful to the faithful,
to the blameless you show yourself blameless,
and to the pure you show yourself pure,

but to the crooked you show yourself shrewd,
for you save humble people
but bring low the eyes of the haughty.

Indeed you make my lamp burn;
my God Adonai makes light in my darkness.
Indeed with you I can advance against troops,
with my God I can scale a wall.

Glory…

Antiphon	I love you, Lord, my deliverer. (alleluia)

PSALM 36

Antiphon for Lent	Lord, in your light we see light.
Easter	You, Lord, are the fountain of life, alleluia.

An oracle of sin in the midst of my heart:
There is no fear of God in the eyes of a sinner,
whose own eyes are full of self-flattery,
who hates to detect sin.

Words of this mouth are wicked and deceitful:
Ceasing to be wise or do good,
this one plots evil while still in bed
and commits to a course not good
and rejects nothing that is wrong.

Adonai, to the heavens is your love
and your fidelity to the skies.
Your righteous might is like the mountains,
your justice deep and great;
human and beast you preserve, Adonai.

How priceless is your unfailing love.
High ones and humans find refuge
in the shadow of your wings.

They feast on the abundance of your house;
in the river of your delights you give them drink.
With you is the fountain of life,
and in your light we see light.

Continue your love to those who know you
and your righteousness to the upright of heart.
Let the foot of pride not come to me
nor the hand of wicked ways drive me away.

See, doers of evil lie fallen;
they are thrown down, unable to rise.

Glory...   Repeat antiphon.

JUDITH 16:1,13-15

Antiphon for Lent   O Lord, you are great and glorious,
wonderful in strength, invincible.

Easter   You sent forth your Spirit,
and all creatures were created,
alleluia.

Begin a song to my God with timbrels;
sing to my Lord with cymbals.
Sing to my Lord a new song;
exalt and acclaim the name.

I will sing to my God a new song;
O Lord, you are great and glorious,
wonderful in strength and unbeatable.

Let your every creature serve you,
for you spoke, and they were made.
You sent forth your spirit, and they were created;
no one can resist your word.

Mountain foundations are shaken by waters
and rocks melt like wax at your glance.
But to those who fear you, you show mercy.

Glory...

Antiphon for Lent   O Lord, you are great and glorious,
wonderful in strength, invincible.

Easter   You sent forth your Spirit,
and all creatures were created, alleluia.

PSALM 47

Antiphon for Lent — Sing praises to God, sing praise.

Easter — God is King over all the earth;
make music with all your skill,
alleluia.

All you nations, clap your hands!
Shout to God with cries of joy!
How awesome, Most High Adonai.

The great King over all the earth
subdued nations under us
and peoples under our feet,
and chose for us an inheritance,
the pride of Jacob the beloved.

God ascended with shouts of joy,
Adonai amid sound of trumpet.
Sing praises to God, sing praises.
Sing praises to our King, sing praises.

For God, King of all the earth, sing praises.
God reigns over the nations,
God sits on the holy throne.

Nobles of nations assemble,
the people of the God of Abraham.
God, shield of the earth, is greatly exalted.

Glory…

Repeat antiphon.

WEEK I
WEDNESDAY EVENING

PSALM 17

Antiphon for Lent   Lord, hold my steps to your paths.

Easter   Alleluia, alleluia, alleluia.

Hear, Adonai, a righteous plea; listen to my cry.
Give ear to my prayer, from lips without deceit.
May my vindication come from you;
may my eyes see right things.

You probe and examine my heart in the night,
you test me and will find nothing.
By resolve my mouth will not sin.

By the word of your lips
my human deeds are kept from violent ways.
Holding my steps to your paths my feet did not slip.

I call on you, El, for you will answer me.
Give your ear to me and hear my prayer.
Show the wonder of your great saving love,
at your right hand those taking refuge from foes.

Keep me as the apple daughter of your eye.
You hide me in the shade of your wings
from those who assail me in enmity,
surrounding around my life.
They close their callous hearts,
they speak their arrogant mouth.

Now they surround our tracks;
their eyes are alert, ready to throw to the ground.
They are like a lion, hungry to tear prey,
like a great lion crouching undercover.

Rise up, Adonai!
Confront and bring down their ways.
Rescue my self by your sword, Adonai,
by your hand from humans,
humans of the world whose reward is this life.

As for those who are cherished by you,
their belly is full, sons and daughters are plenty,
and they store up their wealth for their children.

In justice, I will see your faces
and be satisfied waking up to your likeness.

Glory…

Antiphon for Lent — Lord, hold my steps to your paths.

Easter — Alleluia, alleluia, alleluia.

PSALM 27

Antiphon for Lent The Lord is my light and my salvation;
Whom shall I fear?

Easter God has raised him up as king and savior,
alleluia.

Adonai is my light and my salvation.
Whom shall I fear?
Adonai is the stronghold of my life.
Of whom shall I be afraid?

When people acting evil advance
against me to devour my flesh,
when enmity and foes go against me,
they will stumble and fall.

Though an army besiege against me,
my heart will not fear.
Though war break out against me,
in this I will be confident.

One thing I ask of Adonai:
to seek and to dwell in Adonai's house,
to gaze on Adonai's beauty
all the days of my life
as a seeker in the temple.

I will be kept safely dwelling,
hidden in the shelter of the tabernacle,
on the day of trouble set high upon rock.

Then will my head be exalted above enmity,
and I will sacrifice at the tabernacle
the sacrifice of shouts of joy.

I will sing and make music to Adonai.
Hear, Adonai, my voice calling;
be merciful; answer me.
To you my heart says, "My face seeks you."

Your faces, Adonai, I will seek.
Hide not your faces from me;
turn not away from your servant in anger.

You are my help;
neither reject nor forsake me,
God of my salvation.
Even if my father and my mother forsake me,
you, Adonai, will receive me.

Teach me your way, Adonai,
and lead me through oppression to straight paths.
Do not give me over to the desire
of foes who rise with false witnesses
and breathers of violence.

Still I am confident: I will see
the goodness of Adonai in the land of the living.
Wait for Adonai!
Be strong and strengthen your heart.
And wait for Adonai!

Glory…

Repeat antiphon.

PSALM 28 :1-3,6-9

Antiphon for Lent   My heart trusts in the Lord
and I am helped.

Easter   Alleluia, alleluia, alleluia.

To you I call, my Rock Adonai,
turn not to me a deaf ear.
For if you remain silent, away from me,
then I will be like one going into the pit.

Hear the sound of my cries for mercy
calling to you for help as I lift my hands
toward the Holy Place of your Holiness.

Do not drag me away with those who do bad,
who speak cordiality with their neighbors
but with malice in their heart.

Praised be Adonai,
who heard the sound of my cries for mercy.
Adonai, my strength and my shield,
in whom my heart trusts,
I am helped and my heart leaps for joy
and in my song I will give thanks.

Adonai is the strength
and the saving fortress of the anointed.
Save your people! Bless your inheritance!
Be their shepherd and carry them to forever!

Glory…

Repeat antiphon.

COLOSSIANS 1:12-20

Antiphon for Lent   He is the firstborn of all creation;
he is before all things
and in him all things hold together.

Easter   From him, through him, and in him
all things exist: glory to him forever,
alleluia.

Give joyful thanks to the Father who made you fit
for your part of the lot of the saints in light,

who delivered us out of the authority of darkness
and transitioned us into the kingdom of the beloved Son,
in whom we have redemption, the forgiveness of our sins.

The Son is the image of the invisible God,
the firstborn of all creation.
In him all things were created,
in the heavens and on the earth,
the visible and the invisible,
whether thrones, lordships, rulers or authorities.

All things have been created through him and for him.
He is before all things,
and in him all things hold together.

He is the head of the body, the church,
and the beginning, the firstborn from the dead,
so that in all things he may hold the first place.

COLOSSIANS 1:12-20, continued

In him all the fullness was well pleased to dwell,
and through him reconciliation to himself of all things,
things on earth and things in the heavens,
making peace through the blood of his cross.

Glory...

Antiphon for Lent   He is the firstborn of all creation;
he is before all things
and in him all things hold together.

Easter   From him, through him, and in him
all things exist: glory to him forever,
alleluia.

WEEK I
THURSDAY MORNING

PSALM 18:31-51

Antiphon Adonai is alive; may our Rock be exalted,
the God of our salvation.
(alleluia)

The ways of God are perfect,
the word of Adonai is flawless,
a shield for all who need refuge.
For who is God besides Adonai?
And who is the Rock except our God?

God arms me with strength,
makes perfect my way,
makes my feet like the deer
and makes me to stand on my heights,
training my hands for the battle;
my arms can bend a bow of bronze.

You give to me your shield of victory,
your right hand sustains me,
and in stooping you make me great.
You broaden my path beneath me
so my ankles do not turn.

I pursued enemies and overtook them
and did not turn back until their defeat…
They fell beneath my feet.

PSALM 18:31-51, continued

You armed me with strength for the battle
and made the adversity bow at my feet.
You turned back enmity
and brought defeat to foes.

They cried for help, but no one saved them.
Adonai did not answer them.
I beat them as dust on surfaces of wind;
like mud in the streets I poured them out.

You delivered me from attacks of people,
you made me as a head of nations;
people I knew not are subject to me.

Hearing me in their ear they obey;
sons and daughters of foreigners cringe before me.
They lose heart
and they tremble from their strongholds.

Adonai is alive and praised;
may my Rock be exalted, the God of my salvation.
God gives victory to me
and subdues nations under me,

saving me from enmity,
exalting me above foes,
and rescuing me from violence.
For this I will praise Adonai among the nations,
and to your name I will sing praise.

You make great victories of your king
and show unfailing kindness to David your anointed
and his descendants to forever.

Glory...

WEEK I - THURSDAY MORNING

Antiphon   Adonai is alive; may our Rock be exalted,
            the God of our salvation.
            (alleluia)

PSALM 57

Antiphon for Lent   Awake, my soul; awake the harp and lyre;
                     I will awaken dawn.

Easter   Be exalted, O God, above the heavens,
          alleluia.

Have mercy on me, God, have mercy on me,
for in you my soul takes refuge
and in the shade of your wings I take refuge
until disasters pass.

I cry out to God Most High,
to El who fulfills me,
who sends from the heavens and saves me
and rebukes the one pursuing me.

God sends love and fidelity to my self;
in the midst of ravenous lions I lie,
in the midst of human beings with teeth and spear
and arrows and tongues, their sharp swords.

Be exalted, God, above the heavens,
your glory over all the earth.

PSALM 57, continued

For my feet they spread a net
and my self was bowed down.
Before me they dug a pit
and fell inside it themselves.

My heart is steadfast, Elohim, my heart is steadfast;
I will sing and make music.
Awake, my liver! Wake up the harp and the lyre;
I will wake up the dawn.

I will praise you among the nations, Lord;
I will sing of you among the peoples,
for great to the heavens is your love
and to the skies is your fidelity.

Be exalted above the heavens, God,
your glory over all the earth.

Glory…

Antiphon for Lent	Awake, my soul; awake the harp and lyre; I will awaken dawn.
Easter	Be exalted, O God, above the heavens, alleluia.

JEREMIAH 31:10-14

Antiphon for Lent	My people will be filled with my bounty, declares the Lord.
Easter	The Lord has redeemed the flock, alleluia.

JEREMIAH 31:10-14

Hear, nations, the word of Adonai;
proclaim it to distant coastlands and say:
"The One who scattered Israel
　will gather them and watch them
　as one who is shepherd to a flock."

For Adonai will ransom and redeem Jacob
from the hand of those with more strength.

They will come and they will shout
up on the height of Zion
and they will rejoice in the bounty of Adonai,
the grain and new wine and oil,
and younglings of the flock and herd;
and they themselves like a well-watered garden
will sorrow no more, not again.

Then the maiden will be glad in dance,
and young men together with the old.
I will turn their mourning into gladness;
I will comfort them and give joy instead of sorrow.
I will satisfy with abundance the self of the priests
and my people will be filled with my bounty,
declares Adonai.

Glory…

Antiphon for Lent	My people will be filled with my bounty, declares the Lord.
Easter	The Lord has redeemed the flock, alleluia.

PSALM 48

Antiphon for Lent — Great is the Lord, greatly being praised
in the city of our God.

Easter — This is our God, our guide to forever, alleluia.

Great is Adonai, greatly being praised
in the city of our God, on the holy mountain,
beautiful loft, the joy of all the earth,

Mount Zion, the upmost heights,
sacred mountain, the city of the Great King.
God in the citadels is shown as a fortress when,
see, the kings join forces and advance together.

They saw, were astounded, and fled in terror;
trembling seized them, pain like a woman in labor.
By the east wind you destroyed ships of Tarshish;

just as we heard, so we saw in the city
of Adonai Sabaoth, in the city of our God.
God makes her secure to forever.

In your temple we meditate on your unfailing love.
Like your name, God, so your praise
goes to the ends of the earth;

your right hand is filled with justice.
Mount Zion rejoices because of your judgments;
the villages of Judah are glad.

Walk about Zion! Go around! Count her towers!
Consider at heart her ramparts! View her citadels!

So that you may tell to the next generation:
This God, our God, forever and ever
will guide us even to the end.

Glory…

Repeat antiphon.

WEEK I
THURSDAY EVENING

PSALM 25

Antiphon for Lent — Turn to me, Lord,
and be gracious in my lonely affliction.

Easter — Alleluia, alleluia, alleluia.

To you, Adonai, I lift up my soul;
in you, my God, I trust;
let me not be shamed
and let enmity not triumph over me.
Indeed all who hope in you will not be shamed;
shamed will be those doing defenseless treachery.

Show me your ways, Adonai; teach me your paths.
Guide me in your truth and teach me,
for you are my saving God;
you are my hope all the day.

PSALM 25, continued

Remember your mercies, Adonai,
and your loves, for they are from of old.
The sins of my youth and rebellious ways
you do not remember, as you are loving.

You do remember me, for you are good, Adonai.
Good and upright is Adonai,
who instructs sinners in the way,
guides humble ones in rightness,
and teaches the way to the humble.

All the ways of Adonai are loving and faithful
for those who keep the covenant demands.
For the sake of your name, Adonai,
now you forgive my iniquity, great as it is.

Who is the human who fears Adonai?
The one being instructed in the Lord's chosen way,
whose life will be days spent in prosperity,
whose descendants will inherit the land,
the confidence of Adonai is with those thus fearing;
the covenant is made known to them.

My eyes are ever on Adonai,
who will release my feet from the snare.
Turn to me! Be gracious to me!
For I am lonely and afflicted.

Troubles of my heart have multiplied;
free me from my anguish!
Look upon my affliction and distress!
Take away all of my sins!

See the enmity,
the increase of fierce hate!
Guard my life! Rescue me!
Let me not be shamed, for I take refuge in you.
May integrity and uprightness protect me
because I hope in you.

Redeem Israel, God, from all our troubles.

Glory...

Antiphon for Lent   Turn to me, Lord,
and be gracious in my lonely affliction.

Easter   Alleluia, alleluia, alleluia.

PSALM 30

Antiphon for Lent   Lord my God,
I cried to you for help and you healed me.
I will thank you to forever.

Easter   You have turned my mourning into joy,
alleluia.

I will exalt you, Adonai, for you lifted me
and did not let enmity gloat over me.

Adonai, my God, I cried to you for help
and you healed me.
Adonai, you brought my self up from Sheol;
you spared me from going into the pit.

PSALM 30, continued

Sing to Adonai, you saints!
Sing praise to the holy name!
One moment in anger: lifetimes in the Lord's favor;
in the night weeping remains,
but in the morning rejoicing

when I said in my security,
I will be unshaken to forever.
In your favor, Adonai,
you made my mountain stand firm;
you hid your faces and I was dismayed.

To you, Adonai, I called
and to you, Lord, I cried for mercy.
What would be the gain in my destruction?
What is gained if I go into the pit?

Will the dust praise you?
Will the dust proclaim your fidelity?
Hear, Adonai! Be merciful to me!
Be my one helper, Adonai!

You turned my wailing into dancing for me;
you removed my sackcloth and clothed me in joy
so that my heart may sing to you, and not be silent.
My God Adonai, I will thank you to forever.

Glory…

Antiphon for Lent   Lord my God,
I cried to you for help and you healed me.
I will thank you to forever.

Easter   You have turned my mourning into joy, alleluia.

PSALM 32

Antiphon for Lent
Blessed are human beings
whose sin the Lord counts not,
where transgressions are forgiven.

Easter
We have been reconciled to God
by the death of the Son,
alleluia.

Blessed is the one forgiven of transgression,
who was covered with sin.
Blessed is the human
against whom Adonai does not count sin,
and in whose spirit there is no deceit.

When I kept silent, my bones wasted away
through my groaning all day.
For by day and night your hand was heavy upon me;
my strength was sapped as in summer heat.

I acknowledged my sin to you,
and did not cover up my iniquity;
I said I will confess my transgressions to Adonai
and you forgave the guilt of my sin.

For this let every godly one pray to you
at the time to find you.
Surely the rising of mighty waters
will not reach this one.
You are the hiding place for me;
you will protect me from trouble
and surround me with deliverance song.

PSALM 32, continued

I will instruct you and I will teach you
and counsel you in the way you should go;
My eye is over you.

Do not be like a horse,
like your mule with no understanding;
by bit and bridle and harness they are controlled
or else they will not even come to you.

Many woes have the bad doers,
but the truster in Adonai
is surrounded in unfailing love.

Rejoice in Adonai! Righteous ones, be glad!
And sing, all you upright of heart!

Glory…

Antiphon for Lent	Blessed are human beings whose sin the Lord counts not, where transgressions are forgiven.
Easter	We have been reconciled to God by the death of the Son, alleluia.

REVELATION 11:17-18, 12:10-12a

Antiphon for Lent — Now have come the salvation, the power,
and the kingdom of our God.

Easter — Lord, who is your equal in power?
Who is like you, majestic in holiness?
Alleluia.

We thank you, Lord God Almighty,
the One who is and who was;
you have taken your great power and reign.

The nations raged and your anger came,
and the time to judge the dead
and to reward your slaves and prophets,
the saints, and those fearing your name,
the small and the great…

Now have come the salvation and power
and kingdom of our God
and the authority of Christ.
The accuser of our brothers and sisters was cast,
accusing them before our God day and night.

Their victory was because of the blood of the Lamb
and by the word of their witness.
They loved their life into their death,
and so be glad, you heavens,
and all you dwelling in them.

Glory…

Repeat antiphon.

WEEK I
FRIDAY MORNING

PSALM 35:1-2c,3c,9-19,22-23,27-28

Antiphon
Awake, and rise to my defense;
my God and Lord, contend for me.
(alleluia)

Contend, Adonai, with my contenders!
Restrain those who would attack!
Take up shield and buckler and arise to my aid!...
Say to my soul, "I am your salvation."...

Then my soul will rejoice in Adonai
and take delight in salvation.
All of my bones will exclaim, "Adonai!
　Who, like you, rescues the poor from the strong?
　Or the poor and the needy from the robbers?"

Ruthless witnesses come forward;
on things I do not know they question me.
They repay me evil for good; forlorn is my soul.

Yet when they were ill I clothed myself in sackcloth
and humbled myself with fasting
when my prayer had returned
to my breast unanswered.
As a friend and a sibling I went about weeping,
bowing down like a grieving mother.

But they took glee at my stumbling
and they gathered and gathered attackers
and did not cease to slander me unaware,
an ungodly circle of mockers
gnashing their teeth against me.

Until when, Lord? How long will you look on?
Rescue my life from the ravages,
my precious life from the lions.
I will give you thanks in the great assembly;
among people thronging I will praise you.

Let enmity neither gloat without cause or reason
nor wink the eye at me...

You have seen, Adonai; be not silent.
Be not far from me, Lord.
Awake!, my God and Lord,
and rise to contend to my defense.
Vindicate me in your righteousness, Adonai...

May those who delight in my vindication
shout and be glad and always say,
"May Adonai be exalted,
  who delights in the well being of the servant."
And my tongue will speak your righteousness
and praise of you all the day.

Glory...

Antiphon	Awake, and rise to my defense;
	my God and Lord, contend for me.
	(alleluia)

PSALM 51

Antiphon for Lent Lord, open my lips
and my mouth will declare your praise.

Easter Remember me, Lord God,
when you come into your kingdom,
alleluia.

Have mercy on me, God,
in accord with your unfailing love;
in accord with the greatness of your compassion
blot out my transgressions.

Wash me of my many iniquities
and cleanse me from my sin,
for I know my transgressions
and my sin is before me always.

Against you yourself I sinned;
what I did is evil in your eyes.
You are proven right when you speak
and justified when you judge.
Surely we are sinners from birth,
from conception in a mother's womb.

Surely you desire truth in our inner parts;
in my inmost place you teach me wisdom.
You cleanse me with hyssop and I will be clean;
you wash me and I will be whiter than snow...

WEEK I - FRIDAY MORNING

You let me hear joy and gladness;
let the bones you let be crushed now rejoice.
Hide your faces from my sins
and blot out all my iniquities.

A pure heart create in me, God!
Renew inside me a spirit to be steadfast.
Do not cast me from your presences,
nor take from me your Holy Spirit.

Restore to me the joy of your salvation
and sustain in me a willing spirit.
I will teach transgressors your ways
and sinners will turn back to you.

Save me from bloodguilt, God,
God of my salvation;
my tongue will sing of your righteousness.
Lord, open my lips
and my mouth will declare your praise.

Sacrifices give you no delight;
I could bring a burnt offering,
but it would give you no pleasure.
The sacrifices, God, you will not despise
are a broken spirit and a contrite heart.

Make Zion prosper in your pleasure,
and build up the walls of Jerusalem.
Then you will delight in the sacrifice of the just,
burnt offerings and whole offerings,
bulls offered on your altar.

Glory... Repeat antiphon.

ISAIAH 45:15-25

Antiphon for Lent
God fashioned and made
and formed the earth,
creating it to be not an empty waste,
but to be inhabited.

Easter
Truly you are a hidden God,
the God of Israel, the Savior,
alleluia.

Truly, God, you hide yourself,
Saving God of Israel.
Makers of idols will know shame and disgrace,
all going off together in disgrace.

Israel will be saved by Adonai, salvation everlasting.
You will not know shame or disgrace to the ages.

For this says Adonai, the one creating the heavens,
God who fashioned and made
and formed the earth,
creating it to be not an empty waste,
but formed to be inhabited,

"I am Adonai, and there is no other.
 Not in secret did I speak,
 from some place in a dark land,
 not saying to descendants of Jacob,
 'seek me in vain.'
 I, Adonai, speak truth and delare right things.

Gather together and come!
Assemble together, fugitives of the nations.
Those who carry idols of wood do not know:
they are praying to no-gods that cannot save.

Declare and present! Let them counsel together!
Who foretold this from long ago?
Who declared this from the distant past?
Not I, Adonai? There is no god apart from me,
God righteous and Saving; there is none but me.

Turn to me and be saved, all you ends of the earth,
for I am God and there is no other.

By myself I swore integrity out of my mouth,
the word that will not be revoked.

Indeed, in front of me every knee will bow,
and every tongue will swear, and say,
'In Adonai alone are justice and strength,'

to whom will come and be shamed
all who have raged otherwise."
In Adonai they will be found righteous
and all the descendants of Israel will exult.

Glory…

Antiphon for Lent	God fashioned and made and formed the earth, creating it to be not an empty waste, but to be inhabited.
Easter	Truly you are a hidden God, the God of Israel, the Savior, alleluia.

PSALM 100

Antiphon for Lent   Come before the Lord with joyful song.

Easter   Serve the Lord with gladness,
alleluia.

Shout for joy to Adonai, all you earth!
Serve Adonai with gladness!
Come into the presence with joyful song.

Know that Adonai is God, who made us,
whose people we are,
in whose pasture we are the sheep.

Enter the gates with thanksgiving,
go into the courts with praise!
Give thanks and give praise to the Name!

Good is Adonai, and loving to forever,
and faithful through generations and generation.

Glory…

Antiphon for Lent   Come before the Lord with joyful song.

Easter   Serve the Lord with gladness,
alleluia.

WEEK I
FRIDAY EVENING

PSALM 26

Antiphon for Lent   I trust in the Lord; I do not waver.

Easter   Alleluia, alleluia, alleluia.

Vindicate me, Adonai,
for I have walked blameless in my life
and in Adonai I trusted without waver.

Test me, Adonai! And try me!
Examine my heart and my mind!
For your love is before my eyes
and I walk in your truth.

I do not sit with humans of deceit
nor consort with hypocrites.
I abhor the assembly of those who do evil
and do not sit with those who do wicked.

I wash my hands in innocence
and go about your altar, Adonai,
to proclaim a voice of praise
and to tell of all your wonderful deeds.

Adonai, I love the living place of your house,
the dwelling place of your glory.

PSALM 26, continued

Take not my soul away with sinners
nor my life with people doing bloody things,
those who scheme in their hands
with their right hand full of bribes.

But I walk blameless in my life.
Redeem me! Be merciful to me!
My foot stands on level ground;
in great assemblies I will praise Adonai.

Glory...

Antiphon for Lent   I trust in the Lord; I do not waver.

Easter   Alleluia, alleluia, alleluia.

PSALM 41

Antiphon for Lent   Lord, have mercy on me
and heal my being.

Easter   Christ became poor for our sake,
that we might become rich,
alleluia.

Blessed is the one who gives regard to the weak.
In the time of trouble Adonai will deliver.
Adonai will protect that one's life,
preserve it blessed in the land,
and give no surrender to the desire of foes.
Adonai will sustain on the sickbed,
and restore on that bed from all illness.

Adonai, have mercy on me!
Heal my self for I have sinned against you!
Enmity asks in malice:
"When will that one die and the name perish?"
When they come to see me,
they speak with false hearts, gather slander,
and then go out to the outside to speak.

Together against me they whisper,
imagining the worst for me:
"A vile disease has set in;
  that one will not recover."
Even my close friend has lifted the heel against me,
the human being I trusted, who ate my own bread.

But you, Adonai, have mercy on me
and raise me up that I may repay them.
In this I know that you are pleased with me,
for enmity does not triumph over me;
in my integrity you hold me up
and set me in your presences to forever.

Praised be Adonai, God of Israel,
from everlasting to the everlasting.
Amen and amen.

Glory…

Antiphon for Lent Lord, have mercy on me
and heal my being.

Easter Christ became poor for our sake,
that we might become rich,
alleluia.

PSALM 46

Antiphon for Lent　　The Lord of hosts is with us,
　　　　　　　　　the God of Jacob a fortress to us.

Easter　　The river streams make glad the city of God,
　　　　alleluia.

God is our refuge and strength,
our help in troubles, ever present.
And so we will not fear,
even if earth were to give way,
even if mountains were to fall
into the heart of the sea,
even if sea waters foam
or mountains quake with that surging.

A river has streams that make glad God's city,
the holy dwelling place of the Most High.
God is inside her and she will not fall.
God will help her at the break of day.
Nations are in uproar, kingdoms fall;
the earth melts at the voice of God.

Adonai Sabaoth is with us;
the God of Jacob is our fortress.

Come and see the works of Adonai,
the desolations brought on the earth:
making wars to cease to the ends of the earth,
breaking the bow and shattering the spear
and burning with fire the chariot and shield.

"Be still! And know that I am God.
 I will be exalted among the nations;
 I will be exalted on the earth."

Adonai Sabaoth is with us;
the God of Jacob is our fortress.

Glory…

Repeat antiphon.

REVELATION 15:3b-4

Antiphon for Lent   All the nations will come
and worship before you,
Lord God Almighty.

Easter   Let us sing to the Lord,
glorious in the triumph,
alleluia.

Great and wonderful are your works,
Lord God Almighty.
Just and true are your ways,
King of the nations.

Who will not fear, O Lord,
or glorify your name?

Only you are holy.
All the nations will come and worship before you;
your ordinances are shown to all.

Glory…

Repeat antiphon.

WEEK I
SATURDAY MORNING

PSALM 105

Antiphon for Lent   Look to the Lord, the strength of the Lord;
seek always the faces of the Lord.

Easter   The Lord was true to the sacred promises,
and led us to freedom and joy,
alleluia.

Praise Adonai!
Give thanks to Adonai; call on the name.
Make known among the nations the Lord's deeds!

Glory be to the holy name;
let the heart of the seeker of Adonai rejoice.
Look to Adonai, to the strength;
seek always the faces of the Lord.

Remember the deeds of wonder done,
the miracles and the judgments mouthed,
you descendants and servants of Abraham,
you chosen ones of Jacob.

Adonai is our God, judge in all the earth,
remembering the covenant to forever
commanded for a thousand generations,
the word made with Abraham and the oath to Isaac

confirmed to Jacob as a decree,
to Israel as an everlasting covenant:
"I will give to you land of Canaan,
 a portion of your inheritance."

When they were few, few in numbers,
with strangers in their midst,
then they wandered from nation to nation,
from one kingdom to another people.

No one was allowed to oppress them
and for their sake kings were rebuked:
"Do not touch my anointed ones;
 do not harm my prophets."

Famine was allowed onto the land
and the king's food supply was destroyed.
A man Joseph was sent before them,
sold as a slave;
they bruised his foot with the shackle

and his neck entered the irons
till the time foretold of him came to pass.
The word of Adonai proved him true.
The king sent for him and released him;

the ruler of the peoples set him free
and made him master of his household
and ruler over all his possessions
to discipline the princes as was his pleasure
and to teach the elders.
Then Israel entered Egypt;
Jacob lived as an alien in the land of Ham.

PSALM 105, continued

This people became very numerous,
more fruitful than their foes.
The hearts of the rulers were turned to hate
and conspired against this servant people.

Moses was sent as servant of the Lord
and Aaron as chosen of the Lord.
They performed the deeds of the Lord,
signs and wonders in the land of Ham.

The Lord sent darkness and it was dark;
for they rebelled against the word.
Their waters were turned into blood
which caused their fish to die.

Their land was teemed with frogs,
even the bedrooms of their rulers.
Swarms of flies were sent at a word,
gnats through all of their country.

Their rains were turned into hail
and lightning flamed through their land.
Their vine and fig tree were struck down
and the trees of their country were shattered.

Locusts came at the word
and grasshoppers without number.
Every green thing in their land was eaten up,
eaten up with the produce of their soil.

Then their firstborn were struck down, all of them,
the firstfruit of their humanity in all of their land.
The Lord brought them out with silver and gold
and no one faltered among the tribes.
Egypt was glad when they left, glad with dread.

A cloud as a cover was spread out
and fire to give them light at night.
They asked for quail and the Lord brought it
and satisfied them with bread from heaven.

The rock was opened and waters gushed out
flowing in the desert as a river,
for the holy promise was remembered,
the promise made to servant Abraham,
and the people were brought out rejoicing,
the chosen ones with shouts of joy.

They received the lands of nations
and inherited the toil of peoples
so that they might keep the precepts
and observe the laws of the Lord.

Praise Adonai!

Glory…

Antiphon for Lent — Look to the Lord, the strength of the Lord;
seek always the faces of the Lord.

Easter — The Lord was true to the sacred promises,
and led us to freedom and joy,
alleluia.

PSALM 119:145-152

Antiphon for Lent I rise before dawn and cry for help;
in your word I put my hope.

Easter Lord, in your love, give me life,
alleluia.

I call with all my heart: answer me, Adonai;
your decrees I will obey.
I call to you: save me,
and I will keep your statutes.

I rise before dawn and I cry for help;
in your word I put my hope.
My eyes stay open in the night watch
to meditate on your promise.

Hear my voice, as you are loving, Adonai,
as your law makes me alive.
Scheming devisers are near,
but they are far from your law.

You are near, Adonai,
and all your commands are true.
I learned long ago from your statutes
that you established them to forever.

Glory…

Antiphon for Lent I rise before dawn and cry for help;
in your word I put my hope.

Easter Lord, in your love, give me life, alleluia.

EXODUS 15:1b-4,8-13,17-18

Antiphon for Lent
> The Lord, my strength and my song,
> has become to me salvation.

Easter
> Those who were victorious
> sang the hymn of Moses, the servant of God,
> and the hymn of the Lamb,
> alleluia.

I will sing to Adonai, exalting exaltation,
who hurled horse and rider into the sea.

My strength and my song,
Yah has become to me salvation.
I will praise my God
and exalt the God of my ancestors.

Adonai the warrior, named Adonai,
hurled Pharaoh's army of chariots into the sea...
By the blast of your nostrils the waters piled up;
like a wall they stood firm in the heart of the sea,
raging deep waters congealed.

The enemy boasted, "I will pursue and overtake,
 divide the spoils and gorge on them myself;
 I will draw my sword;
 my hand will destroy them."
You blew with your breath
and the sea covered them;
they sank like lead in the mighty waters.

Who is like you among "gods," Adonai?
Who like you is majestic and holy,
awesome in glory and working wonders?
You stretched your right hand
and the earth swallowed them.

You will lead in your love
the people you redeemed.
You will guide them in strength
to your holy dwelling...

You will bring them in and you will plant them
on the mountain of your inheritance,
the dwelling place you made, Adonai,
the sanctuary, Lord, that your hands established.
Adonai will reign forever and ever.

Glory...

Antiphon for Lent	The Lord, my strength and my song, has become to me salvation.
Easter	Those who were victorious sang the hymn of Moses, the servant of God, and the hymn of the Lamb, alleluia.

PSALM 117

Antiphon for Lent   Praise the Lord, all you nations.

Easter   Strong and steadfast is God's love for us, alleluia.

Praise Adonai, all nations;
and extol, all peoples.

Great is this steadfast love toward us,
the fidelity of Adonai to forever.

Praise Adonai!

Glory...

Antiphon for Lent   Praise the Lord, all you nations.

Easter   Strong and steadfast is God's love for us, alleluia.

WEEK II
VIGIL OF SUNDAY
(Saturday Evening)

PSALM 34

Antiphon for Lent   Taste and see that the Lord is good,
seek and pursue peace.

Easter   Alleluia, alleluia, alleluia.

I will extol Adonai at all times,
praise always on my lips.
My soul she will boast in Adonai,
let afflicted ones hear and let them rejoice.

Glorify Adonai with me!
Let us exalt the name together.
I sought Adonai, who answered me
and delivered me from all my fears.

They look to the name and are radiant;
their faces are never covered with shame.
This poor human called and Adonai heard,
and saved this one from all troubles.

An angel encamps around those who fear Adonai
and delivers them.
Taste and see that Adonai is good!
Blessed is the one who takes this refuge.

Fear Adonai, you saints;
for those who do so there is no lack.
Lions may grow weak and may grow hungry,
but seekers of Adonai lack no good thing.

Come, children! Listen to me!
I will teach you the fear of Adonai.
Who is the human who loves living?
Who desires days to see the good?

Keep your tongue from evil
and your lips from speaking the lie.
Turn from evil! And do good!
Seek and pursue peace!

The eyes of Adonai are on righteous ones
with ears open to their cry.
The faces of Adonai turn from those doing evil
to cut off from the earth their memory.

They cry and Adonai hears
and delivers them from all their troubles.
Close is Adonai to the brokenhearted,
saving those whose spirit is crushed.

Many are the troubles of the righteous
but Adonai delivers them from all of them,
protecting all of their bones;
not one of them will be broken.

PSALM 34, continued

Evil will slay the wicked and condemned will be
those who stay foes of the righteous.
The servants of Adonai are being redeemed
and the lives of any who take this refuge
will not be condemned.

Glory…

Antiphon for Lent	Taste and see that the Lord is good, seek and pursue peace.
Easter	Alleluia, alleluia, alleluia.

PSALM 119:105-112

Lent, 2nd Sunday	Jesus took Peter, James, and his brother John and led them up a high mountain where he was transfigured before them.
Lent, Palm Sunday	Day after day I sat teaching you in the temple and you did not lay hands on me. Now you come to scourge me and lead me to the cross.
Easter, 6th Sunday	The human of truth welcomes the light, alleluia.

PSALM 119:105-112

Your word is the lamp to my foot
and the light for my path.
I have made an oath and confirmation
to follow your righteous laws.

I have suffered much, Adonai;
make me alive as is your word.
Accept the willing praise of my mouth!
And now, Adonai, teach me your laws!

My life is constantly in my hand,
but I will not forget your law.
Doers of badness set a snare for me,
but I did not stray from your precepts.

I have your statutes as a heritage to forever,
they are indeed the joy of my heart.
I set my heart to keep your decrees
to forever, the very end.

Glory...

Repeat antiphon.

PSALM 16

Lent, 2nd Sunday His face was radiant as the sun
and his clothing white as snow.

Lent, Palm Sunday The Lord God is my help;
no shame can harm me.

Easter, 6th Sunday God freed Jesus from the pangs of death
and raised him up to life,
alleluia.

Keep me safe, El, for I take refuge in you.
I said to Adonai, "You are my Lord;
 I have no good apart from you."

As for saints who are in the land,
even glorious ones, all of my delight is in them.
Those who run after others
will increase their sorrows;
I will not pour out their blood libations,
nor take up their names on my lips.

Adonai, you assign my portion and my cup;
you make my lot secure.
Boundary lines fall for me in the pleasant places;
surely this inheritance is my delight.

WEEK II - VIGIL OF SUNDAY (Saturday Evening)

I will praise Adonai who counsels me;
even the nights instruct my heart.
With Adonai before me, always at my right hand,
I will not be shaken.

And so my heart is glad and my tongue rejoices.
My body will rest in security
because you will not abandon my self to Sheol;
you will not let your holy one see decay.

You will make known to me the path of living,
fullness of joy in your presences,
eternal pleasures at your right hand.

Glory…

Lent, 2nd Sunday	His face was radiant as the sun and his clothing white as snow.
Lent, Palm Sunday	The Lord God is my help; no shame can harm me.
Easter, 6th Sunday	God freed Jesus from the pangs of death and raised him up to life, alleluia.

PHILIPPIANS 2:6-11

Lent, 2nd Sunday   Moses and Elijah were speaking to him
of the death he would endure in Jerusalem.

Lent, Palm Sunday   The Lord Jesus humbled himself
by showing obedience
even when this meant death on the cross.

Easter, 6th Sunday   Was it not necessary for Christ to suffer
and so enter into his glory? Alleluia.

Christ Jesus, subsisting in the form of God,
did not deem equality with God something to grab,
but emptied himself, taking the form of a slave,
becoming in human likeness.

And being found in human fashion,
he humbled himself,
becoming obedient until death,
and death on a cross.

And so God highly exalted him,
and gave to him the name above every name,
that in the name of Jesus every knee should bend,
of heavenly beings and earthly beings,
and beings under the earth;

And every tongue acknowledge
to the glory of God the Father
that Jesus Christ is Lord.

Glory…

Repeat antiphon.

WEEK II
RESURRECTION VIGIL

1 TIMOTHY 3:16

Antiphon
>In Christ who rose from the dead
>our hope of resurrection dawned.

We confess that great
is the mystery of our fidelity:

Who was manifested in flesh,
justified in Spirit,
seen by angels,
proclaimed among nations,
believed in the world,
and taken up in glory.

We confess that great
is the mystery of our fidelity.

Glory...

Antiphon
>In Christ who rose from the dead
>our hope of resurrection dawned.

FOR SUNDAY OF WEEK 2

MARK 16:1-20

And when the sabbath was past, Mary the Magdalene,
   and Mary the mother of James, and Salome
bought spices that they might come and anoint him.

MARK 16:1-20, continued

And very early on the first day of the week,
they came upon the tomb at the rising of the sun.
And they asked themselves,
"Who will roll away the stone
out of the door of the tomb for us?"
And looking up they beheld
that the stone had been rolled back,
for it was great exceedingly.
And entering into the tomb, they saw
a young man sitting on the right clothed in a white robe,
and they were greatly astonished. But he said to them,
"Be not greatly astonished. Jesus you seek,
the Nazarene who was crucified;
he was raised, he is not here.
Behold, the place where they put him.
But you go tell his disciples and Peter
that he goes before you to Galilee;
there you will see him, as he told you."
And going forth they fled from the tomb;
trembling and bewilderment had them,
and they told no one anything, for they were afraid.
And rising early on the first day of the week,
he appeared first to Mary the Magdalene,
from whom he had expelled seven demons.
She going reported to those who had been with him,
mourning and weeping.
And hearing that he lives and was seen by her,
they disbelieved.

And after these things,
to two of them walking he showed himself
in a different form, going into the country.
And those going reported to the rest,
and were not believed.
And later to the eleven as they reclined
he showed himself and reproached their disbelief
and their hardness of heart for not believing
the ones beholding him having been raised.
And he said to them, "Going into all the world,
you proclaim the gospel to all the creation.
The one believing and being baptized will be saved,
but the one disbelieving will be condemned.
And the ones believing will follow these signs:
In my name they will expel demons,
they will speak with new tongues,
they will take serpents
and if they drink anything deadly
by no means will it hurt them,
and they will place hands on the sick
who will recover."
And so the Lord Jesus after speaking to them
was taken up into heaven
and sat at the right hand of God.
But those going forth proclaimed everywhere,
while the Lord worked with them
and confirmed the word
through accompanying signs.

•

FOR SUNDAY OF WEEK 6

JOHN 20:1-18

Now on day one of the week, Mary the Magdalene
    came in the early darkness to the tomb,
and saw the stone having been taken out of the tomb.
    She ran therefore and came to Simon Peter
    and to the other disciple whom Jesus loved,
and said to them, "They took the Lord out of the tomb,
    and we do not know where they put him."
        Peter and the other disciple
        went forth and came to the tomb.
            The two ran together,
and the other disciple ran before Peter more quickly
        and came first to the tomb,
    and stooping saw the linens lying,
            but did not enter.
    Simon Peter also came following him,
        and entered into the tomb,
        and behold, the linens lying,
and the cloth which had been on his head,
not lying with them, but apart in one place,
            having been rolled up.
    Then the other disciple also entered,
        having come first to the tomb,
          and he saw and believed,
    for they did not yet know the scripture,
that he deemed it fitting to rise again from the dead.
And so the disciples went away again to themselves.

But Mary stood outside the tomb weeping.
And so as she was weeping,
she stooped into the tomb
and behold, two angels in white, sitting,
one at the head and one at the feet
where the body of Jesus lay.
And they said to her, "Woman, why do you weep?"
She said to them, "They took my Lord,
and I do not know where they put him."
Saying these things, she turned back,
and behold, Jesus standing.
She did not know it was Jesus. Jesus said to her,
"Woman, why do you weep? Whom do you seek?"
Thinking that it was the gardener, she said to him,
"Sir, if you did carry him, tell me where you put him,
and I will take him."
Jesus said to her, "Mary."
Turning, she said to him in Hebrew, "Raboni,"
which means "Teacher."
Jesus said to her, "Do not hold on to me,
for I have not yet ascended to the Father.
But you go to my brothers and sisters and tell them,
I ascend to my Father and your Father
and my God and your God.'"
Mary the Magdalene came announcing to the disciples,
"I have seen the Lord"
and these things he said to her.

•

WEEK II
SUNDAY MORNING

PSALM 104

Antiphon for Lent — The Lord brings forth bread from the earth,
and wine to warm human hearts.

Easter — Alleluia,
the stone was rolled back
from the entrance to the tomb,
alleluia.

Soul of me, praise Adonai!
My God, Adonai, you are beyond measure.
Splendor and majesty clothe you,
wrapped in light as a garment,

stretching out over the heavens like the tent,
laying beams on the waters of the upper chambers.
You make a chariot of the clouds,
riding on wings of wind,
making messengers of the winds
and servants of flaming fire.

You have set foundations on earth,
unmoveable for ever and ever.
Deep is your garment, covering the earth;
above the mountains the waters stood.

At your rebuke, they then fled;
at the sound of your thunder they took flight.
They flowed over mountains
and went down into valleys
to the places you assigned for them.
You set a boundary they are not to cross;
never again are they to cover the earth.

You make springs of water pour into ravines;
between the mountains they flow.
They give water to all beasts of the field;
they quench the thirst of donkeys.
Birds of the air nest in branches beside them;
they give you their song.

You water mountains from your upper chambers;
by the fruit of your works the earth is satisfied.
You make grass grow for the cattle
and plants for human beings to cultivate

to bring forth food from the earth,
wine to make glad the human heart,
oil to make faces shine,
and bread to sustain the human heart.

They are all Adonai's well watered trees,
cedars of Lebanon planted
where birds make their nests,
and the pine tree where the stork makes a home,
mountains, the high ones, for wild goats,
and crags, a refuge for rock-badgers.

PSALM 104, continued

You mark off seasons by the moon,
and know the going down of the sun.
You bring darkness
and all beasts of the forest prowl in the night.
The lions roar for prey
seeking their food from God.

The sun rises, they steal away,
and into their dens they lie down.
Human beings go out to do their work
and labor until the evening.

How many are your works, Adonai!
All of them in wisdom you made.
The earth is full of your creatures.

There is the sea, vast and spacious;
living creatures countless there,
small ones and large ones.
There ships go about
and leviathan which you formed for frolic.

All of them look to you
to give them food at their time.
You give to them and they gather,
you open your hands
and they are goodly satisfied.

You hide your face and they are terrified,
you take away their breath and they die
and to their dust they return.
You breathe your Spirit, and they are created,
and you renew the faces of earth.

May the glory of Adonai endure to forever.
May Adonai rejoice in the works:
looking at the earth, she trembles,
touching the mountains, they smoke.

I will sing to Adonai during my life
and sing praise to my God while I still am.
May my meditation be found pleasing.
I rejoice in Adonai.
May sin vanish from the earth
and the wicked be so no more.

Praise, my soul, Adonai!

Glory…

Antiphon for Lent	The Lord brings forth bread from the earth, and wine to warm human hearts.
Easter	Alleluia, the stone was rolled back from the entrance to the tomb, alleluia.

PSALM 118

Lent, 2nd Sunday

The right hand of the Lord
has shown its power;
the right hand of the Lord has raised me up.

Lent, Palm Sunday

The great crowd that had gathered
for the feast cried out to the Lord:
Blessed is he
who comes in the name of the Lord.
Hosanna in the highest.

Easter, 6th Sunday

This is the day the Lord has made,
alleluia.

Give thanks to Adonai who is good,
whose love is to forever.

Let Israel now declare:
this love is to forever.
Let the house of Aaron declare:
this love is to forever.
Let those who fear Adonai declare:
this love is to forever.

In anguish I cried to Adonai
who answered me with freedom.
Adonai is with me, I will not be afraid.
What can any human do to me?
Before enmity I keep this in mind:
Adonai is with me, ready to help me.

Better to take refuge in Adonai
than to trust in the human;
Better to take refuge in Adonai
than to trust in a prince;

All of the nations surrounded me,
indeed did they surround me;
in the name of Adonai indeed I cut them.
They swarmed around me like bees,
they crackled like thorns in a fire;
in the name of Adonai indeed I cut them.

To push back they pushed me back to fall
but Adonai helped me.
Adonai became my strength and my song
and became to me salvation.
Shout joy and victory in your tents, you righteous.

Adonai's right hand does a mighty thing,
Adonai's right hand lifted high.
Adonai's right hand does a mighty thing.
I will not die; I will live
and proclaim these deeds indeed.
To chasten, Adonai let me be chastened,
but did not give me to death.

PSALM 118, continued

Open for me the gates of righteousness;
I will enter through them
and give thanks to Adonai.
This is Adonai's gate,
where righteous ones may enter.
I will give thanks to you for you answered me
and you became to me salvation.

The stone they rejected as builders
became the cornerstone.
With Adonai this happened
and it is marvelous in our eyes.
This is the day Adonai made;
let us rejoice and be glad.

Adonai, save now!
Adonai, grant success now!
Blessed is the one coming in the name of Adonai;
We bless you from Adonai's house.
Our El Adonai has shined light onto us.

Join with boughs the festal procession
up to the horns of the altar.
To you, my God, I will give thanks.
You, my God, I will exalt.
Give thanks to Adonai who is good,
whose love is to forever.

Glory...

Lent, 2nd Sunday	The right hand of the Lord has shown its power; the right hand of the Lord has raised me up.
Lent, Palm Sunday	The great crowd that had gathered for the feast cried out to the Lord: Blessed is he who comes in the name of the Lord. Hosanna in the highest.
Easter, 6th Sunday	This is the day the Lord has made, alleluia.

DANIEL 3:52-57

Lent, 2nd Sunday	Let us sing the hymn of the three youths which they sang in the fiery furnace, giving praise to God.
Lent, Palm Sunday	God grant that we may be faithful with the angels and the children singing to the conqueror of death: Hosanna in the highest.
Easter, 6th Sunday	Blessed are you, Lord our God, in the dome of heaven, worthy of praise forever, alleluia.

DANIEL 3:52-57

Blessed are you, O Lord, God of our ancestors,
praiseworthy and exalted above all forever.

Blessed is your glorious and holy name,
praiseworthy and exalted above all forever.

Blessed are you in the temple of your sacred glory,
praiseworthy and exalted above all forever.

Blessed are you who sit high on the cherubim
   and look into the depths,
praiseworthy and exalted above all forever.

Blessed are you on your royal throne,
praiseworthy and exalted above all forever.

Blessed are you in the dome of heaven,
to be hymned and glorified forever.

Bless the Lord, all you works of the Lord,
sing praise and high exaltation forever.

Glory…

Lent, 2nd Sunday	Let us sing the hymn of the three youths which they sang in the fiery furnace, giving praise to God.
Lent, Palm Sunday	God grant that we may be faithful with the angels and the children singing to the conquerer of death: Hosanna in the highest.
Easter, 6th Sunday	Blessed are you, Lord our God, in the dome of heaven, worthy of praise forever, alleluia.

PSALM 150

Lent, 2nd Sunday — Praise the Lord in the heavenly power.

Lent, Palm Sunday — Blessed is the one
who comes in the name of the Lord;
peace in heaven and glory in the highest.

Easter, 6th Sunday — Worship God who is seated on the throne;
sing to God in praise: Amen, alleluia.

Praise Adonai!
To El in the sanctuary, give praise.
In the mighty heavens, give praise.
For the works of power, give praise.
For surpassing greatness, give praise.

With sounding of trumpet, give praise.
With harp and lyre, give praise.
With tambourine and dance, give praise.
With flute and string, give praise.

With cymbals clashing, give praise.
With cymbals resounding, give praise.
Let all that has breath praise Adonai!
Praise Adonai!

Glory…

Repeat antiphon.

WEEK II
SUNDAY EVENING

PSALM 23

Antiphon for Lent In pastures of greenness
the Lord makes me lie down.

Easter Alleluia, alleluia, alleluia.

Adonai is my shepherd; nothing do I lack.
My Lord lays me down in green pastures
and leads me beside still quiet waters,
restoring my soul and guiding me
in paths of justice for the Lord's own namesake.

So when I walk in the deep dark valley
I will not fear for you are with me,
your rod and staff a comfort to me.

A table you prepare before me
in the presence even of enmity.
My head you anoint with oil
and my cup is overflowing.

Surely goodness and love will follow me
all the days of my life
and I will dwell in the Lord's own house
for length of days.

Glory…

Repeat antiphon.

PSALM 110:1-6a,7

Lent, 2nd Sunday   The Lord will send forth from Zion
your mighty sceptor in holy splendor.

Lent, Palm Sunday   Christ was scourged
and treated with contempt,
but God's right hand has raised him up.

Easter, 6th Sunday   God raised up Christ from the dead and gave
him a place at his right hand in heaven, alleluia.

Adonai said to my Lord:
"Sit at my right hand
  until I make enmity as a footstool for your feet."

A scepter of your might
Adonai will extend from Zion,
and rule in the midst of enmity!

Your troops are willing on the day of your battle.
In majesties of holiness from the womb of the dawn
to you is the dew of your youth.
Adonai swore and this mind will not change,
"You are a priest to forever
  in the order of Melchizedek."

The Lord is at your right hand
and will crush kings on the day of wrath,
will judge the nations…,
and will drink from a brook on the way
with head lifted up because of all this.

Glory…

Repeat antiphon.

PSALM 115

Lent, 2nd Sunday We worship the one true God
whose made heaven and earth.

Lent, Palm Sunday The blood of Christ washes away our sins
and makes us worthy to serve the living God.

Easter, 6th Sunday You have been turned from your idols
and to faith in the living God, alleluia.

Not to us, Adonai, not to us,
but to your name give glory
because of your love, because of your fidelity.
Why say the nations, "Where now is their God?"

Our God now is in the heavens
and does all that God pleases.
Their idols are silver and gold,
made of human hands.

Made with a mouth, they cannot speak;
made with eyes, they cannot see;
made with ears, they cannot hear;
made with a nose, they cannot smell;

made with hands, they cannot feel;
made with feet, they cannot walk,
and they utter no sound with their throat.
Like them will become those who make them,
and all who trust in them.

Israel, trust Adonai, your help and your shield.
Aaron, trust Adonai, your help and your shield.
Ones fearing Adonai, trust Adonai,
your help and your shield.

Adonai remembers us and will bless us,
will bless the house of Israel,
will bless the house of Aaron,
will bless ones fearing Adonai,
the small ones with the great ones.

May Adonai make an increase to you,
to you and to your children.
You are blessed by Adonai,
Maker of heavens and earth.

Heavens, the heavens are to Adonai,
but earth is given to humanity.
The dead ones do not praise Adonai,
and not all those who go down in silence.

But we, we extol Adonai,
from now and to forevermore.
Praise Adonai!

Glory…

Repeat antiphon.

(Easter) REVELATION 19:1b,2a,5b,6b,7

Easter, 6th Sunday   Alleluia, salvation and glory and power
are to our God, alleluia.

Alleluia! Praise the Lord!
Salvation and glory and power are to our God,
whose judgments are true and just.

Alleluia! Praise the Lord!
Praise our God, all you slaves of the Lord,
you small and you great, who hold God in awe.

Alleluia! Praise the Lord!
The Lord is reigning, our God, the Almighty.
Let us rejoice and let us exult,
and we will give the glory to the Lord.

Alleluia! Praise the Lord!
The day has come
for the marriage of the Lamb,
and the bride has prepared herself.

Glory…

Easter, 6th Sunday   Alleluia, salvation and glory and power
are to our God, alleluia.

(Lent) 1 **PETER** 2:21-24

Lent, 2nd Sunday — God did not spare God's own Son
but gave him up for us all.

Lent, Palm Sunday — Christ bore our sins
in his own body on the cross
so that we might die to sin
and be alive to all that is good.

To this you were called,
for indeed Christ suffered on behalf of you,
leaving to you an example to follow in his steps:

He did not sin, nor was guile found in his mouth;
he was reviled and did not revile in return;
suffering he did not threaten,
but delivered himself to the one judging justly.

Our sins he carried in his body up onto the tree,
that dying to sins, we might live for justice.
By his bruises, you are cured.

Glory…

Lent, 2nd Sunday — God did not spare God's own Son
but gave him up for us all.

Lent, Palm Sunday — Christ bore our sins
in his own body on the cross
so that we might die to sin
and be alive to all that is good.

WEEK II
MONDAY MORNING

PSALM 31:*1-17,20-25*

Antiphon   Lord, shine your faces on your servant.
(alleluia)

In you, Adonai, I take refuge;
let me not be shamed to forever.
Deliver me in your righteousness.
Quickly turn to me your ear! Rescue me!

Be for me a rock of refuge,
a fortress house to save me.
Since you are my rock and my fortress,
for the sake of your name
you lead me and guide me.

You free me from the trap they set for me,
for you are my refuge.
Into your hand I commit my spirit;
you redeem me, Adonai God of truth.

I hate when folks cling to worthless idols,
and I trust in Adonai.
I will be glad and rejoice in your love
for you saw my affliction;
you knew the anguishes of my soul.

You do not put me into the hand of enmity;
you set my feet into the spacious place.

Be merciful to me, Adonai, in my distress;
my eyes and my soul and my body
grow weak with sorrow.

My life is consumed by anguish
and my years with groaning.
My strength fails because of my guilt
and my bones grow weak.

Because of enmity I am
the utter contempt of even my neighbors
and a dread to my friends
who see me on the street and flee.

I am forgotten as though dead;
my heart became like broken pottery,
for I hear the slander of many
and terror on every side
when they conspire together against me
and plot to take my life.

But I trust in you, Adonai;
I say you are my God;
my times are in your hand.
Deliver me from the hands
of enmity and pursuers.

Shine your faces on your servant!
Save me in your unfailing love!…

How great is the goodness
you store up for ones who fear you
and bestow on those taking refuge in you
in the sight of the children of humanity.

PSALM 31, continued

You hide them in the shelter of your presence;
from human intrigues you keep them
in a dwelling safe from the strife of tongues.

Adonai is praised for showing wonderful love
to me in the city besieged, and I said in my alarm,
"I am cut off from before your eyes."
Yet you heard the sound of my cries for mercy
when I called to you for help.

Love Adonai, all you saints,
Adonai faithful and preserving,
but paying back in full the arrogant.

Be strong and strengthen your heart,
all you hoping in Adonai!

Glory…

Antiphon   Lord, shine your faces on your servant.
(alleluia)

PSALM 42

Antiphon for Lent   When can I go and meet the face of God?

Easter   As a deer pines for flowing water
so my soul longs for you, my God,
alleluia.

As a deer breathes heavy for streams of water,
so my soul throbs for you, God.

My soul she thirsts for God, the living God.
When can I go and meet the faces of God?

My tears were food for me by day and by night,
while all day they said to me, "Where is your God?"

These things I remember
as my soul pours out before me:
How I would go with the multitude
to lead them to the house of God
sounding shouts of joy and thanksgiving,
a festive throng!

Why are you downcast, my soul,
and disturbed within me?
Put hope in God, whom I will yet praise,
the saving help and presence.

My God, within me my soul she is downcast.
For this I will remember you
from the land of Jordan and the heights of Hermon,
from the Mount of Mizar:

Deep calls to deep in the roar of your waterfalls.
All your waves and breakers are swept over me.

By day Adonai directs love
and at night the song within me
is a prayer to the God of my life.

I say to El my Rock, "why do you forget me?
  Why must I go about mourning,
  oppressed by enmity?"

PSALM 42, continued

With mortal agony in my bones,
taunted by foes,
while all day they say to me, "Where is your God?"

Why are you downcast, my soul?
Why are you disturbed within me?
Put hope in God, whom I will yet praise,
my saving help and God.

Glory…

Antiphon for Lent	When can I go and meet the face of God?
Easter	As a deer pines for flowing water so my soul longs for you, my God, alleluia.

SIRACH 36:1-6,13-22

Antiphon for Lent	Show mercy, Lord, to the people called by your name.
Easter	Fill Zion with your praises, Lord, and let your wonders be proclaimed, alleluia.

Come to our aid, God of all;
let all the nations be in fear of you.
Raise your hand to the foreign nations,
that they may see your might.

As you have used us to show them your holiness,
so now use them to show us your glory.
They will know as we know
that there is no God but you.

Give new signs and work new wonders;
show the splendor of your right hand and arm…

Gather all the tribes of Jacob,
that they may inherit the land as at the beginning.
Show mercy to the people called by your name:
Israel, whom you named your firstborn.

Have pity on your holy city, Jerusalem,
the foundation for your throne.
Fill Zion with your majesty,
and your temple with your glory.

Give witness of your deeds of old;
fulfill the prophecies spoken in your name.
Reward those who have hoped in you,
and let your prophets be proven true.

Hear the prayers of your servants,
as you are good to your people.
Thus all will know to the ends of the earth
that you are God eternal.

Glory…

Antiphon for Lent	Show mercy, Lord, to the people called by your name.
Easter	Fill Zion with your praises, Lord, and let your wonders be proclaimed, alleluia.

PSALM 19

Antiphon for Lent — The heavens are declaring the glory of God.

Easter — The glory of God illumines the city
and the Lamb of God is its light,
alleluia.

The heavens declare the glory of God,
and the sky proclaims the work of God's hands.
Day after day, speech pouring forth,
and knowledge on display night after night.

There is no speech, there is no language,
and no sound is heard.
Into all the earth their line goes out
and their words to the ends of the world.

There God has pitched a tent for the sun,
and like a bridegroom coming forth,
and like a champion running the course, rejoices.

At the end of the heavens is the rising,
to their furthest ends is the circuit,
and nothing is hidden from its heat.

The law of Adonai is perfect, reviving the soul;
statutes of Adonai are trustworthy,
making wise of the simple;
precepts of Adonai are right ones,
giving joy of heart;

the command of Adonai is radiant,
giving light to eyes;
the fear of Adonai is pure, enduring to forever;
ordinances of Adonai are sure and altogether just;

more precious than gold,
much more than pure gold,
more sweet than honey, the honey of honeycombs.

Your servant is being warned by them;
to keep them is a great reward.
Who can discern errors?
From those hidden from me, forgive me!

And keep your servant from willful sins!
May they not rule over me;
then will I be blameless
and innocent of great transgression.

May the words of my mouth be as pleasing
and the meditation of my heart be as pleasing
before you, Adonai,
my Rock and my Redeemer.

Glory…

Antiphon for Lent	The heavens are declaring the glory of God.
Easter	The glory of God illumines the city and the Lamb of God is its light, alleluia.

WEEK II
MONDAY EVENING

PSALM 12

Antiphon for Lent   Words of the Lord are flawless words,
like silver refined in a furnace of clay.

Easter   Alleluia, alleluia, alleluia.

Help, Adonai, for the godly are no more;
the faithful vanish from humanity's children.
They speak the lie to each of their neighbors,
lips of flattering with heart and heart.

May Adonai close all flattering lips
and tongues speaking the boast that say:
"With our tongues we will triumph,
   our lips are with us; who is our master?"

But because of oppression of the weak,
because of groaning of needy ones,
now Adonai says, "I will arise and protect them."

Words of Adonai are flawless words,
like silver refined in the furnace of clay,
and being purified seven times over.

You, Adonai, you will keep them safe;
you are our protection to forever.
But doers of badness will still strut about
when vileness is honored among human beings.

Glory...   Repeat antiphon.

PSALM 40 :2-14,17-18

Antiphon for Lent My food is that I may do
the will of the one who sent me. John 4:34

Easter Alleluia, alleluia, alleluia.

Waiting, I waited for Adonai,
who turned to me and heard my cry,

who lifted me from the slime pit
and from the muddy mire,
and set my feet on rock,
making firm my standing place,

and put in my mouth a new song,
a hymn of praise to our God.
Many will see and fear and trust Adonai.

Blessed is the one who trusts in Adonai
and looks not to the proud
or those turning to false "gods."

Adonai, my God, many are your deeds of wonder
and your plans cannot be equaled.
Should I speak and tell of them
they would be too many to declare.

Sacrifice and offerings you did not desire,
but my ears you pierced open for me.
Burnt offering and sin offering you did not require.
Then I said, "Here, I have come;

PSALM 40:2-14,17-18, continued

in the scroll, in the book, it is written of me.
To do your will, my God, is my desire,
and your law is within my heart."

I proclaim righteousness in the great assembly.
See my lips unsealed. You, Adonai, you know!

Your righteousness I do not hide in my heart;
your faithfulness and your salvation I speak.
I do not conceal your love and your truth
from the great assembly.

Adonai, withhold not your mercies from me,
may your love and your truth protect me always
for countless troubles surround around me.

My sins overtook me and I cannot see.
They are more than the hairs of my head
and my heart fails me.

Be pleased, Adonai, to save me;
Adonai, come quickly to help me!…

May all who seek you rejoice in you and be glad
and may lovers of your salvation say always,
"Let God be exalted."

Yet I am poor and needy.
May the Lord think of me and not delay,
my help and my deliverer, my God.

Glory…

| Antiphon for Lent | My food is that I may do the will of the one who sent me. | John 4:34 |

Easter — Alleluia, alleluia, alleluia.

PSALM 45

Antiphon for Lent
You, my king,
excel among humanity
with anointing of grace on your lips.

Easter
Blessed are those called
to the wedding feast of the Lamb,
alleluia.

My heart is stirred, a noble theme;
I recite my verses for the king;
my tongue is a pen of a skillful scribe.

You were anointed with grace on your lips,
more excellent among children of humanity.
For thus has God blessed you to forever.

Gird your sword upon your side, mighty one,
your splendor and your majesty.
Your majesty, be victorious!
Ride forth on behalf of truth and humility
and let righteousness display
awesome deeds of your right hand.

Your arrows are sharp;
let nations fall beneath you into the heart
of ones who choose enmity with the royal one
on God's throne forever and ever.
A scepter of justice is the scepter of the kingdom.

PSALM 45, continued

You love righteousness
and hate when people do bad things;
for this your God anointed you
above your companions with oil of joy,
with myrrh and aloes and cassias on your robes,
and from ivory palaces strings make you glad.

Children of royalty are honored among you
and the queen bride stands at your right hand,
honored in gold of Ophir.

Listen, daughter, and consider!
Give your ear and forget your people
and the house of your parents.
The king is enthralled for your beauty;
he is your lord, so honor him!
With the gift of your face, daughter of Tyre,
wealthy people will seek you.

The all-glorious daughter of the king is within
with interweavings of gold in her gown.
In embroidered garments she is led to the king;

her virgin companions following her
are being brought to you.
They are led in with joy and gladness;
they enter the palace of the king.

In the place of your parents will your children be,
as princes and princesses through all the land.
I will make perpetual the memory of your name
through all generations and generation.
For this the nations will praise you
ever and to forever.

Glory…

Antiphon for Lent You, my king,
excel among humanity
with anointing of grace on your lips.

Easter Blessed are those called
to the wedding feast of the Lamb,
alleluia.

EPHESIANS 1:3-10

Antiphon for Lent The mystery of God's will
in the fullness of time
is the heading up of all things in Christ.

Easter From his fullness we have all received
grace upon grace, alleluia.

Blessed be the God and Father
of our Lord Jesus Christ,
who has blessed us in Christ
with every spiritual blessing in the heavens.

EPHESIANS 1:3-10, continued

God chose us in Christ
before the foundation of the world,
to be holy and free of blemish before him.

In love, God gave us a destiny:
as sons are adopted, through Jesus Christ himself,
in accord with the good pleasure of God's will
to the praise of the glory of grace
by which we are favored as God's beloved.

In Christ we have the redemption
through his blood, the forgiveness of sins,
in accord with the riches of his grace
which he made abound to us.

In all wisdom and intelligence
the mystery of God's will is made known to us
in accord with God's good pleasure and purpose:

A stewardship of the fullness of time,
heading up all things in Christ,
the things in the heavens and the things on earth.

Glory...

Antiphon for Lent	The mystery of God's will in the fullness of time is the heading up of all things in Christ.
Easter	From his fullness we have all received grace upon grace, alleluia.

WEEK II
TUESDAY MORNING

PSALM 37

Antiphon
    Wait patiently for the Lord;
    the meek will inherit the land.
    (alleluia)

Fret not over those who do badness;
envy not those who do wrong.
For like grass their efforts will soon wither,
and like the green plant they will die away.

Trust in Adonai and do good!
Dwell in the land and enjoy safe pasture!
Delight in Adonai
who will give the desires of your heart.

Commit your way and your trust
to Adonai who will do it:
making your righteousness shine like the dawn
and your justice like the noonday sun.

Be still before Adonai and wait with patience.
Fret not over the ways of the successful,
over schemes carried out by human beings.

Refrain from anger and turn from wrath!
Fret not; it brings only evil,
for humans doing badness will be cut off,
but those who hope in Adonai will inherit the land.

PSALM 37, continued

A little while and bad doings will be no more;
you will look and not find them in their places.
But the meek will inherit the land
and they will enjoy greatness of peace.

Plotters of bad things to do to the righteous
gnash their teeth at them.
But the Lord laughs at them,
knowing their day is coming.

They draw their sword and they bend their bow
to bring down the poor and the needy,
to slay those of the upright way.
Their sword will pierce into their own heart
and their bows will be broken.

Better the little bit of the righteous
than the wealth of many who do bad things,
for the powers of bad doers will be broken
while Adonai upholds the righteous.

Adonai knows the days of the blameless
and their inheritance will endure to forever.
They will not wither in times of disaster
and in days of famine they will enjoy plenty.

But wicked ways will perish
and those who choose enmity with Adonai
will vanish like the beauty of fields;
like smoke they will vanish.

A doer of badness borrows and does not repay,
but a righteous one is generous and giving.
The blessing on the righteous is to live in the land;
the curse of doing badness is to be cut off.

The steps of human beings are made firm
by Adonai who delights in their way.
Though we stumble, we will not fall
for Adonai upholds us by the hand.

I was young and now I am old,
yet never have I seen the righteous forsaken
or their children begging bread.
Generous and lending all the day,
their children are a blessing.

Turn from evil and do good! Then live to always!
For Adonai loves the just
and will not forsake the faithful.
They will be protected to forever...
Righteous ones will inherit the land
and they will dwell in her to forever.

The mouth of the righteous he utters wisdom
and the tongue she speaks justice.
The law of their God is in their heart
and their feet do not slip.

Wicked ways lie in wait for the righteous
seeking to kill them;
Adonai will not leave them under this power
nor let them be condemned when on trial.

PSALM 37, continued

Wait for Adonai and keep to the way
of the one who will exalt you to possess the land,
and you will see wicked ways cut off.

I saw a ruthless human flourishing
like a native green tree,
but passing away is seen no more;
though I looked he was not to be found.

Consider the blameless and observe the upright
for the future is for the person of peace.
But sinners sinning will be destroyed together;
the future of wicked ways will be cut off.

The salvation of the righteous is from Adonai,
their stronghold in times of trouble.
Their help and deliverance and salvation,
their deliverance from ways that are wicked,
is Adonai in whom they take refuge.

Glory…

Antiphon   Wait patiently for the Lord;
the meek will inherit the land.
(alleluia)

PSALM 43

Antiphon for Lent — Lord, send forth your light and your truth.

Easter — You have come to Mount Zion
and to the city of the living God, alleluia.

God, vindicate me;
plead my cause against a nation not godly;
rescue me from humans deceitful doing wicked.

God, my stronghold, why am I rejected?
Why must I go about mourning,
oppressed by enmity?

Send forth your light and your truth;
let them guide me to your dwellings
and bring me to your holy mountain.

Then I will go to the altar of God,
to El, my joy and delight,
and I will praise you with harp, God, my God.

Why are you downcast, my soul?
Why are you disturbed within me?
Put hope in God, whom I will yet praise,
the saving help of my face, my God.

Glory…

Antiphon for Lent — Lord, send forth your light and your truth.

Easter — You have come to Mount Zion
and to the city of the living God, alleluia.

ISAIAH 38:10-14,17b-20

Antiphon for Lent   Lord, save us all our days.

Easter   Lord,
you have kept my soul from destruction,
alleluia.

I asked, "Must I go in the prime of my days
through the gates of Sheol;
must I be robbed of the rest of my years?"

I said, "I will no longer see Adonai,
Adonai in the land of the living.
As a dweller of the place of cessation
I will look on humanity no longer."

My house was pulled down
and taken from me like the tent of my shepherd;
I rolled up my life,
as a weaver cuts off from a loom.

From day to night you made an end of me.
I waited till dawn;
all my bones are broken as by a lion.
From day to night you made an end of me.

Like a swift or thrush I cried;
I moaned like the dove.
My eyes to the heavens grew weak.
Lord, troubles are at me; come to my aid...

In your love you have kept my self
out of the pit of destruction;
indeed you put behind your back all my sins.

Sheol cannot praise you
and death cannot sing to you praise,
nor can those going down the pit
hope for your faithfulness.

The living alive praise you, as I do this day.
Fathers and mothers tell the children
all about your faithfulness.

Adonai saves us;
we will play our stringed instruments
and sing in the temple of Adonai
all the days of our lives.

Glory…

Antiphon for Lent — Lord, save us all our days.

Easter — Lord,
you have kept my soul from destruction,
alleluia.

PSALM 65

Antiphon for Lent
For you, O God, silence,
and praise in Zion.

Easter
You care for the earth and water her
for a rich abundance,
alleluia.

For you, O God, silence and praise in Zion,
and to you will our vow be fulfilled.

To you hearing our prayer all humanity will come.
Matters of sin overwhelmed over me;
you atoned for our transgressions.

Blessed are the ones you choose
and bring near to live in your courts.
We are filled with the goodness of your house
and the holiness of your temple.

Deeds awesome and righteous are your answer,
God of our salvation,
hope of all the ends of the earth and of the far seas.

You form mountains by your power,
arming yourself with strength.
You still the roar of the seas, the roar of their waves
and the turmoil of nations.

Those who live in far away places
fear your wonders;
in dawns of morning and in the evening
you call forth songs of joy.

You care for the land and water her;
with an abundance you enrich her.
God's stream is as you ordain the earth:
filled with waters, providing grain.
You drench its furrows and level its ridges;
you soften her with showers and bless the crops.

You crown the year with your bounty;
carts overflow with your abundance.
The desert grasslands are overflowing
and the hills are clothed with gladness.

The meadows are covered with the flock
and valleys are coated with grain.
They shout for joy; for joy they sing.

Glory...

Antiphon for Lent   For you, O God, silence,
and praise in Zion.

Easter   You care for the earth and water her
for a rich abundance,
alleluia.

WEEK II
TUESDAY EVENING

PSALM 53

Antiphon for Lent
When God restores
the fortunes of the people of God,
let Jacob rejoice, let Israel be glad.

Easter
Alleluia, alleluia, alleluia.

In the heart of a fool is said, "There is no God."
The evil way is vile and corrupt;
there is no one doing good.

God looks from the heavens
on children of humanity
to see if there is one who understands,
one who is seeking God.

All of them turned away together;
they became corrupt;
there is no one doing good, not even one.

Will the ones doing evil never learn?
Devouring my people, they eat bread;
they do not call on God.

There they dreaded and dread was not there,
for God scattered the bones of attackers
put to shame in God's rejection.

Who would be brought from Zion
for the salvation of Israel?
When God restores the fortunes of God's people,
let Jacob rejoice, let Israel be glad.

Glory…   Repeat antiphon.

PSALM 54 :1-6,8-9

Antiphon in Lent   See! God is helping me;
the Lord sustains my very self.

Easter   Alleluia, alleluia, alleluia.

God, save me by your name
and by your might vindicate me.
God, hear my prayer!
Listen to the words of my mouth!

For strangers attack me
and ruthless people seek my life
without regard for God before them.
See, God is helping me!
The Lord is among those sustaining my self…

With a freewill offering I will sacrifice to you;
I will praise, Adonai, your good name,
for you delivered me from all trouble
and my eye has looked
on those who would be foes.

Glory…   Repeat antiphon.

PSALM 49

Antiphon in Lent
You cannot serve God and mammon.
Where your treasure is
there also will your heart be.

Matthew 6:24b,21

Easter
Seek the things of heaven,
not those of earth,
alleluia.

Hear this all peoples! Listen all alive in the world!
Men and women, all sons and daughters,
rich and poor alike:

My mouth will speak words of wisdom
and my heart utter the understanding of things.
I will turn an ear to a proverb;
I will expound my riddle with a harp.

Why should I fear in days of evil
the badness of deceivers who surround me,
the trusters of wealth,
and the boasters of the greatness of their riches?

No human can redeem redemption of another,
nor for oneself give a ransom to God.
Ransom of a life is costly;
no ransom is ever enough
for one to live to forever
and not see the decay.

For we see that wise people die;
like the foolish and the senseless they perish,
and leave all their wealth to others.
Their thoughts are of their houses to forever
as their dwelling for generations and generation,
and so they call lands by their own names.

The human, despite riches, does not endure,
but perishes just like the beasts.

This is their fate who trust in themselves
and their followers who give them approval.
Like the sheep they are destined for Sheol,
and death will feed on them too.

Upright ones will rule over them in the morning
and their form will decay in Sheol, their mansion.
But God will redeem my soul
and take me from the hand of Sheol.

Be not overawed when human beings grow rich,
when they increase the splendor of their houses.
For in death they will take none of it;
with none of their splendor will they descend.

Though during their lives they blessed themselves,
and people do praise you when you prosper,
they will go to the generation of their ancestors
and never see light to forever.

Like the beast that must perish
so is a human with riches
but still poor in understanding.

Glory… Repeat antiphon.

REVELATION 4:8b,11; 5:9,10,12,13b

Antiphon in Lent Worthy is the Lamb, slain to receive
the power and riches
and wisdom and strength
and honor and glory and blessing.

Easter The Lord has rescued my life
from the power of hell,
alleluia.

Worthy are you, our Lord and our God,
to receive the glory and honor and power,
because you have created all things,
and by your will all things were created and are.

Worthy are you to receive the scroll
and to open its seals,
because you were slain
and purchased for God by your blood
from every tribe and tongue and people and nation.

You made of them to our God
a kingdom and priests,
and they will reign over the earth.

Worthy is the Lamb, slain to receive
the power and riches and wisdom and strength
and honor and glory and blessing.

Glory…

Repeat antiphon.

WEEK II
WEDNESDAY MORNING

PSALM 39

Antiphon
We ourselves groan in ourselves,
eagerly expecting adoption,
the redemption of our body.
(alleluia)

I said, "I will watch my ways
  of sinning with my tongue;
  I will put on my mouth a muzzle
  as long as temptation is in my presence."
So in silent stillness I said nothing good,
and still my anguish increased.

My heart grew hot inside me;
in my meditation a fire burned.
I spoke with my tongue,
"Show me, Adonai, my end,
  what is the number of my days;
  let me know how fleeting I am.

See the handbreadths you made!
My days and my span are as nothing before you.
Indeed, each of all humanity stands as a breath.
Indeed, as a phantom the human goes out.
Indeed, vainly bustling about, heaping up wealth
without knowing who will get it."

PSALM 39, continued

But what am I looking for now, Lord?
My hope she is in you.
Save me from all my transgressions!
Make me not the scorn of fools.
I was silent and opened not my mouth,
for you, you have done it.

Remove your scourge from me;
from the blow of your hand I am overcome.
With a rebuke for sin you discipline the human
and you consume our wealth like a moth;
indeed we are each but a breath.

Hear my prayer, Adonai, and my cry for help;
listen, El, and be not deaf to my weeping.
For I am with you as an alien,
a stranger like all of my ancestors.
Look away from me that I may rejoice
before I depart and am no more.

Glory…

Antiphon   We ourselves groan in ourselves,
eagerly expecting adoption,
the redemption of our body.
(alleluia)

PSALM 77

Antiphon for Lent   God, in your holiness way,
what "god" is as great as God?

Easter   The waters saw you, O God;
          you led your people through the sea, alleluia.

PSALM 77

My cry is for God, indeed I cried for help.
My cry is for God to hear me.

In the day of my distress I sought the Lord,
my hand was stretched in the night without tiring;
my soul refused to be comforted.
I remembered God and I groaned;
I mused and my spirit grew faint.

You kept open the lids of my eyes;
I was troubled and could not speak.
I thought of former days and of years long ago.
I remembered my song in the night;
my heart mused and inquired of my spirit,

"Will the Lord reject to forever,
  never to show favor again?
  Is the unfailing love vanished to forever?
  Has the promise failed for all generations?
  Has God forgotten to be merciful
  or withheld compassion in anger?"

Then I thought, "My appeal is this,
  the years at the right hand of the Most High."
I will remember the deeds of Adonai;
yes, I will remember your long-ago miracles.
I will meditate on all of your works
and consider your mighty deeds.

PSALM 77, continued

God in your holiness way,
what "god" is as great as God?
You are the God who does miracles;
you display among the peoples your power.
You redeemed your people with your arm,
the descendants of Jacob and Joseph.

The waters saw you, God,
the waters saw you and writhed;
indeed the depths were convulsed.
Clouds poured down waters,
thunder resounded in the skies,
and your arrows flashed around.

Your thunder sounded in the whirlwind,
lightnings lit up the world;
the earth trembled and quaked.
Through the sea is your path,
and your way through mighty waters,
though your footprints were not seen.

You led your people like the flock
by the hand of Moses and Aaron.

Glory…

Antiphon in Lent	God, in your holiness way, what "god" is as great as God?
Easter	The waters saw you, O God; you led your people through the sea, alleluia.

1 SAMUEL 2:1-10

Antiphon in Lent My heart rejoices in the Lord,
who humbles and exalts.

Easter The Lord allows death
and raises to life,
alleluia.

My heart rejoices in Adonai,
my horn is lifted high in Adonai.

My mouth boasts over enmity,
for I delight in being delivered.
There is no Holy One like Adonai,
indeed there is no one who compares;
there is no Rock like our God.

Arrogant pride is coming from their mouth.
Do not keep talking so proudly
or proudly let arrogance come from your mouth,
for Adonai is God who knows,
by whom all deeds are weighed.

Bows of warriors are broken
but those stumbling are armed with strength.
The full hire themselves out for more food,
but the hungry ones hunger no more.
She who was barren bore seven sons;
blessed with many sons, she is pining away.

1 SAMUEL 2:1-10, continued

Adonai allows death and is making alive,
brings down to Sheol and is raising up.
Adonai allows poverty and is sending wealth,
humbling and exalting,
raising the poor from the dust
and the needy from ash-heaps
to sit with princes and inherit thrones of honor.

For Adonai's are the foundations of the earth,
setting the world upon them.
The feet of the saints will be guarded
but doers of badness will be silenced in darkness.

For not by strength does the human prevail;
Adonai shatters opposition,
thundering from the heavens.
Adonai will judge the ends of the earth,
give strength, and exalt the horn
of the one chosen and Anointed.

Glory…

Antiphon in Lent	My heart rejoices in the Lord, who humbles and exalts.
Easter	The Lord allows death and raises to life, alleluia.

PSALM 97

Antiphon in Lent	The Lord reigns; let the earth be glad.
Easter	A light has dawned for the just; joy has come to the upright of heart, alleluia.

PSALM 97

Adonai reigns; let the earth be glad.
Let all the distant shores rejoice.
Clouds and thick darkness surround the throne
founded on righteousness and justice.

Fire goes before, consuming foes on every side.
Lightnings light up the world;
the earth sees and trembles.

Mountains melt like wax before Adonai,
before the Lord of all the earth.
The heavens proclaim righteousness
and all peoples see the glory.

Let those who worship idols be shamed,
those boasting in their images.
Worship God, all you "gods."

Zion hears and rejoices
and the villages of Judah are glad
because of your judgments, Adonai.

For you, Adonai, are Most High over all the earth,
far exalted above all the "gods."

Evil is despised by lovers of Adonai,
who guards the lives of faithful ones
and delivers them from the hands of doers of bad.

Light is shed upon the righteous
and joy on the upright of heart.
Rejoice in Adonai, righteous ones,
and praise the holy name.

Glory...   Repeat antiphon.

WEEK II
WEDNESDAY EVENING

PSALM 52

Antiphon in Lent   I trust in God's unfailing love
forever and ever.

Easter   Alleluia, alleluia, alleluia.

Why, mighty one, do you boast of evil
to the disgrace of El all the day?
Your tongue plots destruction
like a sharpened razor, practicing deceit.

You love evil rather than good,
falsehood rather than speaking truth.
Your tongue of deceit loves every harmful word.

Surely El will bring you down,
snatch you from your tent,
and uproot you from the land of the living.

Then the righteous will see and fear,
and they will laugh at you.
See the one who did not see God as the stronghold,
but grew strong by destruction
and trusted in the greatness of wealth.

But I am like an olive tree
flourishing in the house of God;
I trust in God's unfailing love forever and ever.

I will praise you to forever for what you have done,
and in the presence of your saints I will hope in you
for your name is good.

Glory…

Repeat antiphon.

PSALM 62

Antiphon in Lent — Rest, my soul, in God alone;
from God is my salvation

Easter — Do not let your hearts be troubled;
have faith in me, alleluia. *see John 14:1*

My soul finds rest in God alone,
from whom is my salvation,
alone my salvation and my rock,
my fortress never to be shaken greatly.

Until when will you assault a human being,
will you throw down, all of you,
like a leaning wall or a tottering fence?

They fully intend to topple from the lofty place;
they delight in lies
and bless with their mouth and curse in their heart.

My soul finds rest in God alone,
from whom is my hope,
alone my salvation and my rock,
my fortress not to be shaken.

PSALM 62, continued

From God is my salvation and my honor;
my mighty rock and refuge.
Trust in God at all times, people;
pour out your heart to God our refuge.

Sons and daughters of humanity are but a breath;
the so-called great ones are an illusion.
On balanced scales they both rise;
together they are only a breath.

Trust not in extortion
and take no pride in stolen things;
even when riches increase
do not set your heart on them.

One thing God has spoken,
two things I have heard:
that to God is strength and to you, Lord, is love;
and surely you will reward to each
as are our deeds.

Glory…

Antiphon in Lent	Rest, my soul, in God alone; from God is my salvation	
Easter	Do not let your hearts be troubled; have faith in me, alleluia.	see John 14:1

PSALM 67

Antiphon in Lent   May God be gracious to us, bless us,
and shine the holy face upon us.

Easter   May the peoples praise you, God,
and rejoice in your salvation,
alleluia.

May God be gracious to us and bless us,
may God's faces shine upon us.
How else can your ways be known on the earth
and your salvation among all the nations?

May the peoples praise you, God,
may the peoples praise you, all of them.

May the nations be glad and sing for joy
for you rule the peoples
and guide nations of the earth into justice.

May the peoples praise you, God,
may the peoples praise you, all of them.

The land will yield her harvest, God will bless us,
and all the ends of the earth will revere our God.

Glory...

Antiphon in Lent   May God be gracious to us, bless us,
and shine the holy face upon us.

Easter   May the peoples praise you, God,
and rejoice in your salvation,
alleluia.

COLOSSIANS 1:12-20

Antiphon for Lent   All things have been created through him;
he is before all things
and in him all things hold together.

Easter   His glory covers the heavens
and his praise fills the earth, alleluia.

Give joyful thanks to the Father who made you fit
for your part of the lot of the saints in light,

who delivered us out of the authority of darkness
and transitioned us into the kingdom of the beloved Son,
in whom we have redemption, the forgiveness of our sins.

The Son is the image of the invisible God,
the firstborn of all creation.
In him all things were created,
in the heavens and on the earth,
the visible and the invisible,
whether thrones, lordships, rulers or authorities.

All things have been created through him and for him.
He is before all things,
and in him all things hold together.

He is the head of the body, the church,
and the beginning, the firstborn from the dead,
so that in all things he may hold the first place.

In him all the fullness was well pleased to dwell,
and through him reconciliation to himself of all things,
things on earth and things in the heavens,
making peace through the blood of his cross.

Glory…

Repeat antiphon.

WEEK II
THURSDAY MORNING

PSALM 44

Antiphon

> For they won victory
> not by their sword and their arm,
> but by your right hand and arm
> and the light of your faces.
> (alleluia)

With our ears, God, we have heard,
our fathers told us the deed
you did in their days, in days long ago.

You drove out nations by your hand
and you planted them;
you crushed peoples and made them flourish.
For they won victory not by their sword and arm,
but by your right hand and arm
and the light of your faces, for you loved them.

PSALM 44, continued

You are my King and my God;
decree the victories of Jacob.
Through you we push back enmity;
through your name we trample opposition.

Indeed I trust not in my bow
and my sword does not bring me victory,
but you give to us victory over enmity
and shame the adversity.
In God we boast all the day
and we will praise your name to forever.

But you let us be rejected and humbled
and you do not go out with our armies.
You turned us back before enmity
and adversaries plundered from us.

You gave us up like sheep devoured;
among the nations you scattered us.
You sold your people for no great price,
gaining nothing from their sale.

You made us a reproach to our neighbors,
scorn and derision to those around us.
You made us a byword among the nations,
a shaking of heads among the peoples.

All the day my disgrace is before me
and my shame covers my face
at taunts of reproachers and revilers
because of avenging enmity.

All of this happened though we did not forget you
and were not false to your covenant.
Our hearts did not turn back
and our feet did not stray from your path,
but you pushed us into haunts of jackals
and you covered us over with deep darkness.

If we forgot the name of our God,
if we spread out our hands to a foreign "god,"
would God not have discovered this,
the One knowing the secrets of the heart?
Yet for you we face death all the day;
we are considered as sheep for slaughter.

Wake up, Lord! Why do you sleep?
Rouse yourself! Do not reject us to forever.
Why do you hide your faces
and forget our misery and oppression?

Indeed our self is brought down to the dust;
our body clings to the ground.
Rise up as our help and redeem us!
because of your unfailing love.

Glory…

Antiphon For they won victory
not by their sword and their arm,
but by your right hand and arm
and the light of your faces.
(alleluia)

PSALM 80

Antiphon in Lent Shepherd of Israel,
awaken your might;
bring us to salvation.

Easter I am the vine,
you are the branches;
alleluia.   John 15:5a

Hear us, One Shepherd of Israel,
you who lead Joseph like a flock.
From your throne on the cherubim, shine forth
before Ephraim, Benjamin and Manasseh!
Awaken your might! Come to our salvation!

O God, restore us!
Make your faces shine that we may be saved!

Until when, Adonai, God of Hosts,
will you smolder against the prayer of your people?
You fed them with bread of tears
and you made them drink tears by the bowlful.
You made us a contention to our neighbors,
and enmity mocks us.

God of Hosts, restore us!
Make your faces shine that we may be saved!

Out from Egypt, you brought a vine;
you drove out the nations and you planted it.
You cleared the ground before her;
her roots took root and she filled the land.

Mountains were covered by her shade
and the mighty cedars by her branches.
She sent out her branches to the Sea,
and her shoots as far as the River.

Why have you broken down her walls?
All who pass by the way pick at her.
The boar from the forest ravages her,
and creatures of the field feed on her.

God of Hosts, return now!
Look down from heaven!
See and watch over this vine,
this root that your right hand planted,
and the son you raised up for yourself.
Some would burn it or cut it down;
at the rebuke of your faces may those plans perish.

Let your hand be on the one at your right hand,
the descendent of Adam you raised up for yourself.
Then we will not turn away from you;
you revive us and we will call on your name.

Adonai, God of Hosts, restore us!
Make your faces shine that we may be saved!

Glory…

Antiphon in Lent   Shepherd of Israel,
awaken your might;
bring us to salvation.

Easter   I am the vine,
you are the branches; alleluia.   John 15:5a

ISAIAH 12:1b-6

Antiphon in Lent
Make known among the nations
the deeds of the Lord.

Easter
You will rejoice and draw water
from the well of the Savior,
alleluia.

I will praise you, Adonai.
Though you were angry with me,
your anger turned away and you comforted me.

Surely God is my salvation!
I will trust and will not be afraid
for Yah is my strength and my song.

Adonai became for me salvation
and you will draw with joy
waters from wells of salvation…

Give thanks to Adonai! Call on the name!
Make the deeds known among the nations!
Proclaim that the name is exalted!

Sing to Adonai, who has done glory!
Let this be known to all the world.

Shout! And sing for joy, dwellers of Zion!
For great in your midst
is the Holy One of Israel.

Glory…

Repeat antiphon.

PSALM 81

Antiphon in Lent — Sing for joy to God our strength.

Easter — The Lord feeds us with finest of wheat, alleluia.

Sing for joy to God our strength!
Shout to the God of Jacob!

Begin the music! Strike the tambourine,
the melodious harp and the lyre!
Sound the ram horn at the new moon,
the full moon, the day of our feast!

For this is a decree for Israel,
an ordinance of the God of Jacob,
a statute established for Joseph
when time to go out from the land of Egypt
and the language we did not understand:

"I removed the burden from their shoulders,
their hands were freed from the basket.
In distress you called and I rescued you;

I answered from the thundercloud
and tested you at the waters of Meribah.
Hear, my people, and I will warn you, Israel,
if you will listen to me:

PSALM 81, continued

'No foreign "god" shall be among you;
you shall bow to no alien "god."
I am Adonai, your God,
who brought you out of the land of Egypt.
Open wide your mouth and I will fill it!'

But my people did not listen to my voice,
and Israel did not submit to me.
So I gave them to their stubborn heart
and they followed their devices.

If my people were listening to me,
if Israel would follow my ways,
as quickly would I subdue the enmity
and turn a firm hand to the foes.

Anyone hating Adonai would cringe
under punishment lasting to forever.
But I will feed my people with finest of wheat
and satisfy you with honey out of rock."

Glory…

Antiphon in Lent	Sing for joy to God our strength.
Easter	The Lord feeds us with finest of wheat, alleluia.

WEEK II
THURSDAY EVENING

***PSALM** 56:2-7,9-14*

Antiphon in Lent   In God I trust,
I will not be afraid;
what can humanity do to me?

Easter   Alleluia, alleluia, alleluia.

Be merciful to me, my God!
Human beings pursue me all the day,
attacking with oppression
and with slander all the day.

Indeed in their pride do the many attack me.
On the day I am afraid, in you I trust.
My praise is of God's word, in God I trust.
I will not be afraid; what can a mortal do to me?

All the day they twist my words against me;
all their plots are for harm.
They conspire, they lurk, they watch my steps;
they are eager for my life…

Record my lament, put my tears in your wineskin;
are they not in your record?
Enmity will turn back on the day I call;

PSALM 56:2-7,9-14, continued

I will know that God is for me.
In God whose word I praise,
in Adonai whose word I praise, in God I trust.
I will not be afraid; what can a human do to me?

Upon me, God, are my vows to you;
I will present thank offerings to you
for you delivered my soul from death
and my feet from stumbling,
to walk in God's presence
in the light of the living.

Glory…

Antiphon in Lent

In God I trust,
I will not be afraid;
what can humanity do to me?

Easter

Alleluia, alleluia, alleluia.

PSALM 60:3-14a

Antiphon in Lent

O God, you burst forth upon us;
you were angry, now restore us.

Easter

Alleluia, alleluia, alleluia.

God you rejected us and burst forth upon us;
you were angry, now restore us.

You shook the land and tore her open;
mend her fractures, for she quakes!
You showed your people a desperate time;
you made us drink wine to staggering.

For those who fear you, you raised a banner
to be unfurled against the bow,
that your beloved ones may be delivered.
Help us with your right hand and save us!

God spoke from the sanctuary:
"I will triumph and parcel out Shechem,
 and measure out the valley of Succoth;
 mine are Gilead and Manasseh,

 Ephraim my head helmet, Judah my scepter,
 and Moab my washbasin;
 On Edom I toss my sandal
 and over Philistia I shout in triumph."

Who will bring me to the Rock City?
Who will lead me to Edom?
Have you, God, not rejected us,
and not gone out, God, with our armies?

Against enmity give to us aid,
for worthless is human help.
In God will we gain the victory...

Glory...

Antiphon in Lent O God, you burst forth upon us;
you were angry, now restore us.

Easter Alleluia, alleluia, alleluia.

PSALM 72

Antiphon in Lent   I will make you
a covenant of the people,
a light for the Gentiles.

Isaiah 42:6b

Easter   God has appointed him
to judge the living and the dead,
alleluia.

God, endow your justice to King Solomon
and your righteousness to the royal heir,
to judge your people in righteousness
and your afflicted with justice.

Mountains will bring prosperity to the people,
the hills too in righteousness.
He will defend people afflicted,
save the children of the needy,
and crush the oppressor.

They will fear you as long as the sun,
as long as the moon,
from generation to generations.
He will be like rain falling on a mown field,
like showers watering the earth.

In his days the righteous will flourish
in prosperous abundance til the moon is no more.
He will rule from sea to sea
and from the River to the ends of the earth.

Before him will desert tribes bow
and enmity will lick dust.
The kings of Tarshish and the distant shores
will bring tribute and present gifts,
with kings of Sheba and Seba.
They will bow down to him;
all the kings of all the nations will thus serve.

For he will deliver the needy one crying out
and the afflicted one when no one is helping.
He will take pity on the weak and the needy
and will save the lives of the needy ones;

he will rescue their lives
from oppression and violence,
for their lifeblood is precious in his eyes.

May he live and be given gold of Sheba,
and may all ever pray
that he be blessed all the day.

May grain be abundant throughout the land,
on tops of hills, swaying like the fruit of Lebanon,
and people flourish and thrive like grass in a field.

May his name endure to forever
and continue as long as the sun;
being thus blessed, may the nations bless him.

Praised is God, Adonai, God of Israel,
alone doing marvelous deeds.
Praised is the glory of the name to forever;
may the earth be filled with the glory of God.

Amen and amen. *Glory…* Repeat antiphon.

REVELATION 11:17-18, 12:10-12a

Antiphon for Lent Our God, who is and who was,
has taken great power to reign.

Easter Christ yesterday, today,
and the same forever,
alleluia.

We thank you, Lord God Almighty,
the One who is and who was;
you have taken your great power and reign.

The nations raged and your anger came,
and the time to judge the dead
and to reward your slaves and prophets,
the saints, and those fearing your name,
the small and the great…

Now have come the salvation and power
and kingdom of our God
and the authority of Christ.
The accuser of our brothers and sisters was cast,
accusing them before our God day and night.

Their victory was because of the blood of the Lamb
and by the word of their witness.
They loved their life into their death,
and so be glad, you heavens,
and all you dwelling in them.

Glory…

Repeat antiphon.

WEEK II
FRIDAY MORNING

PSALM 38

Antiphon I confess my iniquity;
do not forsake me, Lord my salvation.
(alleluia)

Adonai, rebuke me not in your anger
nor discipline me in your wrath,
for your arrows have pierced into me
and your hand has come down upon me.

There is no health in my body
because of your wrath;
my bones are unsound because of my sin.
Indeed my guilts overwhelm my head
like a heavy burden, too heavy for me.

I loathe them and they fester my wounds
because of my sinful folly.
I am bowed down and brought very low;
all the day I go about mourning.

Indeed my backside is filled with searing
and there is no health in my body.
Feeble and utterly crushed,
my heart groans in anguish.

PSALM 38, continued

Lord, before you is all of my longing;
my sighing is not hidden from you.
My heart pounds, my strength fails me,
and my eyes are without their light.

My friends and companions from the past
avoid being present to my woundedness,
and my neighbors stay far away.
People seeking my life set traps;
wanting to harm me, they talk of ruins
and plot deceptions all the day.

I am like a deaf man and cannot hear,
like a mute unable to open my mouth.
I became like one who does not hear,
like one whose mouth gives no reply.

Indeed, I wait for you, Adonai;
you will answer, Lord my God.
For I said, "let them not gloat over me;
 when my foot does slip, let them not exalt."

For my fall is ready for me
and my pain is ever with me.
Indeed I confess my iniquity;
I am troubled by my sin.

Vigorous ones seek enmity and for no reason,
many and numerous hating me.
Repaying the good with evil,
they slander me when I seek the good.

Forsake me not, Adonai;
my God, be not far from me.
Come quickly to my help,
Lord of my salvation.

Glory…

Antiphon   I confess my iniquity;
do not forsake me, Lord my salvation.
(alleluia)

PSALM 51

Antiphon for Lent   A broken spirit and a contrite heart, O God, you will not despise.

Easter   Have courage, my son;
your sins are forgiven,
alleluia.   Matt 9:2b

Have mercy on me, God,
in accord with your unfailing love;
in accord with the greatness of your compassion
blot out my transgressions.

Wash me of my many iniquities
and cleanse me from my sin,
for I know my transgressions
and my sin is before me always.

Against you yourself I sinned;
what I did is evil in your eyes.
You are proven right when you speak
and justified when you judge.
Surely we are sinners from birth,
from conception in a mother's womb.

Surely you desire truth in our inner parts;
in my inmost place you teach me wisdom.
You cleanse me with hyssop and I will be clean;
you wash me and I will be whiter than snow…

You let me hear joy and gladness;
let the bones you let be crushed now rejoice.
Hide your faces from my sins
and blot out all my iniquities.

A pure heart create in me, God!
Renew inside me a spirit to be steadfast.
Do not cast me from your presences,
nor take from me your Holy Spirit.

Restore to me the joy of your salvation
and sustain in me a willing spirit.
I will teach transgressors your ways
and sinners will turn back to you.

Save me from bloodguilt, God,
God of my salvation;
my tongue will sing of your righteousness.
Lord, open my lips
and my mouth will declare your praise.

Sacrifices give you no delight;
I could bring a burnt offering,
but it would give you no pleasure.
The sacrifices, God, you will not despise
are a broken spirit and a contrite heart.

Make Zion prosper in your pleasure,
and build up the walls of Jerusalem.
Then you will delight in the sacrifice of the just,
burnt offerings and whole offerings,
bulls offered on your altar.

Glory…   Repeat antiphon.

HABAKKUK 3:2-4,13a,15-19

Antiphon for Lent   Even in wrath
you remember compassion.

Easter   You go forth to save your people,
to save your anointed one,
alleluia.

Adonai, I heard your fame;
I stand in awe of your deeds, Adonai.
Now, in the midst of years, renew them!
In the midst of years, make them known!
Even in wrath you remember mercy.

Eloah came from Teman,
the Holy One from the Mount of Paran.
The heavens are covered with glory
and the earth is filled with praise

like the splendor of the rays of the sunrise
or the hand from a hiding place of power…
You came out to deliver your people,
to deliver your anointed one…

You trample on the sea,
your horses churning up the great waters.
I heard my heart and she trembled,
at the sound my lips quivered;

decay crept into my bones and my legs trembled.
Yet, I will wait patiently for the day,
calamity to come on the nation invading.

Though the fig tree does not bud
and there is no grape on the vine,
the crops of the olive fail
and fields produce no food,

the sheep cut themselves off from the pen
and there are no cattle in the stalls,
yet will I rejoice in Adonai
and be joyful in the God of my salvation.

Sovereign Adonai, my strength,
makes my feet like that of the deer,
makes me go to the heights.

Glory…

Antiphon for Lent   Even in wrath
you remember compassion.

Easter   You go forth to save your people,
to save your anointed one, alleluia.

PSALM 147:1-11

Antiphon for Lent   Extol the Lord, Jerusalem!

Easter   Zion, give praise to your God
who has brought peace to your borders,
alleluia.

Hallelujah! Praise Adonai!
How good it is to sing praise to our God!
How pleasant and fitting to give praise!

PSALM 147:1-11, continued

Adonai builds up Jerusalem,
gathers Israel's exiles,
heals the ones with broken hearts
and binds up their wounds,
determines the number of the stars,
and calls to each of them by name.

Great and mighty in power is our Lord,
with unlimited understanding.
Adonai sustains the humble
and throws wickedness to the dust.
Sing to Adonai with thanksgiving!

Make music on the harp to our God,
who covers the skies with clouds
and supplies rain to the earth,
making grass to grow on the hills,
providing food for cattle
and young ravens when they call.

Adonai finds pleasure
not in the strength of the horse
nor delight in the legs of the human,
but is delighting in those who fear Adonai
who hope in this unfailing love.

Glory…

Antiphon for Lent	Extol the Lord, Jerusalem!
Easter	Zion, give praise to your God who has brought peace to your borders, alleluia.

WEEK II
FRIDAY EVENING

PSALM *59 :2-5,10-11,17-18*

Antiphon for Lent   You protect me, my God.

Easter   Alleluia, alleluia, alleluia.

Deliver me from enmity;
protect me, God,
from those who rise up against me.
Deliver me from those who do evil
and save me from people of bloody ways.

See, they lie in wait for my self;
fierce people conspire against me
for no offense of me nor sin, Adonai.
For no wrong they make ready to attack;
arise to help me and look!...

For you, my Strength, I watch,
for you God, my fortress, you God are my love.

God will go before me
and gloat over ones who slander...

But I will sing of your strength
and I will sing in the morning of your love,
for you are my fortress
and my refuge in times of trouble.

To you, my Strength, I sing praise
for you God, my fortress, you God are my love.

Glory…

Antiphon for Lent You protect me, my God.

Easter Alleluia, alleluia, alleluia.

PSALM 116:1-9

Antiphon for Lent Lord, deliver my soul from death
and my feet from stumbling.

Easter The Lord has rescued my self
that I may walk in the land of the living.

I love Adonai
who heard my voice and my cries for mercy
and turned an ear to me,
so all during my days I will call.

Cords of death entangled me
and anguishes of Sheol came upon me;
trouble and sorrow came over me.
Then I called on the name of Adonai:
"Oh, Adonai, save my self!"

Adonai is gracious and righteous,
our God the compassionate one.
Adonai protects the simple hearted;
I was in need and then I was saved.

Return, my soul, to your rest,
for good to you has been Adonai,
who delivered my soul from death,
my eyes from tears,
and my feet from stumbling,

that I may walk before Adonai
in the land of the living.

Glory… Repeat antiphon.

PSALM 121

Antiphon for Lent
My help is from the Lord,
the Maker of heavens and earth.

Easter
The Lord watches over the people of God
and protects them as the apple of God's eye,
alleluia.

I lift up my eyes to the hills.
From where does my help come?
My help is from and with Adonai,
Maker of heavens and earth,

who will not let your foot slip
nor slumber when watching over you.
Indeed the one watching over Israel
will not slumber and will not sleep.

Adonai watches over you,
the Most High at your right hand.
By day the sun will not harm you,
nor the moon by the night.

PSALM 121, continued

Adonai will keep you from all harm
and watch over your life.
Adonai will watch over your going and coming
from now and to forevermore.

Glory…

Antiphon for Lent   My help is from the Lord,
the Maker of heavens and earth.

Easter   The Lord watches over the people of God
and protects them as the apple of God's eye,
alleluia.

REVELATION 15:3b-4

Antiphon for Lent   King of the nations,
just and true are your ways.

Easter   The Lord my strength
has become to me salvation, alleluia.

Great and wonderful are your works,
Lord God Almighty.
Just and true are your ways,
King of the nations.

Who will not fear, O Lord,
or glorify your name?

Only you are holy.
All the nations will come and worship before you;
your ordinances are shown to all.

Glory…   Repeat antiphon.

WEEK II
SATURDAY MORNING

PSALM 106:1-16,19-48

Antiphon   The Lord remembered the covenant for them
and relented.
(alleluia)

Praise Adonai!
Give thanks to Adonai who is good,
whose love is to forever.

Who can proclaim the mighty acts of Adonai?
Who can declare the fullness of praise?
Blessed are they who maintain justice,
doing the right at all times.

Remember me, Adonai, as you favor your people!
In your salvation, come with your aid for me
to enjoy the prosperity of your chosen ones,
to have joy in the joy of your nation,
and to give praise with your inheritance.

We have sinned as did our ancestors;
we have done wrong with wicked acts.
Our ancestors when in Egypt
gave no thought to your miracle deeds,
did not remember your many kindnesses,
and rebelled by *Yam Suf*, the Sea of Reeds.

PSALM 106, continued

Still you saved them for the sake of your name,
to make known your power.
You rebuked the Sea of Reeds; it dried up.
And you led them through the depths as the desert.

You saved them from the hands of foes
and redeemed them from the hand of enmity.

The waters covered the adversaries;
not one of them survived.
Then they believed in the promises made,
and sang out praise.

Soon did they forget those deeds
and would not wait for good counsel.
They craved cravings in the desert
and in the wasteland they tested their El,
who gave them their request
but sent a wasting disease on their life.

They envied Moses in the camp
and Aaron, the consecrated of Adonai...
They made a calf at Horeb
and gave worship to a cast idol.
They exchanged their Glory
for an image of a grass-eating bull.

They forgot El who had saved them,
doing great things in Egypt,
miracle deeds in the land of Ham
and awesome deeds by the Sea of Reeds.

By a word spoken they were to be destroyed,
except that Moses the chosen stood in the breach.
Then they despised the pleasant land
and did not believe the promise made.

They grumbled in their tents
and did not obey the voice of Adonai,
who lifted a hand to let them fall in the desert
and their descendents fall among the nations;
they were scattered through the lands.

They yoked themselves to Baal of Peor
and they ate of sacrifices to lifeless ones.
They provoked anger by their deeds
and a plague broke out among them.

Phinehas stood up and intervened
and the plague was checked;
this was credited to him as righteousness
for generation and generations to forever.

They angered by the waters of Meribah,
the cause of trouble for Moses,
who spoke rashly with his lips
when they rebelled against the Spirit.

They did not defeat the peoples
as Adonai commanded them,
but mingled with the nations
and adopted their customs.
They worshiped their idols
which became to them as a snare.

PSALM 106, continued

They sacrificed their sons and daughters.
They shed the innocent blood
of their own sons and daughters
whom they sacrificed to idols of Canaan,
desecrating the land by this blood.

They defiled themselves by their deeds
and prostituted themselves by their deeds.
Against the people burned the anger of Adonai,
abhorring the promised inheritance.

Into the hands of nations they were given,
ruled by their foes, oppressed by enmity,
and made subject to their power.
Many times were they delivered,
but they rebelled in their decisions
and wasted away in their sins.

On hearing their cry
the Lord took note of their distress
and remembered for them the covenant,
and relented in greatness of love.
They were made pitied by all of their captors.

Save us, Adonai our God!
Gather us from the nations
to give thanks to your holy name
and glory in your praise.

WEEK II - SATURDAY MORNING 313

Praised be Adonai, God of Israel
from everlasting to everlasting
and let all the people say, "Amen!"
Praise Adonai!

Glory...

Antiphon The Lord remembered the covenant for them
and relented.
(alleluia)

PSALM 92:1-9,11,13-16

Antiphon for Lent It is good to proclaim
your love in the morning
and your fidelity at night.

Easter By your deeds, Lord, you have made me glad;
I sing for joy at the works of your hands,
alleluia.

It is good to praise Adonai,
to make music to your name, Most High,
to proclaim in the morning your love
and at night your faithfulness,
on the ten-string and on the lyre,
and the melody of the harp.

PSALM 92:1-9,11,13-16, continued

For you make me glad by your deeds, Adonai;
at the works of your hands I sing for joy.
How great are your works, Adonai;
very profound are your thoughts.
The senseless human does not know
and the fool does not understand.

Though wickedness springs up like grass
and doers of bad things seem to flourish,
their ways will be destroyed to forever.
But you, Adonai, are exalted to forever...

You gave me strength like a wild ox
and I was anointed with fine oil...
The just will flourish like the palm tree,
and grow like a cedar of Lebanon.

Planted in the house of Adonai,
in the courts of our God they will flourish.
In old age they will still bear fruit,
fresh and green they will stay,
to proclaim, "Adonai is upright,
in my Rock there is no wrong."

Glory...

Antiphon for Lent   It is good to proclaim
your love in the morning
and your fidelity at night.

Easter   By your deeds, Lord, you have made me glad;
I sing for joy at the works of your hands,
alleluia.

DEUTERONOMY 32:1-12

Antiphon for Lent   Praise the greatness of our God.

Easter   It is I who allow death and I who give life;
I allow injury and I bring healing,
alleluia.

Listen, heavens, and I will speak:
Hear, earth, the words of my mouth.
Let my teaching fall like the rain,
let my word descend like the dew,
like showers on grass, like abundant rains on plants.

The name of Adonai I will proclaim,
and praise the greatness of our God.
The work of the Rock is perfect indeed;
all the ways of our faithful God are just
and without wrong, upright and just.

The children acted corruptly with no shame,
a generation warped and crooked.
Foolish and unwise people,
you repay Adonai in this way?
Did not your Father create you
and make you and form you?

Remember the days of old!
Consider the years of generation and generation!
Ask your parents and they will tell you!
Ask your elders and they will explain to you

DEUTERONOMY 32, continued

how the Most High gave inheritance to nations,
dividing sons and daughters of humanity
and setting up boundaries of peoples
by numbers of sons and daughters of Israel.

For the portion of Adonai is the people,
Jacob the allotment of inheritance,
found in desert land, a barren and howling waste,
shielded with care, guarded as the apple of the eye,

like an eagle stirring up the nest
and hovering over the young ones,
spreading wings to catch them
and carrying them on its flight feathers.

Led by Adonai alone,
no foreign "god" was with them.

Glory…

Antiphon for Lent Praise the greatness of our God.

Easter It is I who allow death and I who give life;
I allow injury and I bring healing,
alleluia.

PSALM 8

Antiphon for Lent Our Lord, how awesome,
how majestic is your name in all the earth.

Easter You have crowned your Anointed One
with glory and honor, alleluia.

WEEK II - SATURDAY MORNING

PSALM 8

Adonai, our Lord!
How majestic is your name in all the earth!

Your glory is set above the heavens!
From lips of children and infants
you ordained strength to bring to silence
enmity, opposition and vengeance.

When I consider your heavens,
the works of your fingers,
the moon and stars which you set in place,
what is a human that you would be mindful,
a child of Adam and Eve that you would care?

And you made us little lower than a "god"
crowning us with glory and honor,
making us to rule over works of your hands,
putting everything under our feet,

flocks and herds, all of them,
and also beasts of the field,
birds of the air and fishes of the sea,
swimming through the paths of the seas.

Adonai, our Lord!
How majestic is your name in all the earth!

Glory…

Antiphon for Lent	Our Lord, how awesome, how majestic is your name in all the earth.
Easter	You have crowned your Anointed One with glory and honor, alleluia.

WEEK III
VIGIL OF SUNDAY
(Saturday Evening)

PSALM 61

Antiphon for Lent God, you are my refuge
and my tower of strength.

Easter, 3rd Sunday Alleluia, alleluia, alleluia.

The 7th Sunday of Easter is the Solemnity of the Ascension in most Dioceses, page 101

Hear, God, my cry! Listen to my prayer!
From the end of the earth I call to you
as my heart grows faint.

To the high rock you lead me
for you are my refuge and tower of strength
against the Foe (of death).

I would dwell in your tent for forevers
and take refuge in the shelter of your wings.
For you, God, hearing my vows,
gave inheritance to those fearing your name.

You increase the days upon days of the royal one,
and the years for generation and generation,
enthroned in God's presences forever,
appointed and protected in God's love and fidelity.

I will sing praise of your name forever
to fulfill my vows day by day.

Glory...   Repeat antiphon.

PSALM 113

Lent, 3rd Sunday

The Lord says: Turn away from sin
and open your hearts to the Gospel.

Easter, 3rd Sunday

The Lord our God is high above the heavens,
raising up the lowly from the dust, alleluia.

Praise Adonai!
Praise, you who serve Adonai!
Praise the name Adonai!

Let Adonai be praised by name
from now and to forevermore.
From the rising of the sun to its setting
praised be the name Adonai.

Exalted over all the nations is Adonai,
the glory above the heavens.
Who is like our God Adonai,
sitting enthroned on high,
leaning to look down
on the heavens and the earth?

The One who raises the poor from dust
and lifts up the needy from ash heaps
to sit with princes, the princes of the people,
who settles the barren woman in a home,
a happy mother of children.

Praise Adonai!

Glory…

Repeat antiphon.

PSALM 116:10-19

Lent, 3rd Sunday
I will offer the sacrifice of praise
and call on the name of the Lord.

Easter, 3rd Sunday
Lord, you have broken
the chains that held me bound;
I will offer you a sacrifice of praise, alleluia.

I believed it and so said, "I am greatly afflicted."
I said when it dismayed me, "Everyone is a liar."

How can I repay to Adonai all the goodness to me?
I will lift the cup of salvation
and I will call on the name of Adonai.

My vows to Adonai I will now fulfill
in the presence of all the people.
Precious in the eyes of Adonai
are the saints to the death.

O, Adonai, I am truly your servant,
your servant and son of your maidservant;
you freed me from the chains.
I will offer to you the sacrifice of thanksgiving
and I will call on the name of Adonai.

My vows to Adonai I will now fulfill
in the presence of all the people,
in courts of the house of Adonai,
in your midst, Jerusalem.
Praise Adonai!

Glory...   Repeat antiphon.

PHILIPPIANS 2:6-11

Lent, 3rd Sunday
No one takes my life away from me;
I lay it down freely
and I shall take it up again.

Easter, 3rd Sunday
Though he was the Son of God,
Christ learned obedience through suffering;
and for all who obey him,
he has become the source of life, alleluia.

Christ Jesus, subsisting in the form of God,
did not deem equality with God something to grab,
but emptied himself, taking the form of a slave,
becoming in human likeness.

And being found in human fashion,
he humbled himself,
becoming obedient until death,
and death on a cross.

And so God highly exalted him,
and gave to him the name above every name,
that in the name of Jesus every knee should bend,
of heavenly beings and earthly beings,
and beings under the earth;

And every tongue acknowledge
to the glory of God the Father
that Jesus Christ is Lord.

Glory…

Repeat antiphon.

WEEK III
RESURRECTION VIGIL

HOSEA 6:1-6

Antiphon   In Christ who rose from the dead
            our hope of resurrection dawned.

Come and let us return to Adonai,
who let us be torn up but will heal us,
who let us be injured but will bind our wounds,

who will revive us after two days
and restore us on the third day
that we may live in the presence.

So let us know, let us press on to know Adonai,
who will appear coming as the sun rises,
who will come to us like the winter rain,
watering the earth like spring rain.

What can I do with you Ephraim?
What can I do with you Judah?
Your love indeed is like morning mist,
and like the early dew that disappears.

For this I cut to pieces with the prophets
and have slain with words of my mouth
and judgments of lightning flashes:
For it is mercy that I desire and not sacrifice,
knowledge of God rather than burnt offerings.

Glory...   Repeat antiphon.

FOR SUNDAYS OF WEEK 3

LUKE 23:56b–24:12

And on the sabbath, indeed they rested
according to the commandment.
But on day one of the week, while still very early,
they came upon the tomb
carrying spices which they had prepared.
And they found the stone rolled away from the tomb,
and entering they did not find the body of the Lord Jesus.
As they were perplexed about this, behold,
two men stood by them in shining clothing.
And becoming terrified
and bending their faces to the earth, they said to them,
"Why do you seek the living one with the dead?
He is not here, but was raised.
Remember how he spoke to you while yet in Galilee,
saying, 'It is fitting that the Son of humanity be delivered
into the hands of sinful humans and be crucified,
and on the third day to rise again.'"
And they remembered his words,
and returning from the tomb
reported all these things to the eleven
and to all the rest.
Now they were Mary the Magdalene and Joanna
and Mary the mother of James, and the rest with them
told these things to the apostles.
And these words seemed to them as folly,
and they did not believe them.

•

FOR SUNDAYS OF WEEK 7

JOHN 20:19-31

When it was early evening on that day one of the week,
and the doors having been shut where the disciples were
because of fear of the Judeans,
Jesus came and stood in the midst and said to them,
"Peace to you."
And saying this
he showed to them both his hands and his side.
And so the disciples seeing the Lord rejoiced.
And so Jesus said to them again,
"Peace to you;
as the Father has sent me, I also send you."
And saying this he breathed in and onto them saying,
"Receive Holy Spirit.
Of whomever you forgive the sins,
they are forgiven of them;
of whomever you hold, they are held."

But Thomas, one of the twelve called Twin,
was not with them when Jesus came.
And so the other disciples said to him,
"We have seen the Lord."
But he said to them,
"Unless I see in his hands the mark of the nails
and put my finger into the place of the nails
and put my hand into his side,
by no means will I believe."

And after eight days,
again his disciples were within,
and Thomas was with them.
The doors having been shut,
Jesus came and stood in the midst and said,
"Peace to you."
Then he said to Thomas,
"Bring your finger here and see my hands,
and bring and put your hand into my side,
and be not faithless, but faithful."
Thomas answered and said to him,
"My Lord and my God."
Jesus said to him,
"Have you had faith because you have seen me?
Blessed are the ones not seeing and having faith."
And so
Jesus did many and other signs before the disciples,
which have not been written in this scroll.
But these have been written
that you may believe
that Jesus is the Christ, the Son of God,
and that believing
you may have life in his name.

•

WEEK III
SUNDAY MORNING

PSALM 2

Antiphon for Lent Here is a king of my own choosing
who will rule on Mount Zion.

Easter Alleluia, woman, for whom are you looking?
Why seek the living among the dead?
Alleluia.

Why do nations rage and peoples plot vanity?
Kings of the earth make their stand
and ruling ones gather together
against Adonai and Adonai's anointed one:
"Let us break their chains,
  let us throw off their fetters."

The One enthroned in the heavens laughs,
the Lord scoffs and rebukes them.
In anger and in wrath the Lord terrifies them.
"I indeed installed my king
  on my holy hill of Zion.

  I will proclaim a decree of Adonai who said,
   'You are my son, this day I am your father.
    Ask of me and nations are your inheritance,
    and your possession to the ends of earth.
    You will rule them with a scepter of iron
    and dash them to pieces of what potters make.'

Kings, now be wise!
Rulers of earth, be warned!
Serve Adonai with fear; rejoice with trembling!
Kiss my son, lest he be angry
and you be destroyed
for in a moment he can flare up in wrath.

Blessings on all who take refuge in him."

Glory…

Antiphon for Lent — Here is a king of my own choosing
who will rule on Mount Zion.

Easter — Alleluia, woman, for whom are you looking?
Why seek the living among the dead?
Alleluia.

PSALM 93

Lent, 3rd Sunday — Your statutes, O Lord, stand firm;
your truth is greater than the sea-thunders.

Easter, 3rd Sunday — The Lord is king, robed in splendor, alleluia.

Adonai reigns, robed in majesty;
robed is Adonai and armed with strength.

The world is firmly established;
she cannot be moved.
Your throne was set up from long ago;
from eternity you are.

The seas lifted up, Adonai,
the seas lifted up their voice;
the seas lifted up their pounding.

More than thunders of great waters
or mighty breakers of the sea,
mighty in the height is Adonai.

Your statutes stand very firm;
your house, Adonai, is adorned in holiness
for length of days.

Glory…

Lent, 3rd Sunday — Your statutes, O Lord, stand firm;
your truth is greater than the sea-thunders.

Easter, 3rd Sunday — The Lord is king,
robed in splendor,
alleluia.

DANIEL 3:57-90

Lent, 3rd Sunday — Springs and rainwater, bless the Lord;
exalt and sing praise to forever.

Easter, 3rd Sunday — All creation will be freed;
all peoples will know the glory
and freedom of God's children,
alleluia.

DANIEL 3:57-90

Bless the Lord, all you works of the Lord,
exalt and sing praise to forever.
Angels of the Lord, bless the Lord,
You heavens, bless the Lord,
All you waters above the heavens, bless the Lord,
All you powers, bless the Lord,
Sun and moon, bless the Lord,
Stars of heaven, bless the Lord.

All you rain and dew, bless the Lord,
All you winds, bless the Lord,
You fire and heat, bless the Lord,
You ice and cold, bless the Lord,
You dews and falling snows, bless the Lord,
You snows and frosts, bless the Lord,
You nights and days, bless the Lord,
You light and darkness, bless the Lord,
You lightning and clouds, bless the Lord.

Let the earth bless the Lord,
exalt and sing praise to forever.
You mountains and hills, bless the Lord,
All things growing in the ground, bless the Lord,
You seas and rivers, bless the Lord,
You springs and rain, bless the Lord,
You sea monsters and all swimmers, bless the Lord,
All you birds of the air, bless the Lord,
All you wild beasts and cattle, bless the Lord,
You sons and daughters, bless the Lord.

O Israel, bless the Lord,
exalt and sing praise to forever.
You priests of the Lord, bless the Lord,
You servants of the Lord, bless the Lord,
You spirits and souls of the just, bless the Lord,
You holy and humble in heart, bless the Lord,
Hananiah, Azariah, and Mishael, bless the Lord,
exalt and sing praise to forever...

Give thanks to the Lord, who is good,
whose mercy endures to forever.
Bless the God of "gods"
all you who worship the Lord;
sing praise and give thanks to the One God
whose mercy endures to forever.

(No doxology)

Lent, 3rd Sunday	Springs and rainwater, bless the Lord; exalt and sing praise to forever.
Easter, 3rd Sunday	All creation will be freed; all peoples will know the glory and freedom of God's children, alleluia.

PSALM 148

Lent, 3rd Sunday
All rulers and peoples of the earth,
give praise to the Lord.

Easter, 3rd Sunday
The name of the Lord is praised
in heaven and on earth,
alleluia.

Praise Adonai!
Give praise from the heavens!
Give praise in the heights.
Give praise all you angels.
Give praise all you hosts.

Give praise sun and moon.
Give praise all stars shining.
Give praise, you heavens of the heavens
and waters above the skies.

Let them praise the name Adonai,
who commanded and they were created,
who set them in place forever,
to forever the decree Adonai gave,
not to pass away.

PSALM 148, continued

Praise Adonai, you earth,
give praise you sea creatures and all in the deep,
lightning and hail, snow and cloud,
wind of the storm, all who do Adonai's bidding,

the mountains and hills, fruit trees and cedars,
wild animals and all cattle,
small creatures and birds of flight,

kings of the earth and the nations,
princes and all people ruling on earth,
young men and also maidens,
old men and children:

Let them praise the name Adonai
whose name alone is exalted,
whose splendor is above earth and the heavens,

Who raised a horn for the people,
praise of all the saints,
of the sons and daughters of Israel,
of people close to the Lord.

Praise Adonai!

Glory…

| Lent, 3rd Sunday | All rulers and peoples of the earth, give praise to the Lord. |
| Easter, 3rd Sunday | The name of the Lord is praised in heaven and on earth, alleluia. |

WEEK III
SUNDAY EVENING

PSALM 64

Antiphon for Lent   Let the righteous rejoice
and take refuge in the Lord.

Easter   Alleluia, alleluia, alleluia.

Hear my voice, O God, in complaint;
threatened by an enemy, you protect my life.
You hide me from conspiracies,
from the noisy crowd of people doing bad things,

who sharpen their tongue like the sword,
aim their arrow of harmful words,
and shoot from ambush the innocent person;
they shoot suddenly and without fear.

They encourage those who plan harm,
and they talk of hidden snares,
saying, "who will see them?"
They plot injustices they call "the perfect plan!"
Surely the human mind and heart are cunning.

But God will shoot sudden arrows
striking down those plans.
Their ruin will be by their own tongues;
all who see them will shake heads at them.

They will fear all humanity,
then come to proclaim the work of God,
and ponder the deeds of God.
Let the righteous rejoice and take refuge in Adonai;
let all praise the upright of heart.

Glory...

Antiphon for Lent	Let the righteous rejoice and take refuge in the Lord.
Easter	Alleluia, alleluia, alleluia.

PSALM 91

Antiphon for Lent	Have no fear of terror at night; in the shadow of the Almighty, find rest.
Easter	Alleluia, alleluia, alleluia.

One who dwells in the shelter of Elyon,
in the shadow of Shaddai, will find rest.
I will say of Adonai, my refuge, my fortress:
in my God do I trust.

Surely the Lord will save you
from fowler snare, from deadly pestilence.
With the feather of the Lord you will be covered,
and under those wings you will find refuge,
shield and rampart, the faithfulness of the Lord.

You will have no fear of terror at night
nor of arrows flying by day,
of pestilence stalking in the darkness,
nor of plague that destroys at midday.

A thousand may fall at your side,
and ten thousand at your right hand;
near to you they will not come.

Observe with your eyes, simply watch;
punishment of wicked ones you will see.
Make Adonai, who is my refuge,
make Elyon your dwelling.

Harm will not befall you,
nor will disaster come near your tent.
God's own Angels, the Lord will command
to guard you in all of your ways.

In their hands they will lift you up;
your foot will not strike against the stone.
Upon lion and cobra you will tread,
you will trample the great lion and serpent.

"Because you love me, I will rescue you,
  I will protect all who acknowledge my Name.
  You will call upon me and I will answer.
  I am with you in trouble;
  I will deliver you and honor you.

  In length of days I will satisfy you,
  and show you my salvation."

Glory…

Repeat antiphon.

PSALM 110:1-6a,7

Lent, 3rd Sunday
Lord, all powerful King,
free us for the sake of your name.
Give us time to turn from our sins.

Easter, 3rd Sunday
He cleansed us of our sins, and is seated
on high at God's right hand, alleluia.

Adonai said to my Lord:
"Sit at my right hand
 until I make enmity as a footstool for your feet."

A scepter of your might
Adonai will extend from Zion,
and rule in the midst of enmity!

Your troops are willing on the day of your battle.
In majesties of holiness from the womb of the dawn
to you is the dew of your youth.
Adonai swore and this mind will not change,
"You are a priest to forever
 in the order of Melchizedek."

The Lord is at your right hand
and will crush kings on the day of wrath,
will judge the nations...,
and will drink from a brook on the way
with head lifted up because of all this.

Glory...

Repeat antiphon.

PSALM 111

Lent, 3rd Sunday

We have been redeemed
by the precious blood of Christ,
the lamb without blemish.

Easter, 3rd Sunday

The Lord has redeemed his people,
alleluia.

Praise Adonai!
I will extol Adonai with all my heart
in the council of the upright ones
and in the assembly.
Great are the works of Adonai,
pondered by all who delight in them.

Glorious and majestic are the deeds,
and this righteousness endures to forever.
Remembrance is caused of deeds of wonder
by gracious and compassionate Adonai,

providing food for ones fearing the One,
remembering the covenant to forever,
and having shown power at work,
giving the people the land of the nations.

Faithful and just is the handiwork of Adonai,
whose precepts are worthy of trust.
Steadfast are they forever to forever,
done in faithfulness and uprightness.

Redemption is provided for Adonai's people;
ordained to forever is the covenant.
Holy and awesome is the Name.

The beginning of wisdom is fear of Adonai,
good understanding for all who follow this.
Praise endures to eternity.

Glory…

Lent, 3rd Sunday
>
We have been redeemed
by the precious blood of Christ,
the lamb without blemish.

Easter, 3rd Sunday
>
The Lord has redeemed his people,
alleluia.

(Lent) 1 PETER 2:21-24

Lent, 3rd Sunday
>
Ours were the sufferings he bore;
ours the torments he endured.

To this you were called,
for indeed Christ suffered on behalf of you,
leaving to you an example to follow in his steps:

He did not sin, nor was guile found in his mouth;
he was reviled and did not revile in return;
suffering he did not threaten,
but delivered himself to the one judging justly.

Our sins he carried in his body up onto the tree,
that dying to sins, we might live for justice.
By his bruises, you are cured.

Glory…

Repeat antiphon.

(Easter) REVELATION 19:1b,2a,5b,6b,7

Easter, 3rd Sunday   Alleluia, our Lord is king;
let us rejoice and give the glory,
alleluia.

Alleluia! Praise the Lord!
Salvation and glory and power are to our God,
whose judgments are true and just.

Alleluia! Praise the Lord!
Praise our God, all you slaves of the Lord,
you small and you great, who hold God in awe.

Alleluia! Praise the Lord!
The Lord is reigning, our God, the Almighty.
Let us rejoice and let us exult,
and we will give the glory to the Lord.

Alleluia! Praise the Lord!
The day has come
for the marriage of the Lamb,
and the bride has prepared herself.

Glory…

Repeat antiphon.

WEEK III
MONDAY MORNING

PSALM 50

Antiphon   Our God will be shown
and not in silence.
(alleluia)

El Elohim Adonai
speaks and summons earth
from the rising of the sun to its setting.
From Zion, perfect of beauty, God shines forth.

Our God comes and will not be silent,
before whom a fire devours,
around whom a storm is great.
The heavens at above are summoned,
and the earth to judge the people:

"Gather the ones consecrated to me,
  the ones making my covenant by sacrifice."
The heavens proclaim the righteousness of God,
the One who judges.

"Hear, my people, and I will speak, Israel,
  and I will testify against you;
  God, your God, am I.

Not for your sacrifices do I rebuke you,
or your burnt offerings ever before me.
I do not need a bull from your stall
or goats from your pen,

for every animal of the forest is mine,
cattle on the hills, the thousands.
I know every bird of the mountains,
and every creature of fields is mine.

Were I hungry, I would not tell it to you,
for the world is mine and all in her.
Do I eat the flesh of bulls?
Do I drink the blood of goats?

Sacrifice to God thank offerings!
And fulfill your vows to the Most High!
Call upon me in the day of trouble;
I will deliver you and you will honor me."

But God says to those who do the wicked,
"What to you to recite my laws
or to take my covenant on your lip?
For you hate instruction
and you cast my words behind you.

When you see a thief, you join in,
and cast your lot with doers of adultery.
You use your mouth for evil
and harness your tongue to deceit.

PSALM 50, continued

You sit and speak against your brother and sister
and give slander against your mother's children.
You did these, and I kept silent;
you thought me to be like you?

...Consider now this: ...there is no one to rescue
...those who insist on forgetting God.
One sacrificing a thank offering honors me
and prepares the way,
and I will show that one
to the salvation of God."

Glory…

Antiphon Our God will be shown
and not in silence.
(alleluia)

PSALM 84

Antiphon for Lent Blessed are the ones
dwelling in your house,
my King and my God.

Easter My heart and my flesh rejoice in God alive,
alleluia.

How lovely are your dwellings, Adonai Sabaoth!
My soul she yearns and even faints
for the courts of Adonai;
my heart and my flesh cry out for God alive.

Even the sparrow found a home
and the swallow a nest for her
where she may have her young ones
near your altar, Adonai Sabaoth,
my King and my God.

Blessed are the dwellers in your house,
ever they praise you.
Blessed are the ones whose strength is in you,
who make a pilgrimage in their hearts.

Passing through the Baca Valley, springs are made,
pools covered over with autumn rains.
They go from strength to strength
and appear before God in Zion.

Adonai, God Sabaoth, hear my prayer!
Listen, God of Jacob. God, our shield, look!
Look on the face of your anointed one!

Better is a day in your courts
than a thousand elsewhere.
I would rather be doorkeeper in my God's house
than to dwell in tents of those who do bad,

for God Adonai is sun and shield.
Adonai bestows favor and honor,
withholding no good thing from blameless walkers.

Adonai Sabaoth,
blessed is the one trusting in you.

Glory…

Repeat antiphon.

ISAIAH 2:2-5

Antiphon for Lent Come and let us go up
the mountain of the Lord.

Easter The house of the Lord
has been raised on high,
where all the nations
will make their way,
alleluia.

In the last of the days
the mountain of Adonai's temple will be established
as chief of the mountains,
raised above the hills.

All the nations will stream to it.
Many peoples will come and say,
"Come, let us go up to the mountain of Adonai,
to the house of the God of Jacob,
who will teach us the ways
so we may walk in the path."

Indeed, from Zion the law will go out
and from Jerusalem the word of Adonai,
who will judge between the nations
and settle disputes for many peoples.

They will beat their swords into plowshares
and their spears into pruning hooks.
Nations will not take up the sword against nations,
and they will train for war no more.

House of Jacob, come!
Let us walk in Adonai's light.

Glory…

Antiphon for Lent   Come and let us go up
the mountain of the Lord.

Easter   The house of the Lord
has been raised on high,
where all the nations
will make their way,
alleluia.

PSALM 96

Antiphon for Lent   Sing to the Lord and praise the name.

Easter   Say it among the nations:
the Lord rules,
alleluia.

Sing to Adonai a new song!
Sing to Adonai, all the earth!
Sing to Adonai and praise the name!
Proclaim the salvation from day to day!

Declare among the nations the glory of the Lord!
Among all the peoples the marvelous deeds,
for great is Adonai, greatly being praised,
the one being feared above all so-called "gods."

PSALM 96, continued

For all "gods" of the nations are idols,
but Adonai made the heavens,
splendor and majesty and strength and glory
in the holy sanctuary.

Ascribe to Adonai, families of nations!
Ascribe to Adonai glory and strength!
Ascribe to Adonai the glory of the name!

Bring offerings and come into the courts!
Worship Adonai in holy splendor!
Tremble in the presence all the earth!

Say among the nations, "Adonai reigns!"
Firmly established, the world cannot be moved
and peoples will be judged with equity.

Let the heavens rejoice and the earth be glad.
Let the sea resound and all its fullness.
Let the fields and all that is in them be jubilant,
then all the trees of the forests will sing for joy

before Adonai who comes,
who comes to judge the earth,
who will judge the world and its peoples
in justice and in truth.

Glory…

Antiphon for Lent	Sing to the Lord and praise the name.
Easter	Say it among the nations: the Lord rules, alleluia.

WEEK III
MONDAY EVENING

PSALM 71

Antiphon for Lent
You are my hope,
Lord Adonai,
my confidence since my youth.

Easter
Alleluia, alleluia, alleluia.

In you, Adonai, I take refuge;
let me not be shamed to forever.
In your righteousness you rescue and deliver me.
Turn your ear to me and save me!

Be to me as a rock, and a refuge to go to always.
Command that I be saved,
for you are my rock and my fortress.
My God, deliver me from the hands
and grasp of ones who do evil or the cruel,

for you are my hope, Lord Adonai,
my confidence since my youth.
I have relied on you from birth,
from my mother's womb you brought me forth;
my praise is ever to you.

PSALM 71, continued

To many I became like a portent
but you are my strong refuge.
My mouth is filled all the day
with praise of your splendor.
Cast me not away at my time of old age;
forsake me not when my strength is gone.

Enmity speaks against me;
waiting on my life, conspirers together say,
"God has forsaken that one! Pursue to seize,
  for no one is coming to the rescue!"
God, be not far from me.
God, come quickly to help me!

May accusations against me perish in shame.
May scorn and disgrace cover the desire to do harm.

But I will hope always and add to all your praise.
My mouth will tell of your righteousness,
all the day of your salvation,
though I know not its measure;

I will come in mighty acts of Lord Adonai;
I will proclaim the righteousness of you yourself.
You taught me, God, since my youth;
to this day I declare your marvelous deeds.

Even in my old age and gray hair
you do not forsake me, God,
till I delcare your power to this generation,
your might to all who will come,
and your righteousness to the sky,
you, God, who have done great things.
Who, God, is like you?

Though you let me see troubles, many and bitter,
you will again let me live.
And from the depths of the earth
you will again bring me up.
You will increase my honor
and you will again comfort me.

With the harp instrument I will praise you
and your faithfulness, my God;
I will sing praise to you with lyre,
Holy One of Israel.
My lips will shout for joy when I sing praise to you,
even my self whom you redeemed.

Also my tongue will tell all the day of your justice
for desires of some to harm me
are in shame and confusion.

Glory…

Antiphon for Lent	You are my hope, Lord Adonai, my confidence since my youth.
Easter	Alleluia, alleluia, alleluia.

PSALM 123

Antiphon for Lent   Our eyes are to our God
till the Lord shows to us mercy.

Easter   The Lord will be your light forever;
your God will be your glory,
alleluia.

I lift up my eyes to you, sitting in the heavens.
As eyes of slaves are to the hand of their masters,
as the eyes of a maid are to the hand of her mistress,
see, our eyes are to Adonai
till our God shows to us mercy.

Have mercy on us, Adonai, have mercy on us,
for we have endured much contempt.

Much ridicule of the proud ones
and contempt of arrogant ones
have we ourselves endured.

Glory…

Antiphon for Lent   Our eyes are to our God
till the Lord shows to us mercy.

Easter   The Lord will be your light forever;
your God will be your glory,
alleluia.

PSALM 124

Antiphon for Lent
Our help is in the name of the Lord,
the One Making heavens and earth.

Easter
The snare was broken
and we were set free,
alleluia.

If Adonai was not for us, let Israel now say,
if Adonai was not for us
when human beings attacked against us,
then they would have swallowed us alive
when their anger flared against us.

Then the floods would have engulfed us,
the torrents would have swept over our selfs,
and the raging waters would have swept over us.

Praise be to Adonai,
who did not let us be torn by their teeth.
Our selfs, like a bird,
escaped from the snare of fowlers.

The snare being broken we escaped.
Our help is in the name of Adonai,
the Maker of heavens and earth.

Glory…

Repeat antiphon.

EPHESIANS 1:3-10

Antiphon for Lent   God gives us a destiny as sons are adopted.

Easter   When I am lifted up from the earth
I will draw all people to myself, alleluia.

Blessed be the God and Father
of our Lord Jesus Christ,
who has blessed us in Christ
with every spiritual blessing in the heavens.

God chose us in Christ
before the foundation of the world,
to be holy and free of blemish before him.

In love, God gave us a destiny:
as sons are adopted, through Jesus Christ himself,
in accord with the good pleasure of God's will
to the praise of the glory of grace
by which we are favored as God's beloved.

In Christ we have the redemption
through his blood, the forgiveness of sins,
in accord with the riches of his grace
which he made abound to us.

In all wisdom and intelligence
the mystery of God's will is made known to us
in accord with God's good pleasure and purpose:

A stewardship of the fullness of time,
heading up all things in Christ,
the things in the heavens and the things on earth.

Glory…

Antiphon for Lent   God gives us a destiny as sons are adopted.

Easter   When I am lifted up from the earth
I will draw all people to myself, alleluia.

WEEK III
TUESDAY MORNING

PSALM 68

Antiphon   Kingdoms of earth, sing to God;
sing praise to the Lord.
(alleluia)

May God arise
and may foes in enmity flee and be scattered.
As smoke is blown, let it blow;
as wax melts before fire
may wicked ways perish from before God.

But may righteous ones be glad
and rejoice before God;
may they be happy with joy.
Sing to God! Sing praise to the name!
Extol the Rider of the Clouds,
and rejoice in the name Adonai,

PSALM 68, continued

Father of the fatherless
and defender of widows,
God dwelling in holiness.
God sets the lonely into a family
and leads prisoners forth with the songs,
but ones rebelling live on sun-scorched land.

When you went out before your people, God,
when you marched through the wasteland,
the earth shook and heavens poured rain
before the One God of Sinai,
before God, the God of Israel.

You gave a shower of abundances, God,
on your inheritance;
even the weary you refreshed.
Your people settled in her, God;
you provided for the poor from your bounty.

The Lord announced the word,
a great company of proclaimers.
Kings of armies flee, they flee,
and in camps of residence the plunder is divided.

While you sleep among campfires
wings of dove are sheathed with silver
and her feathers with the shine of gold.
When Shaddai scatters the kings,
the scattering is like snow on Zalmon.

A mountain of majesties, the mountain of Bashan,
a rugged mountain is the mountain of Bashan.
Why gaze in envy, you rugged mountains,
at the mountain God chooses for the reign?
Indeed Adonai will dwell to forever.

Chariots of God are tens of thousands,
thousands of the multitude into the Sinai sanctuary.
You ascended to the height and led captive;
you received gifts from human beings,
and even from those rebelling,
to your dwelling, God Adonai.

The Lord is being praised day to day,
bearing our burden is El our Savior.
Our El, the El of salvation,
the Lord Adonai is the escape from death.
Surely God will silence the plans of enmity,
in the crown of their hair where sins go on.

The Lord says, "From Bashan I will bring,
 I will bring from depths of the sea,
 that you may wash your foot in their defeat
 and the tongues of your dogs
 have their share from foes."

They view your processions, God,
processions into the sanctuary
of my God and my King.
Singers are in front, followed by music players
among maidens playing tambourines.

PSALM 68, continued

In great congregations, praise God;
praise Adonai in the assembly of Israel!
There little Benjamin leads the princes of Judah,
their throng the princes of Zebulun and Naphtali.

Your God summoned your power.
Show strength, God, as you did for us!
Because of your temple at Jerusalem,
to you the kings will bring gifts.

Rebuke the beast of the reeds,
the herd of bulls among calves of nations;
being humbled with bars of silver,
nations that delight in wars are scattered.
Envoys from Egypt will come;
Cush will submit their hands to God.

Kingdoms of the earth, sing to God!
Sing praise to the Lord!
To the Rider in the skies, the ancient skies, see!
The voice thunders, the voice of might.

Proclaim the power of God over Israel,
the majesty and power in the skies.
Awesome are you, God, in your sanctuary;
the God of Israel gives power and strengths
to the people praising God.

Glory…

Antiphon   Kingdoms of earth, sing to God;
sing praise to the Lord.
(alleluia)

PSALM 85

Antiphon for Lent

Lord,
you showed favor to your land;
you have forgiven the sins of your people.

Easter

You will turn back, O God,
and revive us again;
may your people rejoice in you,
alleluia.

You showed favor, Adonai, to your land;
you restored the fortune of Jacob.
You forgave the iniquity of your people;
you covered all of their sin.
You set aside all of your wrath;
you turned from your fierce anger.

Restore us, God of our salvation!
And put away your displeasure toward us.
Will you be angry with us to forever?
Will you prolong your anger
to generation and generation?

Will you not revive us again
that your people may rejoice in you?
Show us, Adonai, your unfailing love
and grant us your salvation.

PSALM 85, continued

I will listen to what El Adonai will say,
promising peace to the people, even to the saints,
but not letting them return to folly.
Surely near to ones fearing is salvation,
the glory to dwell in our land.

Love and Faithfulness meet;
Justice and Peace kiss.
Faithfulness springs forth from the earth
and Justice looks down from the heavens.

Indeed Adonai will give the good
and our land will yield her harvest,
Justice going forward to prepare
the way for the steps of the Lord.

Glory...

Antiphon for Lent   Lord,
you showed favor to your land;
you have forgiven the sins of your people.

Easter   You will turn back, O God,
and revive us again;
may your people rejoice in you,
alleluia.

ISAIAH 26:1b-4,7-9,12

Antiphon for Lent   My soul yearns for you in the night;
within me my spirit longs for you.

Easter   We have placed all our hope in the Lord,
who has given us peace, alleluia.

Our city is strong;
salvation makes walls and rampart.
Open gates, so the righteous nation may enter,
the one keeping faiths.

Your steadfast mind will keep peace,
peace because of trusting.
Trust in Adonai to forever,
for in Yah Adonai is the Rock of eternities...

The path of the righteous is level;
the Upright One smooths the way of the righteous.
Yes, in the way of your laws, Adonai, we wait,
for your name and your renown
are the desire of our heart.

My soul yearns for you in the night;
within me my spirit longs for you.
Just as your judgments are on the earth,
so people of the world learn justice...

Adonai, you establish for us peace;
indeed all we have accomplished you did for us.

Glory...

Repeat antiphon.

PSALM 67

Antiphon for Lent May God be gracious to us,
bless us,
and shine the holy face upon us.

Easter The earth has yielded its harvest;
may the nations be glad and sing for joy,
alleluia.

May God be gracious to us and bless us,
may God's faces shine upon us.
How else can your ways be known on the earth
and your salvation among all the nations?

May the peoples praise you, God,
may the peoples praise you, all of them.

May the nations be glad and sing for joy
for you rule the peoples
and guide nations of the earth into justice.

May the peoples praise you, God,
may the peoples praise you, all of them.

The land will yield her harvest, God will bless us,
and all the ends of the earth will revere our God.

Glory…

Repeat antiphon.

WEEK III
TUESDAY EVENING

PSALM 74

Antiphon for Lent   Remember, O God,
your people you purchased of old.

Easter   Alleluia, alleluia, alleluia.

Why, God, do you reject us to forever?
Your anger smolders against sheep of your pasture.
Remember your people you purchased of old
and redeemed, your tribe of inheritance,
Mount Zion where you dwelt.

Lift high your steps through everlasting ruin,
the enmity destruction to the sanctuary.
All who would be foes roared,
and in your meeting place
set up their standard signs.

They behaved like ones wielding at above
axes through a thicket of trees,
and now her carved panels
they smashed with axe and hatchet.
They sent your sanctuary to the ground with fire
and defiled the dwelling place of your Name.

PSALM 74, continued

They said in their heart, "We will crush them."
Completely they burned in the land
all the places to worship God.
We see no miraculous signs;
there is no longer a prophet among us.
Until when? No one knows.

Until when, God, will foes in enmity
mock and revile your name?
To forever?
Why do you hold back your hand,
even your right hand from the fold of your bosom?

But God, my King from of old,
bringing salvation onto the midst of the earth,
you split open the sea by your power,
you break the heads of monsters in the waters.

You crushed the heads of Leviathan,
giving him as food to people and desert creatures.
You opened up streams and springs
and dried up everflowing rivers.

To you is the day and to you is the night,
and you established the moon and the sun.
You set all the boundaries of the earth;
summer and winter were made by you.

Remember those who in enmity mock Adonai
and the foolish people who revile your name.
Do not hand the life of your dove to the wild beast;
remember to forever the life of your afflicted ones.

Dark places of the land are filled with them
and haunts of violence.
Have regard for the covenant.
Let not the oppressed retreat, nor the disgraced;
may the poor and the needy praise your name.

Rise up, God! Defend your cause!
Remember the all-day mockery of fools.
Ignore not the clamor of foes,
nor those in enmity and continual uproar.

Glory…

Antiphon for Lent   Remember, O God,
your people you purchased of old.

Easter   Alleluia, alleluia, alleluia.

PSALM 125

Antiphon for Lent   The Lord surrounds the people of God
from now and to forevermore.

Easter   Peace be with you;   John 20:19
it is I, do not be afraid;   Mark 6:50
alleluia.

Ones trusting in Adonai are like Mount Zion;
not to be shaken, they endure to forever.

As mountains surround around Jerusalem,
so Adonai surrounds around the people
from now and to forevermore.

Indeed the sceptor of badness will not remain
over the lot of the righteous
lest the hands of the righteous be used for bad.

Do good, Adonai, to the good,
even to those upright in their hearts!
But those who turn to evil ways
Adonai will banish with those who do evil.

Peace be upon Israel!

Glory…

Antiphon for Lent   The Lord surrounds the people of God
from now and to forevermore.

Easter   Peace be with you;   John 20:19
it is I, do not be afraid;   Mark 6:50
alleluia.

PSALM 131

Antiphon for Lent
Unless you turn
and become as a child,
by no means
may you enter the kingdom.   see Mark 10:15

Easter
The hope of Israel is the Lord,
alleluia.

Adonai, my heart is not proud
and my eyes are not haughty
and I am unconcerned with the great matters,
with things so wonderful as to be beyond me.

But indeed I have become still and quiet in my soul
like a child with a mother, being weaned.
Like one being weaned is my soul within me.

Israel, put your hope in Adonai
from now and to forevermore.

Glory…

Antiphon for Lent
Unless you turn
and become as a child,
by no means
may you enter the kingdom.   see Mark 10:15

Easter
The hope of Israel is the Lord,
alleluia.

REVELATION 4:8b,11; 5:9,10,12,13b

Antiphon for Lent   Lord, out of every tribe and tongue
and people and nation,
you made to our God
a kingdom and priests.

Easter   Let all creation serve you,
for all things came into being at your word,
alleluia.

Worthy are you, our Lord and our God,
to receive the glory and honor and power,
because you have created all things,
and by your will all things were created and are.

Worthy are you to receive the scroll
and to open its seals,
because you were slain
and purchased for God by your blood
from every tribe and tongue and people and nation.

You made of them to our God
a kingdom and priests,
and they will reign over the earth.

Worthy is the Lamb, slain to receive
the power and riches and wisdom and strength
and honor and glory and blessing.

Glory…

Repeat antiphon.

WEEK III
WEDNESDAY MORNING

***PSALM 89**:2-38*

Antiphon   Wherever you are, Lord,
there is mercy, there is truth.
(alleluia)

Forever will I sing the great love of Adonai;
with my mouth I will make known
your faithfulness to generation and generation.
Indeed I will declare forever love standing firm,
your faithfulness established in the heavens.

"I made a covenant with my chosen ones,
 sworn to my servant David.
 I will establish your line to forever,
 and to generation and generation
 I will make firm your throne."

The heavens praise your wonder, Adonai,
and your faithfulness in the holy assembly.
For who in the sky can compare to Adonai;
who is like Adonai among heavenly beings?

God is greatly feared in the council of holy ones
and is awesome over all who surround around.
Adonai Sabaoth, who is like you?
Mighty Adonai, your faithfulness is around you.

PSALM 89:2-38, continued

You rule over the surging of the sea;
when waves mount up you still them.
You crushed Rahab like the slain
and scattered enmity
with the arm of your strength.

To you are the heavens and to you is the earth;
the world and her fullness you founded.
North and South you created;
Tabor and Hermon sing for joy at your name.

To you is the arm strong with power;
your hand is exalted, your right hand.
Righteousness and Justice
are the foundation of your throne;
Hesed-Love and Faithfulness go before your faces.

Blessed are people who learn to acclaim Adonai;
they walk in the light of your presences.
In your name they rejoice all the day
and in your righteousness they exult,

for you are the glory of their strength
and by your favor you exalt our horn.
Indeed Adonai is our shield
and the Holy One of Israel is our king.

Once in a vision you spoke to your faithful ones:
"I bestowed strength on a warrior;
 I exalted from the people a young man.

I found David my servant,
I anointed him with my sacred oil,
and my hand will sustain him;
surely my arm will strengthen him.

No enemy will subject him to tribute
and no wicked people will oppress him.
Before him I will crush foes
and strike down adversity,

and my faithfulness and my love are with him,
and through my hands will the horn be exalted.
And I will set his hand over the sea
and his right hand over the rivers.

He will call me out: 'You are my Father,
  my God and Rock of my salvation.'
I will also appoint him firstborn
and most exalted among kings of the earth.

I will maintain my love for him to forever
and my unfailing covenant with him.
I will establish his line to forever
and his throne as days of the heavens.

If his sons and daughters forsake my law
and do not follow my statutes,
if they violate my decrees
and keep not my commands,

then I will punish their sins with the rod
and their iniquity with floggings.
But I will not take my love from them,
nor will I ever betray my faithfulness.

PSALM 89:2-38, continued

I will not violate my covenant
nor will I alter the utterance of my lips.
Once I swore by my holiness;
I will not lie to David:

His line will continue to forever
and his throne like the sun before me.
Like the moon it is established forever,
a faithful witness in the sky."

Glory…

Antiphon   Wherever you are, Lord,
               there is mercy, there is truth.
               (alleluia)

PSALM 86

Antiphon for Lent   Bring joy to me, your servant,
                     for to you, Lord, I lift up my soul.

Easter   People of all nations will come
                     and worship before you, O Lord,
                     alleluia.

Hear in your ear, Adonai;
answer me for I am poor and needy.
Guard my life for I am devoted;
save your servant, my God,
the one trusting in you.

Have mercy on me, Lord,
for to you I call all the day.
Bring joy to me, your servant,
for to you, Lord, I lift up my soul.

Indeed, Lord, you are kind and forgiving
and abundant in love for all who call to you.
Hear my prayer, Adonai;
listen to the sound of my cries for mercy.

In the day of my trouble I will call to you
for you will answer me...
There is none like you among so-called "gods"
and there are no deeds like yours, Lord.

All the nations you made will come
and they will worship before you, Lord,
and they will bring glory to your name
for you are great and do marvelous deeds,
you, God, by yourself.

Teach me, Adonai, your way
and I will walk in your truth.
Make my heart undivided
that I may fear your name.

I will praise you, Lord my God, with all my heart
and I will glorify your name to forever
for great is your love of me
and you deliver my soul from the depth of Sheol.

Arrogant ones attack against me, God;
a band of ruthless people seek my life
and do not regard you before them.

PSALM 86, continued

But you, Lord El, Compassionate and Gracious,
are slow of anger and abundant in love and fidelity.
Turn to me! And have mercy on me!

Grant your strength to your servant
and save the child of your maidservant!
Give to me a sign of goodness
that enmity may see and find shame,
for you, Adonai, help me and comfort me.

Glory...

Antiphon for Lent	Bring joy to me, your servant, for to you, Lord, I lift up my soul.
Easter	People of all nations will come and worship before you, O Lord, alleluia.

ISAIAH 33:13-16

Antiphon for Lent	Blessed is the one walking rightly and speaking right things.
Easter	Our eyes will see the King in all his radiant beauty, alleluia.

ISAIAH 33:13-16

Hear what I did, you who are far away!
And acknowledge my power, you who are near.

Sinners are terrified in Zion
and trembling grips the godless.
Who of us can dwell in fire that consumes?
Who of us can dwell in everlasting burning?

One walking rightly and speaking right things,
rejecting the gain of extortions,
keeping hands from accepting the bribe,
stopping ears from hearing of blood,
shutting eyes against contemplation of evil:

That one will dwell on the heights
in a mountain fortress refuge,
supplied with bread and waters unfailing.

Glory…

Antiphon for Lent	Blessed is the one walking rightly and speaking right things.
Easter	Our eyes will see the King in all his radiant beauty, alleluia.

PSALM 98

Antiphon in Lent — Shout for joy
before the Lord, the King!

Easter — All peoples will see
the saving power of our God,
alleluia.

Sing to Adonai a new song
who has done marvelous things,
working salvation at the right hand and holy arm.

Adonai made known salvation,
righteousness revealed for the eyes of the nations.
Love is remembered and faithfulness
to the house of Israel

and all the ends of the earth see
the salvation of our God.
Shout for joy to Adonai, all you earth!
Burst forth, and sing, and make music!

Make music to Adonai with harp,
with harp and the sound of singing,
with trumpets and blast of ram horn:
Shout for joy before the King Adonai!

Let the sea resound, the fullness of the world,
and those living in her.
Let the rivers clap hands,
let the mountains sing together for joy

before Adonai who comes to judge the earth,
who will judge the world in righteousness
and peoples with equity.

Glory…

Repeat antiphon.

WEEK III
WEDNESDAY EVENING

PSALM 70

Antiphon for Lent   To my poverty and need God came quickly.

Easter   Alleluia, alleluia, alleluia.

God, save me; Adonai hasten to help me!
May plans to seek my life be shamed and confused;

may the desire for my ruin turn back in disgrace
and ones saying "aha!, aha!" turn back in shame.

May all who seek you rejoice in you and be glad
and may lovers of salvation say always,
"Let God be exalted."

Yet I am poor and needy, God,
come quickly to me and do not delay,
Adonai, my help and deliverer.

Glory…

Repeat antiphon.

PSALM 126

Antiphon for Lent   Those who sow in tears
will reap a song of joy.

Easter   Your weeping will be turned into joy,
alleluia.

When Adonai returned Zion from captivity
we felt like people in a dream.
Then our mouth was filled with laughter,
and our tongue with a song of joy.

Then they said among the nations
"Their Adonai did greatness for them."
Adonai did greatness for us;
we were full of joy.

Restore our good fortune, Adonai,
like streams in the Negev desert.
Sowers are now in tears;
they will reap with a song of joy.

Going out, the sower goes out weeping,
carrying seeds for the sowing.
Returning, the sower will return
carrying sheaves with a song of joy.

Glory…

Repeat antiphon.

PSALM 127

Antiphon for Lent
Lord, build the house;
Lord, watch over the city.

Easter
Whether we live or die,
we are the Lord's,
alleluia.

If Adonai does not build the house,
the builders labor in vanity.
If Adonai does not watch over the city,
the watcher stands guard in vain.

It is vanity to rise early or stay up late,
or to eat the bread of hard toil;
the Lord provides as the beloved get their sleep.
See, heritage of Adonai!

Sons are a reward, and daughters of the womb.
Like arrows in the hand of a warrior,
so are children of one's youth.

Blessed is the one whose quiver is full of them;
they will not be shamed
when they contend at the gate with enmity.

Glory…

Repeat antiphon.

COLOSSIANS 1:12-20

Antiphon for Lent He is the firstborn of all creation;
he is before all things
and in him all things hold together.

Easter From him, through him, and in him
all things exist;
glory to him forever,
alleluia.

Give joyful thanks to the Father who made you fit
for your part of the lot of the saints in light,

who delivered us out of the authority of darkness
and transitioned us into the kingdom of the beloved Son,
in whom we have redemption, the forgiveness of our sins.

The Son is the image of the invisible God,
the firstborn of all creation.
In him all things were created,
in the heavens and on the earth,
the visible and the invisible,
whether thrones, lordships, rulers or authorities.

All things have been created through him and for him.
He is before all things,
and in him all things hold together.

He is the head of the body, the church,
and the beginning, the firstborn from the dead,
so that in all things he may hold the first place.

In him all the fullness was well pleased to dwell,
and through him reconciliation to himself of all things,
things on earth and things in the heavens,
making peace through the blood of his cross.

Glory...

Repeat antiphon.

WEEK III
THURSDAY MORNING

***PSALM** 89:39-53*

Antiphon

I am the root and stock of David;
I am the morning star.
(alleluia)

Lord, you have rejected and spurned,
you were angry with your anointed one.
You renounced the covenant of your servant,
the crown you defiled in the dust.

You broke through all of the walls
and reduced the strongholds to ruin.
Those passing on the way plundered
and the neighbors were full of scorn.

PSALM 89:39-53, continued

You exalted the right hand of foes
and made all the enemies rejoice.
You turned back the edge of our sword
and did not support us in the battle.

You put an end to the splendor
and cast the throne to the ground.
You cut short the days of youth
and covered us over with shame.

Until when, Adonai?
Will you hide yourself to forever?
Will your wrath burn like fire?
Remember how fleeting am I!
For what futility you created
sons and daughters of Adam and Eve!
What human can live and not see death,
or save the self from the power of Sheol?

Where, Lord, are your former great loves
sworn to David in your faithfulness?
Remember, Lord, the mocking of your servants!
I bear this in my heart from many nations, Adonai:
the mockery of enmity,
the mockery of the steps of your anointed one.

Praised be Adonai to forever. Amen and amen.

Glory…

Antiphon   I am the root and stock of David;
I am the morning star.
(alleluia)

PSALM 87

Antiphon for Lent
Glorious things
are being said of you,
city of God.

Easter
City of God,
you are the source of our life;
with music and dance
we will rejoice in you,
alleluia.

On the holy mountain is the foundation of Adonai,
who loves the gates of Zion
more than all of Jacob's dwellings.
Glorious things are being said of you, city of God.

"I will record Rahab and Babylon
 among those who know me;
 see Philistia and Tyre with Cush:
 this one was born there!"

Indeed of Zion it will be said,
"One and another were born in her,
 and the Most High will establish her."
Adonai will write when registering peoples,
"This one was born there."
And making music the ones will sing,
"All of my fountains are in you."

Glory...

Repeat antiphon.

ISAIAH 40:10-17

Antiphon for Lent See the Sovereign Lord come with power:
with ruling arm, reward, and recompense.

Easter Like a shepherd
he will gather the lambs in his arms
and carry them close to his heart,
alleluia.

See! Sovereign Adonai comes with power,
and with a ruling arm.
See! And with reward
and accompanied with recompense.

Like a shepherd tending the flock
and gathering lambs in the arms,
carrying them in the heart
and leading gently those with young.

Who can measure the waters in a hand's hollow?
Or mark off the heavens with handbreadths?
Or hold the dust of the earth in a basket?
Or weigh mountains on a scale
or hills in a balance?

Who has understood the mind of Adonai?
What human has given counsel or instruction,
or whom was consulted for enlightenment
and teaching about what is right
and teaching knowledge?
Who can show the path of understanding?

Surely nations are like drops in a bucket
and are regarded as dust on a scale.
Surely islands are weighed like fine dust.

Even Lebanon is not sufficient to make fire,
nor their animals sufficient for burnt-offering.
Before God, all the nations are as nothing,
regarded as worthless and less than nothing.

Glory…

Repeat antiphon.

PSALM 99

Antiphon for Lent
Exalt the Lord, our God;
and worship at the mountain
of the Lord's holiness.

Easter
Great is the Lord in Zion,
and exalted over all the nations,
alleluia.

Adonai reigns; let the nations tremble.
The One sits enthroned on the cherubim;
let the earth shake.

Great in Zion is Adonai,
and exalted over all of the nations.
Let them praise your great and awesome name,
"Holy are you, and mighty."

PSALM 99, continued

The King of justice loves you
and establishes equity and justice,
having done what is right in Jacob.

Exalt Adonai our God!
And worship at the feet on the footstool,
"Holy are you, and mighty."

Moses and Aaron are among the priests,
and Samuel among those calling the name,
calling on El Adonai, who answered them,
who spoke to them from the pillar of cloud.
They kept the statutes and decrees given to them.

Adonai, our God, you answered them.
You were the one Forgiving El to them,
though punishing their misdeeds.

Exalt Adonai our God!
And worship at the holy mountain,
for holy is our God Adonai!

Glory…

Antiphon for Lent   Exalt the Lord, our God;
and worship at the mountain
of the Lord's holiness.

Easter   Great is the Lord in Zion,
and exalted over all the nations,
alleluia.

WEEK III
THURSDAY EVENING

***PSALM** 79:1-5,9-11,13*

Antiphon for Lent   Help us, God of our salvation;
                    deliver us and atone for our sins
                    for the sake of your name.

Easter   Alleluia, alleluia, alleluia.

God, the nations invaded into your inheritance,
they defiled your holy temple,
they reduced Jerusalem to rubbles.
They gave the bodies of your servants
as food to birds of the air,
the flesh of your saints to beasts of earth.

They poured out their blood
like the waters around Jerusalem
and no one is there burying.
We are a reproach to our neighbors,
scorn and derision to those around us.
Until when, Adonai, will you be angry?
Will the fire of your jealousy burn to forever?...

Hold not against us the sins of our ancestors;
may your mercies be quick to meet us
for we are in desperate need.
Help us, God of our salvation,
for the glory of your name,
and deliver us and atone for our sins
for the sake of your name.

Why should the nations say, "Where is their God?"
Let vengeance be known among the nations
before our eyes for your servants,
for their blood being poured out.
May the groan of prisoners come before you;
and by your strong arm preserve the condemned…

We your people, the sheep of your pasture,
will praise you to forever.
Generation to generation
will recount your praise.

Glory…

Antiphon for Lent	Help us, God of our salvation; deliver us and atone for our sins for the sake of your name.
Easter	Alleluia, alleluia, alleluia.

PSALM 86:1-7,11

Antiphon for Lent   Bring joy to me, your servant,
for to you, Lord, I lift up my soul.

Easter   Alleluia, alleluia, alleluia.

Hear in your ear, Adonai,
answer me for I am poor and needy.
Guard my life for I am devoted;
save your servant, my God,
the one trusting in you.

Have mercy on me, Lord,
for to you I call all the day.

Bring joy to me, your servant,
for to you, Lord, I lift up my soul.
Indeed, Lord, you are kind and forgiving
and abundant in love for all who call to you.

Hear my prayer, Adonai;
listen to the sound of my cries for mercy.
In the day of my trouble I will call to you
for you will answer me...

Teach me, Adonai, your way
and I will walk in your truth.
Make my heart undivided
that I may fear your name.

Glory...

Repeat antiphon.

PSALM 132

Antiphon for Lent Let us go to dwellings of the Lord;
may your saints sing for joy.

Easter The Lord has given him
the throne of David his father,
alleluia.

Adonai, remember David
and all the hardships he endured,
the oath he swore to Adonai,
the vow he made to the Mighty One of Jacob.

I will not enter into the structure of my house;
I will not go to the mats of my bed;
I will not allow my eyes to sleep
nor let slumber come to my eyelids,
till I find a place for Adonai,
a dwelling for the Mighty One of Jacob.

See, we heard her in Ephrathah;
we came upon her in fields of Jaar.
"Let us go to the dwellings;
 let us worship at the feet on the footstool."

Arise, Adonai, to your rest,
you and the ark of your might.
May your priests be clothed in righteousness
and may your saints sing for joy.
For the sake of your servant David
reject not the face of your anointed one.

Adonai swore an oath to David,
sure and not to be revoked.
"From the descendants of your body
 I will place on your throne.

If your sons and daughters keep my covenant
and my statutes that I teach them
then their children to forever
will sit on your throne."

For Adonai chose Zion
and desired her as a dwelling:
"This is my resting place to forever;
 here I will sit, for I desired her.

To bless I will bless her provisions;
her poor ones I will satisfy with food,
her priests I will clothe in salvation,
and her saints will sing; they will sing for joy.

Here I will make grow a horn for David;
I will set up a lamp for my anointed one.
Enmity will be clothed with shame.
The crown on David will be resplendent."

Glory…

Antiphon for Lent — Let us go to dwellings of the Lord;
may your saints sing for joy.

Easter — The Lord has given him
the throne of David his father,
alleluia.

REVELATION 11:17-18, 12:10-12a

Antiphon for Lent
Now have come
the salvation, the power,
and the kingdom of our God.

Easter
Lord, who is your equal in power?
Who is like you, majestic in holiness?
Alleluia.

We thank you, Lord God Almighty,
the One who is and who was;
you have taken your great power and reign.

The nations raged and your anger came,
and the time to judge the dead
and to reward your slaves and prophets,
the saints, and those fearing your name,
the small and the great...

Now have come the salvation and power
and kingdom of our God
and the authority of Christ.
The accuser of our brothers and sisters was cast,
accusing them before our God day and night.

Their victory was because of the blood of the Lamb
and by the word of their witness.
They loved their life into their death,
and so be glad, you heavens,
and all you dwelling in them.

Glory...

Repeat antiphon.

WEEK III
FRIDAY MORNING

PSALM 69*:2-22,30-37*

Antiphon for Lent   I am worn out from my calling out;
my throat is parched and my eyes fail,
looking for my God.

Easter   Seekers of God, you will live,
alleluia.

Save me, Adonai,
for waters have come to my neck.

I sink into the deep mire; there is no foothold.
I have come into deep waters; floods engulf me.

I am worn out from calling out;
my throat is parched and my eyes fail,
looking for my God.

Those hating me for no reason
are more numerous than the hairs of my head.
Many are the ones destroying me
in enmity for no reason.

What I did not steal then I must restore.
You, God, you know my folly
and my guilts are not hidden from you.

PSALM 69, continued

May those who hope in you, God of Israel,
not be disgraced because of me.
For your sake I endure scorn
and shame covers my face.

I am a stranger to my brothers and sisters,
an alien to the children of my mother.
Zeal for your house consumes me
and insults of your insulters fall on me.

When I weep and fast, my self is a scorn to me.
When I put on my clothing of sackcloth
then I am as sport to them.
Those sitting at the gate mock at me
and drinkers of strong drink in their songs.

But I pray to you, Adonai, in the time of favor;
in the greatness of your love, God,
answer me with your sure salvation.

Rescue me from the mire and let me not sink;
let me be delivered from those who hate
and from the depths of the waters.
Let not the flood of waters engulf me,
nor the depth swallow me
nor the pit close its mouth over me.

Answer me, Adonai, for good is your love!
In the greatness of your mercies, turn to me!
Hide not your faces from your servant;
to my trouble, be quick! Answer me!
Come near because of the foes;
rescue my self and redeem me!

You know my scorn and shame and disgrace;
all in enmity are before you.
Scorn broke my heart and I became helpless
and I looked to have sympathy but there was none,
and for comforters, but found none.

They put gall in my food
and for my thirst gave me vinegar to drink...
I am in pain and suffering;
may your salvation protect me, God.

I will praise God's name in song and glory
with a thanksgiving more pleasing to Adonai
than ox or bull with horn and hoof.

The poor ones will see and be glad;
may your hearts now live, you seekers of God,
for Adonai hears the needy ones
and despises not the captives.

Let heaven and earth give praise
with the seas and all moving in them.
For God will save Zion
and rebuild the cities of Judah;

then they will settle there and possess her
and the children of the servants will inherit her
and lovers of the Name will dwell in her.

Glory...

Antiphon for Lent   I am worn out from my calling out;
my throat is parched and my eyes fail,
looking for my God.

Easter   Seekers of God, you will live, alleluia.

PSALM 51

Antiphon for Lent   Restore to me, Lord,
the joy of your salvation
and sustain in me a willing spirit.

Easter   Lord, wash me of my guilt,
alleluia.

Have mercy on me, God,
in accord with your unfailing love;
in accord with the greatness of your compassion
blot out my transgressions.

Wash me of my many iniquities
and cleanse me from my sin,
for I know my transgressions
and my sin is before me always.

Against you yourself I sinned;
what I did is evil in your eyes.
You are proven right when you speak
and justified when you judge.
Surely we are sinners from birth,
from conception in a mother's womb.

Surely you desire truth in our inner parts;
in my inmost place you teach me wisdom.
You cleanse me with hyssop and I will be clean;
you wash me and I will be whiter than snow...

You let me hear joy and gladness;
let the bones you let be crushed now rejoice.
Hide your faces from my sins
and blot out all my iniquities.

A pure heart create in me, God!
Renew inside me a spirit to be steadfast.
Do not cast me from your presences,
nor take from me your Holy Spirit.

Restore to me the joy of your salvation
and sustain in me a willing spirit.
I will teach transgressors your ways
and sinners will turn back to you.

Save me from bloodguilt, God,
God of my salvation;
my tongue will sing of your righteousness.
Lord, open my lips
and my mouth will declare your praise.

Sacrifices give you no delight;
I could bring a burnt offering,
but it would give you no pleasure.
The sacrifices, God, you will not despise
are a broken spirit and a contrite heart.

Make Zion prosper in your pleasure,
and build up the walls of Jerusalem.
Then you will delight in the sacrifice of the just,
burnt offerings and whole offerings,
bulls offered on your altar.

Glory…   Repeat antiphon.

JEREMIAH 14:17b-22

Antiphon for Lent   Lord, we admit our no-good ways;
indeed we sinned against you.

    Easter   Christ bore our sins in his own body
as he hung upon the cross,
alleluia.

Let my eyes overflow with tears by night, by day,
without cease, for the grievous wounds suffered
by the virgin daughter of my people,
a very crushing blow.

If I go out in the country, see: ones slain by sword!
If I go in the city, see: the ravages of famine!
Indeed, both prophet and priest
have gone to a land they do not know.

To reject you rejected Judah?
Is Zion despised by your self?
Why have you afflicted us so we have no healing?

Our hope is for peace, but no good happens;
for a time of healing, but see: the terror!
We are aware, Adonai, of our no-good ways
and the guilt of our ancestors;
indeed we ourselves sin against you.

For the sake of your Name, neither despise us
nor dishonor the throne of your glory.
Remember, and break not your covenant with us!

Is there one among the worthless nations
that can bring rain or send showers from the skies?
Is that One not you, our God Adonai?
And so we hope in you,
for you do all these things.

Glory…

Repeat antiphon.

PSALM 95

Antiphon for Lent
> The Lord is our God,
> and we are the people
> of the pasture and flock
> and care of our God.

Easter
> Come into the Lord's presence
> singing for joy,
> alleluia.

Come, let us sing to Adonai;
let us shout to our saving Rock.
Come, let us extol Adonai
with thanksgiving and with song.

Adonai is the great El,
the great King above all those little "g" gods,
holding in hand the depths of earth
and peaks of mountains,
the sea and dry land formed in this hand.

PSALM 95, continued

Come, let us worship and bow and kneel
before Adonai who made us.
For God is our God, and we are the people
of the pasture and flock and care of our God.

"If today you hear this voice
 do not harden your heart,
 as at Meribah and the desert day at Massah
 where your ancestors tested me;
 they tried me though they saw my deeds.

For forty years was my anger on that generation,
 the people straying in their heart;
 and so they did not know my ways,
 and so were unable to enter my rest."

Glory…

Antiphon for Lent | The Lord is our God,
and we are the people
of the pasture and flock
and care of our God.

Easter | Come into the Lord's presence
singing for joy,
alleluia.

WEEK III
FRIDAY EVENING

PSALM 22

Antiphon for Lent   My God did not despise, disdain,
nor hide from
the suffering of the afflicted.

Easter   Alleluia, alleluia, alleluia.

My God, my God, why have you forsaken me?
Far from my salvation are the words of my groan.
My God, I cry out by day, but you do not answer;
nor is silent my night.

Yet you Holy One are enthroned, praises Israel.
In you our ancestors trusted and were delivered.
To you they cried and they were saved.
In you they trusted and were not disappointed.

But I am a worm and not human,
the scorn of humanity and despised by people.
All those seeing me mock at me;
they shake their heads in insult:
"In the one you trust, let your Adonai rescue you;
  let the one who 'delights' in you deliver you!"

PSALM 22, continued

You brought me out from the womb,
to trust in you at the breasts of my mother.
From the womb I was cast upon you;
from the womb of my mother, you are my God.
Be not far from me,
for trouble is near with no one to help.

Many bulls surround me;
the strong of Bashan encircle me.
They open wide their mouths against me,
lions tearing up prey and roaring.

Like the waters I am poured out
and my bones are all out of joint.
My heart like wax melts away within my insides.

Like a broken clay pot, my strength is dried up,
and my tongue is stuck in the roof of my mouth;
you lay me in the dust of death.
Dogs indeed surround around me,
a band of bad doers encircles me as a lion
ready to tear into my hands and my feet.

I can count all of my bones;
they stare and they gloat over me.
They divide my garments among them
and for my clothing they cast lots.

But you, Adonai, be not far off;
come quickly to help me, my Strength!
Deliver my precious life from the sword
and from the power of the dog.
Rescue me from the mouth of the lion
and from the horns of wild oxen.

I will declare your name to my brothers and sisters
and praise you within the assembly.

You fearing Adonai, give praise!
All you descendants of Jacob, give honor!
All you descendants of Israel, give reverence
before Adonai, who despised not, nor disdained,
nor hid the holy face from those suffering affliction,
but heard their cry for help.

From you is my praise within the great assembly;
my vows will I fulfill before those who fear you.
The poor ones will eat to satisfaction,
and the seekers will praise Adonai;
may your heart live to forever.

All the ends of the earth will remember
and turn to Adonai,
and all the families of nations will bow down,
for to Adonai is the dominion, ruling over nations.
All those rich on the earth will feast and worship
and kneel, all who go down to the dust,
all who cannot keep their own self alive.

Those to come will be served by being told,
and in the same way serve generations to come.
They will come and they will proclaim
the deeds of the faithfulness of the Lord,
the story, to people yet to be born.

Glory...

Antiphon for Lent   My God did not despise, disdain,
nor hide from the suffering of the afflicted.

Easter   Alleluia, alleluia, alleluia.

PSALM 88

Antiphon for Lent   Day and night I cry out before you;
may my prayer come before you.

Easter   Alleluia, alleluia, alleluia.

Adonai, Elohay, my Savior,
I cry out day and night before you.
May my prayer come before you;
turn your ear to my cry.

My soul is full of troubles
and my life draws near to Sheol.
I am counted among those going down to the pit,
like a human with no strength,

set apart with the dead ones
like slain ones lying in the grave,
whom you no longer remember,
whom are cut off from your care.

You put me in the pit of the lowest,
in the darkest deep.
Your anger lies heavy upon me
and all your waves overwhelm.

You took away my friends
and made me repulsive to them;
in confinement I cannot escape.
My eye is dim from grief;
I call to you, Adonai,
and in every day spread my hands to you.

Is it to the dead ones you show wonder?
Do the dead rise up and praise you?
Is your love declared in the grave
or your fidelity in the no-more?
Is your wonder known in the darkness
or your righteous deeds in the land of oblivion?

But to you, Adonai, I cry for help
and in the morning my prayer comes before you.
Why do you reject my self, Adonai?
Why hide your faces from me?

Afflicted and coming close to death and despairing,
from youth I have suffered your terrors.
Your anger has swept over me
and your terrors have destroyed me.

They surround me all the day like the floods,
engulfing over me completely.
You took far away my loving companion;
my one friend is darkness.

Glory...

Antiphon for Lent	Day and night I cry out before you; may my prayer come before you.
Easter	Alleluia, alleluia, alleluia.

PSALM 135

Antiphon for Lent   I know that our God is great,
greater than all "gods."

Easter   I, the Lord,
am your savior and redeemer,
alleluia.

Praise Adonai!
Praise the name of Adonai!
Servants of Adonai, give praise!
You who minister in the house of Adonai,
in the courts of the house of our God,

praise Adonai, for good is Adonai!
Sing praise to the Name, for it is pleasant!
Adonai has chosen Jacob, Israel the chosen treasure.

For I know that great is our Lord;
greater than all the "gods" is Adonai,
who does as Adonai pleases
in the heavens and on earth and in the deep sea,

making clouds rise from the ends of the earth,
sending lightning with the rain,
and bringing wind from the storehouses,

who struck down the firstborn of Egypt,
from human to animals,
sending signs and wonders to the midst of Egypt
against Pharaoh and against all of his servants,

having struck down many nations and mighty kings:
Sihon, king of the Amorites, and Og of Bashan,
and all the kingdoms of Canaan,
who gave their land as an inheritance,
an inheritance to Israel, the people of Adonai.

Your name, Adonai, is to forever,
your renown to generation and generation,
for you, Adonai, will vindicate your people
and will have compassion on your servants.

Idols of the nations are silver and gold,
the making of human hands.
A mouth to them but they cannot speak.
Eyes to them but they cannot see.

Ears to them but they cannot hear,
and there is no breath in their mouth.
Like them will be their makers
and all who trust in them.

House of Israel, praise Adonai!
House of Aaron, praise Adonai!
House of Levi, praise Adonai!
You who fear Adonai, praise Adonai!

Praised be Adonai from Zion,
dwelling in Jerusalem.
Praise Adonai!

Glory…

Repeat antiphon.

REVELATION 15:3b-4

Antiphon for Lent
All the nations will come
and worship before you,
Lord God Almighty.

Easter
Let us sing to the Lord,
glorious in triumph,
alleluia.

Great and wonderful are your works,
Lord God Almighty.
Just and true are your ways,
King of the nations.

Who will not fear, O Lord,
or glorify your name?

Only you are holy.
All the nations will come and worship before you;
your ordinances are shown to all.

Glory…

Antiphon for Lent
All the nations will come
and worship before you,
Lord God Almighty.

Easter
Let us sing to the Lord,
glorious in triumph,
alleluia.

WEEK III
SATURDAY MORNING

PSALM 107

Antiphon Give thanks to the Lord for unfailing love
and deeds of wonder for all human beings.
(alleluia)

"Give thanks to Adonai, who is good,
  whose love is to forever."

Let this be said by the redeemed of Adonai,
who redeemed them from the hand of the foe
and gathered them from the lands,
from east and west, from north and the south sea.

Some wandered in the desert wasteland,
finding no way to a city for settling.
Hungry and thirsty, their life ebbed away in them.

Then they cried out to Adonai in their trouble,
who delivered them from their distresses,
who led them by a direct way
to go to a city for settling.

Let them give thanks to Adonai for unfailing love,
for deeds of wonder done
for sons and daughters of Adam and Eve,
for satisfying the throats of the thirsty
and filling the hungry with goodness.

Some sit in the dark and deep gloom,
prisoners of suffering and iron,
for they rebelled against the word of El
and despised the counsel of the Most High
who subjected their heart to the bitter labor,
and no one was there to help.

Then they cried in their trouble to Adonai,
who saved them from their distress,
brought them out from the dark and deep gloom,
and broke away their chains.

Let them give thanks to Adonai for unfailing love,
for deeds of wonder done
for sons and daughters of Adam and Eve,
for breaking down gates of bronze
and cutting through bars of iron.

Some were fools through their rebellious ways,
afflicted because of their iniquities.
Loathing all food,
they drew themselves near to the gates of death.

Then they cried in their trouble to Adonai,
who saved them from their distress,
sending forth the word to heal them
and rescue them from their graves.

Let them give thanks to Adonai for unfailing love,
for deeds of wonder done
for sons and daughters of Adam and Eve,
and let them sacrifice offerings of thanksgiving
and tell of the works with songs of joy.

Some went to the sea in ships
to do trade on the mighty waters.
They saw the works in the deep,
the wonderful deeds of Adonai,
who spoke and stirred up the tempest wind
and lifted up the waves.

They mounted up to the heavens
and went down to the deep;
in peril their courage melted away.
They reeled and staggered like drunkards,
all of them at their wits end.

Then they cried in their trouble to Adonai,
who brought them out from their distress,
stilling the storm to a whisper
and hushing the waves.
They were glad when it grew calm
and they were guided to the haven they desired.

Let them give thanks to Adonai for unfailing love,
for deeds of wonder done
for sons and daughters of Adam and Eve,
and let them exalt in the assembly of the people,
and in the council of elders give praise.

PSALM 107, continued

Adonai turned rivers into desert,
springs of waters into thirsty ground,
and land of fruit into a salt waste
because of wicked ways of those living there.

Adonai then turned desert into pools of waters,
parched ground into springs of waters,
and brought hungry ones to live there.

They founded and settled a city,
sowed fields and planted vineyards,
and yielded the fruit of harvest.
They were blessed and they increased greatly,
and their herds were not allowed to diminish.

Then they decreased and were humbled
by oppression, calamity and sorrow.
With contempt poured on them,
nobles were made to wander in a trackless waste.

But the needy were lifted from affliction
and their families increased like a flock.
They see the upright and they rejoice,
but doers of badness shut their mouth.

Whoever is wise, heed these things
and consider the great love of Adonai.

Glory…

Antiphon   Give thanks to the Lord for unfailing love
and deeds of wonder for all human beings.
(alleluia)

PSALM 119:145-152

Antiphon for Lent You are near, Adonai,
and all your commands are true.

Easter The words I have spoken to you
are spirit and life, John 6:63b
alleluia.

I call with all my heart: answer me, Adonai;
your decrees I will obey.
I call to you: save me,
and I will keep your statutes.

I rise before dawn and I cry for help;
in your word I put my hope.
My eyes stay open in the night watch
to meditate on your promise.

Hear my voice, as you are loving, Adonai,
as your law makes me alive.
Scheming devisers are near,
but they are far from your law.

You are near, Adonai,
and all your commands are true.
I learned long ago from your statutes
that you established them to forever.

Glory…

Repeat antiphon.

WISDOM 9:1-6,9-11

Antiphon for Lent
Wisdom of God,
come forth beside me
that I may learn what is pleasing to you.

Easter
Lord,
you have built your temple and altar
on your holy mountain,
alleluia.

God of my ancestors, Lord of mercy,
who made all things by your word
and through your wisdom framed humanity
to be master of the creatures you have created,
and to govern the world in holiness and justice
and judge justly and with an upright heart,

Give me Wisdom, your companion at your throne,
and do not reject me from among your children,
for I am your servant, born of your handmaid,
a feeble human with a short life
and a weak understanding of justice and laws.

Though a human be ever so perfect in human eyes,
without your Wisdom that same one
will be of no account...

With you is Wisdom, who knows your works
and was present when you created the world,
who knows what is pleasing in your eyes
and what is right in accord with your ordinances.

Send her forth from the holy heavens
and dispatch her from your majestic throne,
that she may labor beside me
and I may learn what pleases you.

For she knows and understands all things
and will guide me to prudence in my actions
and guard me in her magnificence.

Glory...

Repeat antiphon.

PSALM 117

Antiphon for Lent   The fidelity of the Lord
is to forever.

Easter   I am the way,
the truth,
and the life,
alleluia.

John 14:6

Praise Adonai, all nations;
and extol, all peoples.

Great is this steadfast love toward us,
the fidelity of Adonai to forever.

Praise Adonai!

Glory...

Repeat antiphon.

WEEK **IV**
VIGIL OF SUNDAY
(Saturday Evening)

PSALM 134

Antiphon for Lent   Praise the Lord
all servants and ministers at night.

Easter   Alleluia, alleluia, alleluia.

See Adonai and give praise,
all you servants of Adonai,
and ministers at night in the house of Adonai.

Lift up your hands in the sanctuary
and praise Adonai!

May you be blessed from Zion by Adonai,
the One Making heavens and earth.

Glory…

Antiphon for Lent   Praise the Lord
all servants and ministers at night.

Easter   Alleluia, alleluia, alleluia.

PSALM 122

Lent, 4th Sunday   Let us go to God's house with rejoicing.

Easter, 4th Sunday   May the peace of Christ
fill your hearts with joy,
alleluia.

I rejoiced with those saying to me,
"Let us go to Adonai's house."
Our feet stand in your gates, Jerusalem.

Jerusalem is built like a city
formed together, a compact.
There the tribes go up, the tribes of Adonai.

Make it in Israel a statute
to praise the name of Adonai,
for there the thrones stand for judgment,
thrones of the house of David.

Pray for the peace of Jerusalem!
May those who love you be secure.
May peace be within your walls,
security within your citadels.

For the sake of my sisters and brothers and friends
I will say, "Now, peace be within you."
For the sake of the house of our God Adonai
I will seek your prosperity.

Glory…

                                                Repeat antiphon.

PSALM 130

Lent, 4th Sunday Awake, sleeper,
rise from the dead,
and Christ will light you up.   Eph. 5:14b

Easter, 4th Sunday With your own blood
you have redeemed us for God,
alleluia.

From the depths I cry to you, Adonai.
Lord, hear my voice.
Let your ears be attentive to my cries for mercy.

If you kept a record of sins, Adonai,
Lord, who could stand?
But with you is the forgiveness,
and so you are revered in awe.

I wait, my soul waits for Adonai,
in whose word I put hope.
My soul waits for the Lord
more than watchers for the morning,
even watchers for the morning.

Put hope, Israel, in Adonai!
For unfailing love is from Adonai,
in whom is full redemption,
who will redeem Israel from all their sins.

Glory…

Repeat antiphon.

PHILIPPIANS 2:6-11

Lent, 4th Sunday
So great was God's love for us
that when we were dead because of our sins,
God brought us to life in Christ Jesus.

Easter, 4th Sunday
Was it not necessary for Christ to suffer
and so enter into his glory?
alleluia.

Christ Jesus, subsisting in the form of God,
did not deem equality with God something to grab,
but emptied himself, taking the form of a slave,
becoming in human likeness.

And being found in human fashion,
he humbled himself,
becoming obedient until death,
and death on a cross.

And so God highly exalted him,
and gave to him the name above every name,
that in the name of Jesus every knee should bend,
of heavenly beings and earthly beings,
and beings under the earth;

And every tongue acknowledge
to the glory of God the Father
that Jesus Christ is Lord.

Glory…

Repeat antiphon.

WEEK IV
RESURRECTION VIGIL

JEREMIAH 7:3b-7

Antiphon   In Christ who rose from the dead
              our hope of resurrection dawned.

This says Adonai Sabaoth, God of Israel:
"Reform your ways and your actions
 and I will let you live in this place!

Trust you not in words of deception to say,
'Temple of Adonai, Temple of Adonai,
 Temple of Adonai are these.'

If indeed to change you change
your ways and your actions,
if to deal you deal with each other with justice,
you oppress no alien, orphan or widow,
you shed no innocent blood in this place,
you follow no other "gods" to your own harm,
then I will let you live in this place
in the land I gave to your ancestors
from ever and to ever."

Glory…

Antiphon   In Christ who rose from the dead
              our hope of resurrection dawned.

FOR SUNDAYS OF WEEK 4   **LUKE 24:13-35**

And, behold, two of them on the same day
were journeying to a village named Emmaus,
sixty stadia *(7 miles)* distant from Jerusalem,
and they were talking to each other
about all these things having occurred.
And it came to pass as they talked and discussed:
Jesus himself drawing near journeyed with them,
but their eyes were held to not recognize him.
And he said to them, "What are these words
which you exchange with each other walking?"
And they stood with sad faces.
And the one named Cleopas answering said,
"You are only a stranger in Jerusalem and do not know
the things happening there in these days?"
And he said to them, "What things?"
And they said to him,
"The things about Jesus the Nazarene,
who was a prophet-man, powerful in work and word
before God and all the people,
how both the chief priests and our rulers
delivered him to judgment of death and crucified him.
But we were hoping
that he was the one about to redeem Israel.
But also with all these things,
this is the third day since these things happened.
But also some of our women astonished us.

Being at the tomb early and not finding his body,
> they came saying they had seen
> a vision of angels who say that he lives.
And some of the ones with us went to the tomb,
> and found as indeed the women said,
> but him they did not see."
And he said to them,
"O foolish ones and slow in heart to believe
> in all things which the prophets spoke.
Did the Christ not deem it fitting to suffer these things
> and to enter into his glory?"
And beginning from Moses and from all the prophets,
> he explained to them in all the scriptures
> the things concerning himself.
And as they drew near to the village
> to which they were journeying,
> he pretended to journey farther.
And they urged him saying, "Remain with us,
because it is toward evening and the day has declined."
And he went in to remain with them.
And it came to pass as he reclined with them,
> taking the bread, he blessed,
> and having broken he handed it to them.
And their eyes were opened and they recognized him;
> and he became invisible to them.
And they said to each other,
> "Was not our heart burning in us
> as he spoke to us on the way,
> as he opened up to us the scriptures?"

And rising up in the same hour,
they returned to Jerusalem and found
the eleven collected and the ones with them saying,
"Truly the Lord was raised and appeared to Simon."
And they related the things on the way,
and how he was known by them
in the breaking of the bread.

•

FOR SUNDAYS OF WEEK 8   **JOHN 21:1-19**

After these things Jesus again
showed himself to the disciples on the sea of Tiberias,
and this is how he showed himself:
There were together Simon Peter and Thomas,
called Twin, and Nathanael from Cana of Galilee, and
the sons of Zebedee, and two others of the disciples.
Simon Peter said to them, "I am going to fish."
They said to him, "We also are coming with you."
They went forth and embarked in the boat,
and in that night they caught nothing.
But when it became morning, Jesus stood on the shore;
however, the disciples did not know that it was Jesus.
And so Jesus said to them,
"Children, have you not any fish?"
They answered him, "No."
So he said to them,

JOHN 21:1-19, continued

"Throw the net on the right side of the boat,
and you will find."
And so they threw,
and they were no longer able to drag
from the multitude of the fishes.
And so the disciple whom Jesus loved said to Peter,
"It is the Lord."
Simon therefore Peter, hearing that it was the Lord,
girded himself with his garment, for he was naked,
and threw himself into the sea.
But the other disciples in the little boat came,
for they were not far from the land
but about two hundred cubits *(100 yards)*,
dragging the net of the fishes.
When they disembarked onto the land,
they saw a coal fire and a fish lying and bread lying.
Jesus said to them,
"Bring from the fishes you caught now."
Simon Peter went up and dragged the net to the land,
full of a hundred fifty-three great fish,
and being so many the net was not torn.
Jesus said to them, "Come, you; break the fast."
Not one of the disciples dared to question him,
"who are you," knowing that it was the Lord.
Jesus came and took the bread and gave it to them,
and the fish likewise.
This was now the third time that Jesus
showed himself to the disciples raised from the dead.

When they had breakfasted, Jesus said to Simon Peter,
"Simon of John,
do you agape-love me more than these?
He said to him,
"Yes, Lord, you know that I philia-love you."
He said to him, "Feed my lambs."
He says to him again secondly,
"Simon of John, do you agape-love me?"
He said to him,
"Yes, Lord, you know that I philia-love you."
He said to him, "Shepherd my sheep."
He says to him the third,
"Simon of John, do you philia-love me?"
Peter is grieved that he said to him the third
'do you love me?' and said to him,
"Lord, you know all things,
you know that I philia-love you."
Jesus said to him, "Feed my sheep:
Amen amen I tell you, when you were younger,
you girded yourself and walked where you wished;
but when you grow old, you will stretch out your hands
and another will gird you and will carry you
where you do not wish."
And this he said signifying by what death
he would glorify God.
And saying this he told him,
"Follow me."

•

WEEK IV
SUNDAY MORNING

PSALM 66

Antiphon for Lent   Let all the earth shout to God,
who has given us life.

Easter   Alleluia,
do not weep, Mary:
the Lord has risen from the dead,
alleluia.

Shout to God all the earth!
Sing the glory of the name!
Offer glory and praise to God!
Say to God, "How awesome are you;
  how great are your deeds."

Before you and your power
those in enmity cringe.
All of the earth bow down to you,
they sing praise to you,
they sing praise to your name.

Come and see the deeds of God who is awesome,
the works on behalf of all sons and daughters.
God turned the sea into dry land;
through the river they passed on foot.

Let us rejoice in God.
God rules forever with power,
with eyes watching the nations.
Let not rebels rise up.

Peoples, praise our God! Make heard the praise!
God preserves our life among the living,
and lets not our foot to slip.

God, you tested us, refined us as silver is refined.
You let us be brought into prison,
you let burdens be put on our backs,
you let human beings ride over our head.

We went through the fire and through the waters
and you brought us to the place of abundance.

I will come to your temple with burnt offerings,
I will fulfill to you my vows, promised on my lips,
spoken in a time of trouble.

Sacrifices of fat animals I will sacrifice to you;
with offerings of rams I will offer bull and goats.

Come! Listen! Let me tell all who fear God
what God has done for my very self.
To God my mouth cried out
with praise on my tongue.

If I cherished sin in my heart
the Lord would not have listened.
Surely God listened and heard my voice of prayer.

God, be praised, who rejected not my prayer
nor took from within me
the Lord's own *hesed* love.   Glory...   Repeat antiphon.

PSALM 118

Lent, 4th Sunday

O God, my God,
I give you thanks;
you are my God,
I shall proclaim your glory.

Easter, 4th Sunday

I will not die; I will live
and proclaim the deeds of the Lord,
alleluia.

Give thanks to Adonai who is good,
whose love is to forever.

Let Israel now declare:
this love is to forever.
Let the house of Aaron declare:
this love is to forever.
Let those who fear Adonai declare:
this love is to forever.

In anguish I cried to Adonai
who answered me with freedom.
Adonai is with me, I will not be afraid.
What can any human do to me?
Before enmity I keep this in mind:
Adonai is with me, ready to help me.

Better to take refuge in Adonai
than to trust in the human;
Better to take refuge in Adonai
than to trust in a prince;

All of the nations surrounded me,
indeed did they surround me;
in the name of Adonai indeed I cut them.
They swarmed around me like bees,
they crackled like thorns in a fire;
in the name of Adonai indeed I cut them.

To push back they pushed me back to fall
but Adonai helped me.
Adonai became my strength and my song
and became to me salvation.
Shout joy and victory in your tents, you righteous.

Adonai's right hand does a mighty thing,
Adonai's right hand lifted high.
Adonai's right hand does a mighty thing.
I will not die; I will live
and proclaim these deeds indeed.
To chasten, Adonai let me be chastened,
but did not give me to death.

Open for me the gates of righteousness;
I will enter through them
and give thanks to Adonai.
This is Adonai's gate,
where righteous ones may enter.
I will give thanks to you for you answered me
and you became to me salvation.

PSALM 118, continued

The stone they rejected as builders
became the cornerstone.
With Adonai this happened
and it is marvelous in our eyes.
This is the day Adonai made;
let us rejoice and be glad.

Adonai, save now!
Adonai, grant success now!
Blessed is the one coming in the name of Adonai;
We bless you from Adonai's house.
Our El Adonai has shined light onto us.

Join with boughs the festal procession
up to the horns of the altar.
To you, my God, I will give thanks.
You, my God, I will exalt.
Give thanks to Adonai who is good,
whose love is to forever.

Glory…

Lent, 4th Sunday

O God, my God,
I give you thanks;
you are my God,
I shall proclaim your glory.

Easter, 4th Sunday

I will not die; I will live
and proclaim the deeds of the Lord,
alleluia.

DANIEL 3:52-57

Lent, 4th Sunday
God of might, deliver us;
free us from the power of the enemy.

Easter, 4th Sunday
Blessed be, O Lord,
your holy and glorious name,
alleluia.

Blessed are you, O Lord, God of our ancestors,
praiseworthy and exalted above all forever.

Blessed is your glorious and holy name,
praiseworthy and exalted above all forever.

Blessed are you in the temple of your sacred glory,
praiseworthy and exalted above all forever.

Blessed are you who sit high on the cherubim
and look into the depths,
praiseworthy and exalted above all forever.

Blessed are you on your royal throne,
praiseworthy and exalted above all forever.

Blessed are you in the dome of heaven,
to be hymned and glorified forever.

Bless the Lord, all you works of the Lord,
sing praise and high exaltation forever.

Glory…

Repeat antiphon.

PSALM 150

Lent, 4th Sunday   Give praise for God's mighty deeds.

Easter, 4th Sunday   Give honor and praise to our God,
whose deeds are perfect
and ways are true,
alleluia.

Praise Adonai!
To El in the sanctuary, give praise.
In the mighty heavens, give praise.
For the works of power, give praise.
For surpassing greatness, give praise.

With sounding of trumpet, give praise.
With harp and lyre, give praise.
With tambourine and dance, give praise.
With flute and string, give praise.

With cymbals clashing, give praise.
With cymbals resounding, give praise.
Let all that has breath praise Adonai!
Praise Adonai!

Glory…

Lent, 4th Sunday   Give praise for God's mighty deeds.

Easter, 4th Sunday   Give honor and praise to our God,
whose deeds are perfect
and ways are true,
alleluia.

WEEK **IV**
SUNDAY EVENING

PSALM 23

Antiphon for Lent   In pastures of greenness
the Lord makes me lie down.

Easter   Alleluia, alleluia, alleluia.

Adonai is my shepherd; nothing do I lack.
My Lord lays me down in green pastures
and leads me beside still quiet waters,
restoring my soul and guiding me
in paths of justice for the Lord's own namesake.

So when I walk in the deep dark valley
I will not fear for you are with me,
your rod and staff a comfort to me.

A table you prepare before me
in the presence even of enmity.
My head you anoint with oil
and my cup is overflowing.

Surely goodness and love will follow me
all the days of my life
and I will dwell in the Lord's own house
for length of days.

Glory…

Repeat antiphon.

PSALM 76

Antiphon for Lent Giving light, you are more majestic
than mountains of game.

Easter Alleluia, alleluia, alleluia.

God is known in Judah; great in Israel is the Name.
In Salem is God's tent, in Zion the dwelling place.
There flashes broke the arrow,
shield and sword, and weapons of war.

Giver of Light, you are,
more majestic than mountains of game.
Human beings of valiant heart lie plundered;
they sleep their sleep
and warriors can no more lift up their hands.
At your rebuke, God of Jacob,
both chariot and horse lie still.

You are feared, you.
Who can stand before you when you are angry?
From the heavens you pronounced judgment;
when God rose for the judgment
to save all the afflicted of the land,
the land feared and she was quiet.

Even the wrath of humanity comes to praise you,
and you hold close the survivor of wrath.
Make vows! Fulfill vows to your God Adonai!
Let all the neighbors of God bring their gift
to the One rightly feared,
who breaks the spirit of rulers of the earth,
the One rightly feared by the kings and the queens.

Glory…

Antiphon for Lent Giving light, you are more majestic
than mountains of game.

Easter Alleluia, alleluia, alleluia.

PSALM 112

Lent, 4th Sunday Happy the one
who shows mercy for the Lord's sake;
that one will stand firm forever.

Easter, 4th Sunday Out of darkness comes the dawn,
a light for upright hearts,
alleluia.

Praise Adonai!
Blessed are the ones who fear Adonai,
and delight greatly in the commandments.
Mighty in the land will that one be,
and blessed with generations of upright children,

PSALM 112, continued

wealth and richness in their houses,
and righteousness enduring to forever.
Light dawns in the darkness
for the upright, gracious,
compassionate and righteous.

The good human, generous and lending,
conducts affairs with justice.
Surely to forever the good one will not be shaken;
remembered forever will the righteous one be.

The good will have no fear of bad news,
being steadfast of heart and trusting Adonai
with heart secure, no fear to the end,
when face to face with enmity.

The good one scatters, giving to the poor,
with righteousness enduring to forever;
the dignity of the good one will be lifted in honor.

The doers of bad things will see this and be vexed
with gnashing of teeth and a wasting away,
wicked longings coming to nothing.

Glory...

Lent, 4th Sunday	Happy the one who shows mercy for the Lord's sake; that one will stand firm forever.
Easter, 4th Sunday	Out of darkness comes the dawn, a light for upright hearts, alleluia.

(Lent) 1 **PETER** 2:21-24

Lent, 4th Sunday

Those things,
which God foretold through his prophets
concerning the sufferings
that Christ would endure,
have been fulfilled.

To this you were called,
for indeed Christ suffered on behalf of you,
leaving to you an example to follow in his steps:

He did not sin, nor was guile found in his mouth;
he was reviled and did not revile in return;
suffering he did not threaten,
but delivered himself to the one judging justly.

Our sins he carried in his body up onto the tree,
that dying to sins, we might live for justice.
By his bruises, you are cured.

Glory...

Repeat antiphon.

(Easter) **REVELATION** 19:1b,2a,5b,6b,7

Easter, 4th Sunday

Alleluia,
salvation and glory and power are to our God,
alleluia.

(Easter) REVELATION 19:1b,2a,5b,6b,7

Alleluia! Praise the Lord!
Salvation and glory and power are to our God,
whose judgments are true and just.

Alleluia! Praise the Lord!
Praise our God, all you slaves of the Lord,
you small and you great, who hold God in awe.

Alleluia! Praise the Lord!
The Lord is reigning, our God, the Almighty.
Let us rejoice and let us exult,
and we will give the glory to the Lord.

Alleluia! Praise the Lord!
The day has come
for the marriage of the Lamb,
and the bride has prepared herself.

Glory…

Easter, 4th Sunday   Alleluia,
salvation and glory and power are to our God,
alleluia.

WEEK IV
MONDAY MORNING

PSALM 73

Antiphon   Surely, the God of Israel
is good to the pure of heart!
(alleluia)

Surely good to Israel is El, to those pure of heart.
But my feet almost slipped,
as nearly lost were my footholds,
for I envied the arrogant
and the prosperity I have seen of the wicked.

None of them struggle with death
and healthy are their bodies.
Human burdens are not theirs, nor human plagues.

And so pride wraps them as a necklace
clothing violence on them.
Their eyes bulge with fat;
their conceits pass the limits of the mind.

They scoff and they speak with malice
and threaten arrogant oppression.
Their mouths lay claim to the heavens,
and their tongues to possession of the earth.

PSALM 73, continued

And so their people turn to here for themselves
and they drink up waters of abundance.
They say, "How does El know?"
and, "Is there knowledge of this to the Most High?"
See these bad doers:
even carefree of Always they increase their wealth.

Surely in vain have I kept my heart pure
and washed my hands in innocence.
But I am plagued all the day
and punished in the mornings.

If I said that I would speak as they do,
see the generation of your children I would betray!

My efforts to understand this
are oppressive to my eyes.
Until! I entered into sanctuaries of God
and understood about their final destiny.

Surely you place them on slippery ground
and cast them down to ruins.
How sudden is their destruction,
swept away complete by terrors.
As with a dream when waking up, Lord,
their fantasy you will despise when you arise.

When my heart was grieved, and my spirits bitter,
and senseless, and unknowing,
I was but a brute beast before you.

Yet I am always with you;
you hold me by my right hand.
With your counsel you guide me
and will take me after the glory.

Who in the heavens is to me?
And with you, nothing on earth do I desire.
My flesh and my heart may fail,
but the strength of my heart is Elohim
and my portion to forever.

For see! Those far from you will perish…
But the nearness of Elohim is my good.
I have made you my refuge, Lord Adonai,
to tell of all your deeds.

Glory…

Antiphon

Surely, the God of Israel
is good to the pure of heart!
(alleluia)

PSALM 90

Antiphon for Lent Each morning, Lord,
you fill us with your kindness.

Easter Let the splendor of the Lord our God
be upon us,
alleluia.

You, Lord, you are our dwelling place
from generation to generation.
Before the mountains were born,
before you brought forth earth,
from eternity to eternity, you are God.

You turn humans back to dust and say,
"Return, sons and daughters of humanity."
A thousand years in your eyes
are like the day yesterday that went by,
like one watch of the night.

You sweep humans into the sleep
like new grass in the morning that sprouts.
In the morning the human springs up and sprouts,
and then by the evening is withered and dry.

Indeed we can be consumed in your anger
and terrified by your indignation.
You set our iniquities before you,
our secrets in the light of your presences.

Indeed all our days pass away under your anger;
we finish our years like a sigh.
Our days last for seventy years
or eighty if given the strength.

The best part of them are trouble and sorrow,
passing quickly, and we fly away.
Who knows the power of your anger,
who fears your wrath?

Number our days aright;
teach, that we may gain hearts of wisdom.
How long, Adonai, until you relent?
Have compassion on your servants.

Satisfy our morning hunger with your unfailing love
that we may sing for joy and be glad all our days.
Make us glad, equal to our affliction,
the years of trouble we have seen.

May your deeds be shown to your servants
and your splendor to their children.
May the favor of the Lord our God rest upon us
and the work of our hands be made good;
yes, make good the work of our hands.

Glory...

Antiphon for Lent	Each morning, Lord, you fill us with your kindness.
Easter	Let the splendor of the Lord our God be upon us, alleluia.

ISAIAH 42:10-16

Antiphon for Lent Praise the Lord
from the ends of the earth.

 Easter I will turn darkness into light before them,
alleluia.

Sing to Adonai a new song,
praise from the ends of the earth!

Ones going down to the sea and all in it,
and the islands, the ones living in them,
and the desert and its towns
and settlements where Kedar lives,
let them arise, let them sing for joy,

and the people of Sela
let them shout from the top of mountains.
Let them give to Adonai the glory
and proclaim praise in the islands.

Adonai will march out like the mighty human
and stir up zeal like a warrior,
and shouting and raising a cry
will triumph over enmity.

I was silent for a long time
and held back in quiet;
like a woman bearing a child,
I cry out and gasp and pant.

I will lay waste mountains and hills
letting all their vegetation dry up;
I will turn rivers into islands and dry up pools.

I will lead blind ones by ways they did not know;
along paths they did not know I will guide them.
I will turn what is dark before them into light
and rough places into smooth.

These things I will do
and I will not forsake them.

Glory…

Antiphon for Lent   Praise the Lord
from the ends of the earth.

Easter   I will turn darkness into light before them,
alleluia.

PSALM 135

Antiphon for Lent   I know that our Lord is great,
greater than all "gods."

Easter   The Lord does as the Lord wills,
alleluia.

Praise Adonai!
Praise the name of Adonai!
Servants of Adonai, give praise!
You who minister in the house of Adonai,
in the courts of the house of our God,

praise Adonai, for good is Adonai!
Sing praise to the Name, for it is pleasant!
Adonai has chosen Jacob, Israel the chosen treasure.

For I know that great is our Lord;
greater than all the "gods" is Adonai,
who does as Adonai pleases
in the heavens and on earth and in the deep sea,

making clouds rise from the ends of the earth,
sending lightning with the rain,
and bringing wind from the storehouses,

who struck down the firstborn of Egypt,
from human to animals,
sending signs and wonders into the midst of Egypt
against Pharaoh and against all of his servants,

having struck down many nations and mighty kings:
Sihon, king of the Amorites, and Og of Bashan,
and all the kingdoms of Canaan,
who gave their land as an inheritance,
an inheritance to Israel, the people of Adonai.

Your name, Adonai, is to forever,
your renown to generation and generation,
for you, Adonai, will vindicate your people
and will have compassion on your servants.

Idols of the nations are silver and gold,
the making of human hands.
A mouth to them but they cannot speak.
Eyes to them but they cannot see.

Ears to them but they cannot hear,
and there is no breath in their mouth.
Like them will be their makers
and all who trust in them.

House of Israel, praise Adonai!
House of Aaron, praise Adonai!
House of Levi, praise Adonai!
You who fear Adonai, praise Adonai!

Praised be Adonai from Zion,
dwelling in Jerusalem.
Praise Adonai!

Glory…

Antiphon for Lent — I know that our Lord is great,
greater than all "gods."

Easter — The Lord does as the Lord wills, alleluia.

WEEK IV
MONDAY EVENING

PSALM 82

Antiphon for Lent   One is the lawgiver and judge,   James 4:12
the one able to save and destroy;
who are you to be judging your neighbor?

Easter   Alleluia, alleluia, alleluia.

God Elohim is presiding in the assembly of El,
giving judgment among little "g" gods:

"Until when will you defend the unjust
and show partiality to the faces of bad doers?
Defend the weak and the orphans!
Maintain the rights of the poor and oppressed!
Rescue the weak and the needy!
Deliver them from the hands of bad doers!"

They know nothing and they understand nothing.
They walk in darkness
and all the foundations of earth are shaken.

"I said, 'you are gods, all of you,
sons and daughters of Elyon Most High,'
but like all humans you too will die
and like other rulers you too will fall."

Rise up, Elohim, and judge the earth!
For you inherit all of the nations!

Glory...   Repeat antiphon.

PSALM 120

Antiphon for Lent   I call on the Lord in my distress
and the Lord answers me.

Easter   Alleluia, alleluia, alleluia.

In my distress I call on Adonai who answers me.
Adonai, save my self from lips of the lie
and from the deceitful tongue.

What will be done to you and what more
will be done to you, deceiful tongue?
Sharp arrows of war,
with coals of broom trees.

Woe to me that I dwell in Meshech
and live among tents of Kedar.

Too long has my self lived
among haters of peace.
I am of peace,
but when I speak they are for war.

Glory...

Antiphon for Lent   I call on the Lord in my distress
and the Lord answers me.

Easter   Alleluia, alleluia, alleluia.

PSALM 136

Antiphon for Lent   Give thanks to the Lord
whose faithful-loyal-steadfast (*hesed*) love
is to forever.

Easter   Whoever is in Christ
is a new creature,
alleluia.

Give thanks for Adonai who is good
  and is loving to forever.
Give thanks to the One who is El of the "els"
  and is loving to forever.
Give thanks to the One who is Lord of the lords
  and is loving to forever,

to the One who has done great wonders alone
  and is loving to forever,
who made the heavens by understanding
  and is loving to forever,
who spread out the earth upon the waters
  and is loving to forever,

who made the great lights
  and is loving to forever,
the sun as governor over the day,
  and is loving to forever,
the moon and stars as governors over the night,
  and is loving to forever,

who struck down Egypt in their firstborn
   and is loving to forever,
who brought Israel out from among them
   and is loving to forever,
with mighty hand and outstretched arm,
   and is loving to forever,

who divided the Reed Sea into halves
   and is loving to forever,
and brought Israel through its midst,
   and is loving to forever,
but swept Pharoah and his army into the Reed Sea,
   and is loving to forever,

who then led the people through the desert
   and is loving to forever,
who struck down great kings
   and is loving to forever,
and killed mighty kings,
   and is loving to forever,

Sihon, king of the Amorites,
   and is loving to forever,
and Og, the king of Bashan,
   and is loving to forever,

who gave the land as an inheritance
   and is loving to forever,
an inheritance to servant Israel,
   and is loving to forever,
who remembered us in our low estate
   and is loving to forever,

PSALM 136, continued

and freed us from enmity,
  and is loving to forever,
who gives food to every creature
  and is loving to forever.
Give thanks to El of the heavens,
  who indeed is loving to forever!

Glory…

Antiphon for Lent	Give thanks to the Lord whose faithful-loyal-steadfast (*hesed*) love is to forever.
Easter	Whoever is in Christ is a new creature, alleluia.

EPHESIANS 1:3-10

Antiphon for Lent	They mystery of God's will for stewardship in the fullness of time is the heading up of all things in Christ.
Easter	From his fullness we have all received, grace upon grace, alleluia.

EPHESIANS 1:3-10

Blessed be the God and Father
of our Lord Jesus Christ,
who has blessed us in Christ
with every spiritual blessing in the heavens.

God chose us in Christ
before the foundation of the world,
to be holy and free of blemish before him.

In love, God gave us a destiny:
as sons are adopted, through Jesus Christ himself,
in accord with the good pleasure of God's will
to the praise of the glory of grace
by which we are favored as God's beloved.

In Christ we have the redemption
through his blood, the forgiveness of sins,
in accord with the riches of his grace
which he made abound to us.

In all wisdom and intelligence
the mystery of God's will is made known to us
in accord with God's good pleasure and purpose:

A stewardship of the fullness of time,
heading up all things in Christ,
the things in the heavens and the things on earth.

Glory…

Repeat antiphon.

WEEK IV
TUESDAY MORNING

PSALM 102

Antiphon   Lord, let my cry for help come to you;
hide not your face.
(alleluia)

Adonai, hear my prayer
and let my cry for help come to you.
Hide not your faces from me
on the day of my distress.
Turn your ear to me on the day I call!
Quickly! Answer me!

My days vanish like smoke
and my bones burn like a glowing ember.
My heart is blighted like the grass
and so withered that I forget to eat my food.
Because of my loud groaning
my bones cling to my skin.

I am like a desert owl;
like an owl of the ruins lying awake,
I became like a bird alone on the housetop.
Enmity taunts me all the day,
railing against me, cursing by me.

I eat ash as food and mingle my drink with tears
because of your anger and your wrath,
for you took me up and threw me aside.
My days are like the long shadow,
and like the grass I wither away.

But you, Adonai, sit enthroned to forever,
and your renown is to generation and generation.
You will arise.
You will have compassion on Zion,
for the time to show favor to her,
the appointed time, has come,
for her stones are dear to your servants
and her dust moves them to pity.

The nations will fear the name of Adonai
and all the kings of the earth your glory,
for Adonai will rebuild Zion and appear in glory
and respond to the prayers of the destitute
and not despise their plea.

Let this be written for future generations
that people yet to be created may praise Yah.
Adonai looked down from the high sanctuary place
viewing from heavens to earth,
to hear the groans of prisoners
and release those to be put to death
to declare in Zion the name of Adonai
and give praise in Jerusalem
when peoples assemble together,
and kingdoms, to give worship.

PSALM 102, continued

Adonai broke my strength in mid-course
and cut short my days, and I said,
"My El,
  take me not away in the midst of my days.
  Your years are through generation of generations.

In the beginning you founded the earth
and the heavens, the work of your hands.
They will perish, but you remain
and they will all wear out like the garment;
like clothing you will change them
and they will be discarded.

But you: the same; your years will never end.
Children of your servants will live
and their descendants
will be established before you."

Glory…

Antiphon   Lord, let my cry for help come to you;
hide not your face.
(alleluia)

PSALM 101

Antiphon for Lent   To you, Lord, I will sing praise;
I will take care to be blameless in life.

Easter   Whoever does the will of my Father
will enter the kingdom of heaven,
alleluia.

PSALM 101

I will sing of *hesed* love and justice;
to you, Adonai, I will sing praise.
I will take care to be blameless in life.
When will you come to me?

I will walk with a blameless heart
in the midst of my house.
I hate and will not set before my eyes
vile things that faithless people do;
they will not cling to me.

The perverse heart will be far from me;
I do not know evil.
I will silence the secret slandering of a neighbor;
haughty eyes and proud hearts I will not endure.

My eyes are on the faithful of the land,
to dwell with me;
one walking in a blameless way
will minister to me.

Anyone practicing deceit
will not dwell in the midst of my house;
nor will one speaking falsehoods
stand before my eyes.

Each morning I will silence bad doers in the land
to cut off doings of bad things
from the city of Adonai.

Glory…

Repeat antiphon.

DANIEL 3:26-27,29,34-41b

Antiphon for Lent   Lord, do not withdraw your mercy.

Easter   Let all the nations, O Lord,
know the depths of your loving mercy for us,
alleluia.

Blessed be you, Lord, God of our ancestors,
your name worthy of praise and glory forever.

For you are just in all you do;
all your deeds are true and your ways right,
and all your judgments are true…

We have sinned and broken your law
in turning from you;
in all ways possible we have sinned…

For the sake of your name,
do not give us up to forever
and do not void your covenant.

Do not take your mercy from us
for the sake of Abraham your beloved,
for the sake of your servant Isaac,
and Israel, your holy one,

to whom you promised to multiply
descendants like the stars of heaven
and like the sand on the shore of the sea.

For we, Lord, have become
least of the other nations
and are brought low in the world this day
because of our sins.

We have in our day no ruler, prophet, or leader,
no burnt offering, sacrifice, oblation or incense,
no place to make an offering before you
and so find your favor.

But with a contrite heart and a humble spirit
may we be accepted
as if they were burnt offerings of rams and bulls
or thousands of fat lambs.
As such may our sacrifice be seen by you today
and may we follow you without reserve,
for no shame will come to those who trust you.

And so we follow you with all our heart;
we fear you and seek your face.

Glory…

Antiphon for Lent   Lord, do not withdraw your mercy.

Easter   Let all the nations, O Lord,
know the depths of your loving mercy for us,
alleluia.

PSALM 144:1-10

Antiphon for Lent   O God, I will sing to you a new song.

Easter   The Lord is my refuge and my savior, alleluia.

Praised be Adonai, my Rock,
who trains my hands for war, my fingers for battle,

my love and fortress, my stronghold and deliverer,
my shield in whom I take refuge,
who subdues peoples under me.

What, Adonai, is a human that you care for us?
Children of humanity, that you think of them?
Like a breath is the human,
whose days like a shadow are fleeting.

Adonai, part your heavens and come down!
Touch the mountains so they smoke!
Send lightning, lightning, and you scatter them!
Shoot your arrows and you rout them!

Reach your hands from on high!
Deliver me! Rescue me from the mighty waters
and from the hand of foreign peoples speaking lies,
whose right hands are the right hand of deceit.

I will sing a new song to you, God,
and on the lyre of ten make music to you,
the One giving victory to the kings,
the One delivering from the deadly sword
your servant David.

Glory…   Repeat antiphon.

WEEK IV
TUESDAY EVENING

PSALM 13

Antiphon for Lent   My heart rejoices, Lord, in your salvation.

Easter   Alleluia, alleluia, alleluia.

Until when, Adonai? Will you forget me forever?
Until when will you hide your faces from me?
Until when must I wrestle with thoughts of my soul
and sorrow in my heart by day?
Until when will an enemy triumph over me?

Look! Answer me, my God Adonai!
Give light to my eyes, or I will sleep the death!
Or enmity will say, "I overcame that one,"
and foes will rejoice when I fall.

But my trust is in your unfailing love;
my heart rejoices in your salvation.
I will sing to Adonai, who is good to me.

Glory…   Repeat antiphon.

PSALM 137:1-6

Antiphon for Lent   If I forget you, Jerusalem,
may my right hand forget what she does.

Easter   Sing for us a Zion song,
alleluia.

By rivers of Babylon, there we sat and wept
as we remembered Zion;
On the poplars in their midst we hung our harps,

for there our captors asked us for words of song,
our tormentors for joy:
"Sing for us from the songs of Zion!"

How can we sing in a foreign land
a song of Adonai?
If I forget you, Jerusalem,
may my right hand forget its skill.

May my tongue cling to the roof of my mouth
if I remember you not,
if I consider any but Jerusalem
as the height of my joy.

Glory…

Antiphon for Lent   If I forget you, Jerusalem,
may my right hand forget what she does.

Easter   Sing for us a Zion song,
alleluia.

PSALM 138

Antiphon for Lent   Before those who would be gods
I will sing praise of You.

Easter   Though I walk in the midst of trouble,
you keep me alive,
alleluia.

I will praise you with all my heart.
Before those who would be "gods"
I will sing praise of you.
I will bow toward your holy temple
and I will praise your name
for your love and your faithfulness.

You are exalted above all,
your name and your word.
On the day I called, then you answered me.
You made me bold and stout in my heart.

May all the kings of the earth praise you, Adonai,
when they hear the words of your mouth.
May they sing of the ways of Adonai,
for great is the glory of Adonai.

Though on high, Adonai looks upon the lowly
and knows the proud from afar.
Though I walk in the midst of trouble,
you keep me alive
against the anger of ones being foes.

PSALM 138, continued

You stretch out your hand, your right hand,
and you save me.
Adonai will fulfill me.
Your love, Adonai, is to forever.
Abandon not the works of your hands.

Glory…

Antiphon for Lent   Before those who would be gods
I will sing praise of You.

Easter   Though I walk in the midst of trouble,
you keep me alive,
alleluia.

REVELATION 4:8b,11; 5:9,10,12,13b

Antiphon for Lent Worthy is the Lamb, slain to receive
the power and riches
and wisdom and strength
and honor and glory and blessing.

Easter Yours, O Lord, is majesty and power,
glory and triumph,
alleluia.

Worthy are you, our Lord and our God,
to receive the glory and honor and power,
because you have created all things,
and by your will all things were created and are.

Worthy are you to receive the scroll
and to open its seals,
because you were slain
and purchased for God by your blood
from every tribe and tongue and people and nation.

You made of them to our God
a kingdom and priests,
and they will reign over the earth.

Worthy is the Lamb, slain to receive
the power and riches and wisdom and strength
and honor and glory and blessing.

Glory…

Repeat antiphon.

WEEK IV
WEDNESDAY MORNING

PSALM 103

Antiphon   Praise the Lord, my soul,
and forget not all of the Lord's benefits.
(alleluia)

My soul, praise Adonai!
All my inmost being, praise the holy Name!
My soul, praise Adonai,
whose benefits are not to be forgotten:

forgiveness of all of your sins,
healing of all your diseases,
redemption of your life from the pit,
crowning you with love and compassion,
satisfying your desire with good,
renewing your youths like the eagle,
working righteousness and justice
for all who are oppressed.

Adonai's ways are made known to Moses
and the deeds to peoples of Israel.

Compassionate and gracious is Adonai,
slow to anger and abundant in love,
neither accusing to always
nor harboring anger to forever,
neither treating us in accord with our sins
nor repaying us in accord with our iniquities.

As high as the heavens are above the earth
so great is the love for ones who fear Adonai.
As far as the east is from the west
so far from us are our transgressions removed.

As a father has compassion on his children,
so has Adonai compassion on ones fearing,
knowing our form and remembering we are dust.

The days of a human are like the grass
flourishing like flowers of the field,
for wind blows over and it is no more
and the place remembers it no more.

But the love for those who fear Adonai
is from everlasting to everlasting.
The righteousness is for children of the children
of those keeping the covenant
and those remembering to obey the precepts.

Adonai established a throne in the heavens
and rules over all the kingdoms.
Praise Adonai, you angels,
you strong and mighty ones doing the bidding,
obeying the voice of the word.

Praise Adonai, you hosts,
you serving and doing the will.
Praise Adonai, all you works,
in all places of the dominion.
My soul, praise Adonai!

Glory…

Repeat antiphon.

PSALM 108

Antiphon for Lent   My heart is steadfast, O God.

Easter   O God, arise above the heavens,
alleluia.

My heart is steadfast, God; I will sing
and even my soul will make music.
Awake the harp and lyre; I will wake up the dawn!

I will praise you among the nations, Adonai,
and I will sing of you among the peoples,
for greater than above the heavens is your love
and to the skies your faithfulness.

Be exalted above the heavens, God,
your glory over all the earth
that your loved ones may be delivered.
Save your right hand, and help me!

God spoke from the sanctuary:
"I will triumph and parcel out Shechem,
and measure the valley of Succoth;

mine are Gilead and Manasseh,
Ephraim my head helmet, Judah my scepter,
and Moab my washbasin;
On Edom I toss my sandals
and over Philistia I shout in triumph."

Who will bring me to the Fortress City?
Who will lead me into Edom?
Have you, God, not rejected us,
and not gone out, God, with our armies?

Against enmity give to us aid,
for worthless is human help.
In God will we gain victory…

Glory…

Repeat antiphon.

ISAIAH 61:10-62:5

Antiphon for Lent   My God has clothed me
in garments of salvation.

Easter   The Lord
will make praise and justice blossom
before all the nations,
alleluia.

To delight, I delight in Adonai,
my soul rejoices in my God,
who clothed me in garments of salvation
and arrayed me in a robe of righteousness,
as a bridegroom dresses his head like a priest
and a bride adorns herself with her jewels,

for as the soil makes the sprout come up
and as a garden makes seeds to grow
so will Sovereign Adonai
make righteousness spring up
and praise before all the nations.

For the sake of Zion, I will not keep silent;
for the sake of Jerusalem I will not remain quiet,
till righteousness comes out like the dawn
and salvation blazes like a torch.

The nations will see your righteousness
and all the kings your glory
and you will be called by a new name
that the mouth of Adonai will bestow.
You will be a crown of splendor
in the hand of Adonai
and a royal diadem in the hand of your God.

No longer will you be called One Being Deserted,
nor will your name be called Desolation,
but you will be called "my delight is in her"
and your land "espoused."
Adonai will delight in you
and your land will be married.

As a young man marries a maiden,
your Builder will marry you;
and as a bridegroom rejoices over a bride,
so will your God rejoice over you.

Glory…

Antiphon for Lent My God has clothed me
in garments of salvation.

Easter The Lord
will make praise and justice blossom
before all the nations,
alleluia.

PSALM 146

Antiphon for Lent I will sing praise to my God
all my life.

Easter Zion, the Lord, your God,
will reign forever,
alleluia.

Praise Adonai, my soul!
I will praise Adonai during my life;
I will sing praise to my God while I still am.

Put your trust not in princes
nor in human beings in whom there is no salvation.
Their spirits depart,
and they return to the ground.
On that day their plans come to nothing.

PSALM 146, continued

Blessed are they whose help is the God of Jacob,
whose hope and God are Adonai,
the maker of heaven and earth
and the sea and all that is in them.

The one staying faithful to forever
defends the cause of the oppressed
and gives food to the hungry.

Adonai sets prisoners free;
Adonai gives sight to the blind;
Adonai lifts those who are bowed down;
Adonai loves the righteous.

Adonai watches over alien strangers,
and sustains the orphan and the widow,
but frustrates the ways that are wicked.
Adonai reigns to forever,
your God, Zion, from generation to generation.

Praise Adonai!

Glory…

Antiphon for Lent	I will sing praise to my God all my life.
Easter	Zion, the Lord, your God, will reign forever, alleluia.

WEEK **IV**
WEDNESDAY EVENING

PSALM 75

Antiphon for Lent   God is the judge, only God.

Easter   Alleluia, alleluia, alleluia.

We give thanks to you, God;
we give thanks for your name is Near,
and they tell of your wonderful deeds.

You choose and appoint the time
to be the upright judge.
The earth quakes, and all its people,
and you hold her pillars firm.

I say to the arrogant, "boast not,"
and to the bad doers, "lift not your horn;
  lift not your horns against the heavens
  nor speak with neck outstretched."

For there is no one from east or from west
and no one from the desert to exalt.
But God is the one judge,
bringing down this one and exalting another.

A cup is full in the hand of Adonai,
and wine foams and mixed spice pours out.
Indeed from this they drink to her dregs,
all the bad doers of the earth.

And I will declare to forever,
and sing praise to the God of Jacob.
All the horns of bad doers will be cut off,
and the horns of the righteous will be lifted up.

Glory…

Antiphon for Lent   God is the judge, only God.

Easter   Alleluia, alleluia, alleluia.

PSALM 94

Antiphon for Lent   The Lord knows human thoughts.

Easter   Alleluia, alleluia, alleluia.

God of vindication,
Adonai, God of vindication, shine forth!
Rise up, One Judge of the earth!
Pay back desserts to the proud!

Until when, bad doers?
Until when, Adonai, will bad doers be jubilant?
They pour out and speak arrogance;
all the bad doers boast.

They crush your people, Adonai,
and they oppress your inheritance.
They slay the widow and alien;
they murder the orphan.

They say Adonai does not see
and the God of Jacob pays no heed.
Take heed, senseless ones among the people;
fools, when will you become wise?

Does the one who implants the ear not hear?
Does the one who forms the eye not see?
Will the one who disciplines nations not punish?
Will the one who teaches have no knowledge?

Adonai knows the thoughts of humans,
that they are futile.

Blessed is the one whom you discipline, Adonai,
the one you teach from your law
to grant relief from days of trouble
till a pit is dug for bad doers,

for the people of Adonai will not be rejected,
the inheritance never forsaken.
Judgment will again be on righteousness,
after which will go all the upright of heart.

Who will rise up for me against people being bad?
Who will take a stand for me against bad doers?
Unless Adonai helps me,
I would as soon dwell in the silence of my self.

When I said, "My foot slips,"
your love, Adonai, supported me.
When my anxieties were great inside me
your consolations brought joy to my soul.

PSALM 94, continued

Can a throne of corruptions be allied with you,
one that brings misery by decree?
They band together against the life of the righteous
and condemn the innocent to blood.

But Adonai became to me as a fortress,
and my God as a rock of refuge.
A rock of refuge is my God,
who will repay their sin to them
and destroy them for their wicked ways.
Our God, Adonai, will destroy them.

Glory…

Antiphon for Lent   The Lord knows human thoughts.

Easter   Alleluia, alleluia, alleluia.

PSALM 139:1-18,23-24

Antiphon for Lent   How precious to me, God,
are your thoughts,
how vast they are,
the sums of them.

Easter   The night will shine as the day,
alleluia.

PSALM 139:1-18,23-24

Adonai, you search me and you know me.
You know my sitting and my rising;
you perceive my thoughts from afar.
You discern my going and my lying down,
and you are familiar with all of my ways.

When a word is not yet on my tongue
you see it, Adonai; you know them all.
Behind and before you hem me in
and you lay your hand upon me.
Too wonderful for me is this knowledge,
more lofty than what I can attain.

Where can I go that is away from your Spirit?
Where could I flee from your presences?
If I go up to the heavens, you are there;
if I make a bed in Sheol, you I see!

If I rise on the wings of dawn,
if I settle on the far side of the sea,
even there your hand will guide me
and your right hand will hold me...

If I say, "Surely darkness will hide me
  and the night will light around me,"
even darkness will not be dark to you
and night will shine as the day;
as the darkness, so the light.

For you created my inmost beings;
you knit me together in my mother's womb.
I praise you because I am full of fear and wonder;
my self knows well how wonderful are your works.

PSALM 139:1-18,23-24, continued

My frame was not hidden from you
when I was made in the secret place,
woven together in the depths of earth.

Your eyes saw my body
and in your book were written and ordained
all the days before the first day was.

How precious to me, El, are your thoughts,
how vast are they, the sums of them;
if countable they number more than the sand.
Awake and still, I am with you.

Search me, El, and know my heart!
Test me, and know my anxious thoughts!
See if there is in me an offensive way,
then lead me in the way everlasting!

Glory…

Antiphon for Lent How precious to me, God, are your thoughts,
how vast they are, the sums of them.

Easter The night will shine as the day,
alleluia.

COLOSSIANS 1:12-20

Antiphon for Lent All things have been created through him;
he is before all things
and in him all things hold together.

Easter　　　His glory covers the heavens
and his praise fills the earth,
alleluia.

COLOSSIANS 1:12-20

Give joyful thanks to the Father who made you fit
for your part of the lot of the saints in light,

who delivered us out of the authority of darkness
and transitioned us into the kingdom of the beloved Son,
in whom we have redemption, the forgiveness of our sins.

The Son is the image of the invisible God,
the firstborn of all creation.
In him all things were created,
in the heavens and on the earth,
the visible and the invisible,
whether thrones, lordships, rulers or authorities.

All things have been created through him and for him.
He is before all things,
and in him all things hold together.

He is the head of the body, the church,
and the beginning, the firstborn from the dead,
so that in all things he may hold the first place.

In him all the fullness was well pleased to dwell,
and through him reconciliation to himself of all things,
things on earth and things in the heavens,
making peace through the blood of his cross.

Glory…

Repeat antiphon.

WEEK IV
THURSDAY MORNING

PSALM 3

Antiphon
You, Lord, shield around me,
my glorious One,
you lift my head.
(alleluia)

How many, Adonai, are the foes,
many rising against me, many saying of me,
"No deliverance by God for this self!"

But you, Adonai, shield around me,
my glorious One, you lift my head.
My voice cries to Adonai
who answers me from the holy hill.

I lie down and I sleep;
and I wake because Adonai sustains me.
I will have no fear of tens of thousands of people
who are drawn up on every side against me.

Arise, Adonai! Deliver me, my God!
You struck the jaw of enmity
and broke the teeth of badness.
From Adonai is the deliverance.
May your blessing be on your people.

Glory…

Repeat antiphon.

PSALM 6

Antiphon Be merciful to me, Lord, and heal me.
(alleluia)

Adonai, do not rebuke me in your anger
nor discipline me in your wrath.
Be merciful to me, Adonai, for I am faint!
Heal me, Adonai, for my bones are in agony
and my soul is in great anguish.

But you, Adonai, how long?
Turn, Adonai, and deliver my soul!
Save me because of your unfailing love!
Not from death are you remembered.
Who can praise you from Sheol?

I am worn out from my groaning;
through all the night I flood my bed with tears,
I drench my couch.
My eye grows weak with sorrow;
she fails because of all foes.

Away from me, all doers of badness,
for Adonai has heard the sound of my weeping.
Adonai has heard my cry for mercy.
Adonai accepts my prayer.
May enmity be ashamed and greatly dismayed,
and turn back in humble confusion.

Glory...

Antiphon Be merciful to me, Lord, and heal me.
(alleluia)

PSALM 143:1-11

Antiphon for Lent   Bring word to me, Lord,
in the morning your unfailing love.

Easter   For the sake of your name, Lord,
keep my self alive,
alleluia.

Adonai, hear my prayer!
Listen in your faithfulness to my cries for mercy!
Relieve me in your righteousness!
Bring not your servant into judgment
for not anyone alive is righteous before you.

Indeed enmity pursues my self
and crushes my life to the ground
and makes me dwell in dark places
like dead ones of long ago.
My spirit grows faint within me;
within me my heart is dismayed.

I remember days of long ago
and meditate on all of your work
and consider the deed of your hands.
I spread out my hands to you;
like land parched is my soul for you.

Be quick! Answer me, Adonai! My spirit faints!
Hide not your faces from me
or I will be like and with ones going down the pit.

Bring in the morning your word of unfailing love,
for in you I put trust.
Show me the way I should go
for to you I lift up my soul!

Rescue me, Adonai, from enmity; in you I hide.
Teach me to do your will, for you are my El.
May your good Spirit lead me on level ground.

For the sake of your Name, Adonai,
you keep me alive in your righteousness;
you bring my self out from trouble.

Glory…

Antiphon for Lent	Bring word to me, Lord, in the morning your unfailing love.
Easter	For the sake of your name, Lord, keep my self alive, alleluia.

ISAIAH 66:7-14a

Antiphon for Lent
> The Lord says, see!
> I extend a river of peace,
> and wealth of nations
> like a flooding stream.

Easter
> I will see you again
> and your heart will rejoice,
> alleluia.

"Before she goes into labor she gives birth;
 before pain comes upon her, she delivers a son.
 Who has heard of such as this?
 Who has seen such as these?

Can a country be born in one day
or a nation be brought forth in one moment?
Yet she is in labor,
then Zion gives birth to her children.

Do I bring to the moment of birth
and not give delivery?"
asks your God Adonai;
"Do I bring one to delivery and then close up?

Rejoice with Jerusalem and be glad for her!
All who love her, rejoice with her!
Rejoice, all who mourn over her,

> for you will nurse and you will be satisfied
> at the breast of her comforts,
> for you will drink deeply and you will delight
> in the overflow of her abundance."

For this says Adonai:
"See, I extend peace to her like a river,
  and wealth of nations like a flooding stream,
  and you will nurse, being carried at her side,
  and you will be playdanced on her knees.

> As a child is comforted by a mother,
> so will I comfort you
> and over Jerusalem you will be comforted.

> When you see, your heart will rejoice
> and your bones will flourish like the grass."

<small>Glory…</small>

<small>Antiphon for Lent</small>   The Lord says, see!
I extend a river of peace,
and wealth of nations
like a flooding stream.

<small>Easter</small>   I will see you again
and your heart will rejoice,
alleluia.

WEEK IV
THURSDAY EVENING

PSALM 128

Antiphon for Lent   May the Lord bless you from Zion
and see to the prosperity of Jerusalem
all the days of your life.

Easter   Alleluia, alleluia, alleluia.

Blessed are all who fear Adonai
and walk in the way.

Indeed you will eat from the labor of your hands.
To you will be blessings and prosperity,
and your spouse like a fruitful vine
inside and outside your house,
sons and daughters around your table
like shoots of the olives.

See: one who fears Adonai is blessed;
may Adonai bless you from Zion.
See and enjoy the prosperity of Jerusalem
all the days of your life,
and the joy of the children of your children.

Peace be upon Israel.

Glory…

    Repeat antiphon.

PSALM 129

Antiphon for Lent — The Lord gains victory over me.

Easter — Alleluia, alleluia, alleluia.

"From my youths they oppressed me greatly,"
let Israel now say.
"From my youths they oppressed me greatly,
but gained no victory over me.

On my back the plowers plowed;
their furrows they made long.
Righteous Adonai cut free the cords of bad doers."

May all haters of Zion be shamed and turned back;
May they be like grass on housetops,
which withers before it grows,

which cannot fill one hand of the reaper
nor an arm of the gatherer,
and passers-by will not say,
"Blessing of Adonai upon you!"

"We bless you in the name of Adonai!"

Glory…

Antiphon for Lent — The Lord gains victory over me.

Easter — Alleluia, alleluia, alleluia.

PSALM 144

Antiphon for Lent Lord who am I that you care for me?
Human heir that you think of me?

Easter The Lord is my stronghold and my savior,
alleluia.

Praised be Adonai, my Rock,
who trains my hands for war, my fingers for battle,

my love and fortress, my stronghold and deliverer,
my shield in whom I take refuge,
who subdues peoples under me.

What, Adonai, is a human that you care for us?
Children of humanity, that you think of them?
Like a breath is the human,
whose days like a shadow are fleeting.

Adonai, part your heavens and come down!
Touch the mountains so they smoke!
You send lightning, lightning, and scatter them!
Shoot your arrows and you rout them!

Reach your hands from on high!
Deliver me! Rescue me from the mighty waters
and from the hand of foreign peoples speaking lies,
whose right hands are the right hand of deceit.

WEEK IV - THURSDAY EVENING 487

I will sing a new song to you, God,
and on the lyre of ten make music to you,
the One giving victory to the kings,
the One delivering from the deadly sword
your servant David.

Deliver me! Rescue me from foreigners' hands,
whose mouths speak the lie,
whose right hands are the right hand of deceit.

Our sons in their youth
are like well nurtured plants,
our daughters like carved pillars adorning a palace,

our barns filled with provisions from kind to kind,
our sheep becoming thousands
and tens of thousands in our fields,
and our oxen drawing loads,

no break in the walls and no exile
nor a cry of distress in the streets:
Blessed are the people of whom all this is true;
blessed are the people whose God is Adonai.

Glory...

Antiphon for Lent	Lord who am I that you care for me? Human heir that you think of me?
Easter	The Lord is my stronghold and my savior, alleluia.

REVELATION 11:17-18, 12:10-12a

Antiphon for Lent Our God, who is and who was,
has taken great power to reign.

Easter Christ yesterday and today:
he is the same forever,
alleluia.

We thank you, Lord God Almighty,
the One who is and who was;
you have taken your great power and reign.

The nations raged and your anger came,
and the time to judge the dead
and to reward your slaves and prophets,
the saints, and those fearing your name,
the small and the great…

Now have come the salvation and power
and kingdom of our God
and the authority of Christ.
The accuser of our brothers and sisters was cast,
accusing them before our God day and night.

Their victory was because of the blood of the Lamb
and by the word of their witness.
They loved their life into their death,
and so be glad, you heavens,
and all you dwelling in them.

Glory…

Repeat antiphon.

WEEK **IV**
FRIDAY MORNING

PSALM 55:2-15,17-24

Antiphon Cast your cares on the Lord,
who will sustain you.
(alleluia)

Listen, Elohim, to my prayer!
Ignore not my plea, but hear me and answer me,
as I am troubled by my thoughts
and distraught at the voice of enmity,
at the stares of the faces of bad doers,
for they bring suffering down upon me
and revile me in anger.

My heart is in anguish within me
and the terrors of death assail me.
Fear and trembling harass me
and horror has overwhelmed me.

And I said, "Would that I had wings like the dove;
 I would fly away and rest.
 See! I would flee far and stay in the desert.
 I would hurry to my place of shelter
 from the storm of the tempetuous wind."

Confuse them, Lord; confound their speech,
for I see violence and strife in the city.
By day and by night they prowl about on her walls;
within her are malice and abuse.

PSALM 55, continued

Destructive forces are within her
and threats and lies never leave her streets.
It is not an enemy insulting me,
nor a foe rising against me
that I endure, from whom I hide;

but it is you, ordered as a human like me,
my companion and my friend with whom
together we shared close companionship
walking with the throng at the house of Elohim...

To Elohim I call and am saved by Adonai
who hears my voice when I cry out in distress
in evening and in morning and at noon,
who ransoms my self in wholeness from the battle
though many are opposite me.

El enthroned forever will hear and let be afflicted
those who never allow themselves to change,
who do not fear God,
who send hands against friends,
and violate covenants.

This one's mouth is smooth as butter,
yet war is in the heart,
speaking words more soothing than oil
that are yet drawn swords.

Cast your cares on Adonai, who will sustain you
and to forever let not the righteous fall.

But you, God, will bring the bloody and deceitful
into the pit of corruption, not living half their days.
And I will trust in you.

Glory…

Antiphon
Cast your cares on the Lord,
who will sustain you.
(alleluia)

PSALM 51

Antiphon for Lent
Create in me a clean heart, O God;
renew in me a steadfast spirit.

Easter
Christ gave himself up for us
as a sacrificial offering to God,
alleluia.

Have mercy on me, God,
in accord with your unfailing love;
in accord with the greatness of your compassion
blot out my transgressions.

Wash me of my many iniquities
and cleanse me from my sin,
for I know my transgressions
and my sin is before me always.

Against you yourself I sinned;
what I did is evil in your eyes.
You are proven right when you speak
and justified when you judge.
Surely we are sinners from birth,
from conception in a mother's womb.

PSALM 51, continued

Surely you desire truth in our inner parts;
in my inmost place you teach me wisdom.
You cleanse me with hyssop and I will be clean;
you wash me and I will be whiter than snow...

You let me hear joy and gladness;
let the bones you let be crushed now rejoice.
Hide your faces from my sins
and blot out all my iniquities.

A pure heart create in me, God!
Renew inside me a spirit to be steadfast.
Do not cast me from your presences,
nor take from me your Holy Spirit.

Restore to me the joy of your salvation
and sustain in me a willing spirit.
I will teach transgressors your ways
and sinners will turn back to you.

Save me from bloodguilt, God,
God of my salvation;
my tongue will sing of your righteousness.
Lord, open my lips
and my mouth will declare your praise.

Sacrifices give you no delight;
I could bring a burnt offering,
but it would give you no pleasure.
The sacrifices, God, you will not despise
are a broken spirit and a contrite heart.

Make Zion prosper in your pleasure,
and build up the walls of Jerusalem.
Then you will delight in the sacrifice of the just,
burnt offerings and whole offerings,
bulls offered on your altar.

Glory…

Antiphon for Lent   Create in me a clean heart, O God;
renew in me a steadfast spirit.

Easter   Christ gave himself up for us
as a sacrificial offering to God,
alleluia.

TOBIT 13:8-11,13-15

Antiphon for Lent   Children of the righteous, rejoice and exult;
gather together and bless the Lord of the ages.

Easter   Jerusalem, city of God,
you will shine as a bright light,
alleluia.

Acknowledge the Lord in Jerusalem.

You Jerusalem, Holy City,
will be scourged for what your children have done.
The Lord will again have mercy
on the children of the righteous.

TOBIT 13:8-11,13-15, continued

Acknowledge the Lord as is deserving
and bless the King of the ages,
that your sanctuary will be built in you again
with joy and cheer by all who were exiles,
and love for all generations
those who were distressed.

A bright light will shine to all the ends of the earth;
many nations will come from far away.
The inhabitants of the most remote parts of earth
will come to your holy Name
bearing in their hands gifts for the King of Heaven.

Generation to generation will give joyful praise
and the name of the Lord will be great forever…

Then, children of the righteous, rejoice and exult;
be gathered together and bless the Lord of the ages.

Happy are those who love you
and happy will be those who rejoice in prosperity.

Happy also are all who grieve over your afflictions
for they will rejoice with you
and give witness to your joy forever.

My soul, praise the Lord, the great King.

Glory…

Antiphon for Lent   Children of the righteous, rejoice and exult;
gather together and bless the Lord of the ages.

Easter   Jerusalem, city of God,
you will shine as a bright light, alleluia.

PSALM 147:12-20

Antiphon for Lent Extol the Lord, Jerusalem!
and hear my prayer.

Easter I saw the new Jerusalem,
coming down from heaven,
alleluia.

Extol Adonai, Jerusalem!
Zion, now give praise!

Your God strengthens the bars of your gates,
blesses your peoples within you,
grants peace to your border,
and satisfies you with finest of wheat.

Your God sends a command to the earth,
and in swiftness runs a word,
spreading snow like the wool
and scattering frost like the ash.

Hail is hurled like pebbles;
who can stand before the icy blast?
The word of the Lord is sent, and they melt;
wind stirs up and the waters flow.

The word of the Lord is revealed to Jacob,
decrees and laws of the Lord to Israel.
Not for any nation did the Lord do this;
they do not know these laws.
Praise Adonai!

Glory…

Repeat antiphon.

496   HINGE HOURS for LENT and EASTER

WEEK IV
FRIDAY EVENING

PSALM 133

Antiphon for Lent　　The multitude of believers
　　　　　　　　　　was heart and soul one.　　　　　　Acts 4:32a

　　　Easter　　Alleluia, alleluia, alleluia.

See how good and how pleasant it is
to live as brothers and sisters,
united together.

Like the precious oil running down
on the head and on the beard of Aaron,
running down on his collar and robes,

as if the dew of Hermon
was falling on Mount Zion,
there Adonai bestows
the blessing of life to forever.

Glory…

Antiphon for Lent　　The multitude of believers
　　　　　　　　　　was heart and soul one.　　　　　　Acts 4:32a

　　　Easter　　Alleluia, alleluia, alleluia.

PSALM 140:1-9,13-14

Antiphon for Lent   Rescue me from evil, my God;
you protect me from violence.

Easter   Alleluia, alleluia, alleluia.

Rescue me, Adonai, from humans doing badness;
protect me from humans of violence
who devise bad things in their hearts
and stir up wars every day.
They make their tongues sharp as a serpent;
viper poison is on their lips.

Keep me, Adonai, from the hands of bad doers;
protect me from humans of violence
who plan to trip up my feet.
Proud ones have hidden a snare for me,
spread a net of cords,
and set a trap for me at the side of the path.

I say to Adonai, "You are my God!"
Hear, Adonai, the cry of my cries for mercy!
Lord Adonai, strength of my deliverance,
you shield over my head in the day of battle.
Grant not, Adonai, the desires of bad doers;
let not their plans succeed
or they will become proud...

I know that Adonai secures justice for the poor
and the cause of the needy.
Surely the righteous will praise your Name;
the upright will live before your faces.

Glory…

Repeat antiphon.

PSALM 145

Antiphon for Lent   Every day I will praise you,
your great deed I will proclaim.

Easter   God so loved the cosmos
that he gave us his only Son,   Jn 3:16
alleluia.

I will exalt you, my God the King,
and I will praise your Name to forever and ever.

In every day I will praise you
and I will extol your Name to forever and ever.
Great is Adonai, and greatly being praised,
an unfathomable greatness.

Generation to generation commend your works
and tell of your mighty acts
and the glorious splendor of your majesty,
and I will meditate on your wonderful deeds.

PSALM 145, continued

They will tell of the power of your awesome works
and I will proclaim your great deed.
They will celebrate and remember
the abundance of your goodness
and they will sing of your righteousness.

Gracious and compassionate is Adonai,
slow of angers and rich in love.
Good to all is Adonai,
whose compassions are on all who are made.

All whom you have made will praise you, Adonai,
and your saints will extol you.
They will tell of the glory of your kingdom
and speak your might to make known

to sons and daughters of humanity your mighty acts
and the glorious splendor of your kingdom.
Your kingdom is the kingdom of all the everlastings
and your dominion is through all
generation and generation.

Adonai is faithful to all the promises
and loving to all who are made.
Adonai upholds all who are falling
and lifts up all who are being bowed.

The eyes of all look to you
and you give them their food at their time,
opening your hand and satisfying the desire
of every living thing.

Righteous is Adonai in all ways,
and loving to all who are made.
Near is Adonai to all who call,
to all who call in truth.

Fulfilled is the desire
of all who fear and love Adonai,
who hears their cry and saves them
and watches over them.
But wicked ways will be destroyed.

My mouth will speak praise of Adonai.
Let every creature praise the holy Name
to forever and ever.

Glory…

Antiphon for Lent	Every day I will praise you, your great deed I will proclaim.
Easter	God so loved the cosmos that he gave us his only Son, alleluia.

Jn 3:16

REVELATION 15:3b-4

Antiphon for Lent King of the nations,
just and true are your ways.

Easter The Lord is my strength,
I shall always praise
the One who has become my savior,
alleluia.

Great and wonderful are your works,
Lord God Almighty.
Just and true are your ways,
King of the nations.

Who will not fear, O Lord,
or glorify your name?

Only you are holy.
All the nations will come and worship before you;
your ordinances are shown to all.

Glory…

Antiphon for Lent King of the nations,
just and true are your ways.

Easter The Lord is my strength,
I shall always praise
the One who has become my savior,
alleluia.

WEEK IV
SATURDAY MORNING

PSALM 78

Antiphon   The children of Israel ate the manna
             and drank the water from the rock. (alleluia)

Give ear, my people, to my teaching.
Turn your ear to words of my mouth.
I will open my mouth in a parable;
I will utter things hidden from of old.

Things we heard and know our ancestors told us,
these we will not hide from their descendents
but tell to the next generation
the deeds of Adonai worthy of praise
and the power and deeds of wonder done.

Statutes decreed for Jacob and laws set up for Israel
command our ancestors to teach their children
so the next generation will come to know;
children born will grow to tell their children.

In God will they put their trust
and never forget the deeds of El
but keep God's commands,
unlike the stubborn generation of their ancestors,
a generation of rebellion and unloyal hearts
and in spirit unfaithful to God.

Children of Ephraim, armed to shoot the bow,
retreated on the day of battle,
refusing to keep and live by God's covenant.

They forgot the deeds of wonder done
shown in the sight of their ancestors,
miracles in the land of Egypt, the plain of Zoan,

dividing the sea and leading them through it,
making the waters stand like a wall,
guiding them with a cloud by day
and all the night by light of fire,

splitting the rock in the desert,
giving water abundant as the deep sea,
bringing streams from the rocky crag,
and making waters flow down like rivers.

But they kept on with the sin
rebellious in the desert against Sabaoth.
They tested God by their will
demanding the food of their craving.

Against God they questioned,
"Can a table be spread in the desert by God,
 whom yes we saw strike a rock
 from where waters gushed and streams flowed,
 and too for the people of God give food or meat?"

Adonai heard and was then angry
and fire broke out against Jacob
and wrath rose up against Israel
for they did not believe in God
nor trust in the deliverance.

And yet God did command the skies above
and opened doors of the heavens
and rained down for them manna to eat
and gave them grain from the heavens.

The humans ate the bread of angels,
food sent to them in abundance.
God set the east wind free from the heavens
and led by power the south wind
and rained down meat on them like dust.

Birds of flight like sand on the seashore
fell around their tents
into the middle of their camp
and they ate to more than enough,
being given all of their cravings.

They did not turn from their cravings
and while their food was still in their mouths
the anger of God rose to slaughter their sturdy
and cut down the strong young of Israel.

Still with all this they sinned
and did not believe in the deeds of wonder done.
So their days vanished in futility
and their years quick as a ghost.

When God slew them they would repent and seek
and be eager for God
and remember that God is their Rock
and God Sabaoth their Redeemer.

PSALM 78, continued

They would flatter with their mouths
and lie to God with their tongues;
their hearts were not loyal
and they were unfaithful to the covenant.

But God was merciful and forgiving
and did not wipe them out,
refraining from nurturing the fullness of wrath
and restraining anger often,
remembering that they were but flesh,
a passing breath that does not return.

How often they rebelled against God in the desert,
giving grief in the wasteland.
Again and again they tested God,
vexing the Holy One of Israel.

They did not remember the power of God
nor the day of their redemption from oppression,
God's miracle signs in Egypt
and wonders in the plain of Zoan.

God turned those rivers to blood
and their streams were undrinkable.
Swarms of insects were sent and devoured,
and frogs for devastation.

Their crops were given to the grasshopper
and their produce to the locust.
With hail their vines were destroyed
and their sycamore figs with sleet.
Their cattle were given over to the hail
and their livestock to the lightning bolts.

God unleashed blazing anger against them,
wrath and indignation and hostility,
a band of angel destruction.

A path prepared for this anger,
they were not spared from death
and the animals were given over to the plague.
All the firstborn of Egypt were struck,
the strong young firstfruits in the tents of Ham.

But the people of God were brought out as a flock
and led like sheep through the desert
guided in safety to be not afraid
while the sea engulfed their enemies.

Thus were they brought to the holy hill,
the mountain won by the right hand of God
who drove out nations from before them
and allotted from their lands an inheritance
and settled in their tents the tribes of Israel.

But they tested and rebelled against God Sabaoth
whose statutes they did not keep.
They were disloyal and faithless like their ancestors
and as unreliable as a bent bow.

With their high-place shrines they angered God
who was jealous because of their idols,
who heard them and became angry
and rejected Israel completely
and abandoned the shrine at Shiloh,
the very tent God set up among humans.

PSALM 78, continued

God gave the ark into captivity,
the glorious ark into the hands of enmity,
and the people to the sword
in anger at this heritage.

Their young men were consumed in fire
and their young women heard no wedding songs;
their priests fell by the sword
and their widows could not weep.

Then the Lord woke up as from sleep,
as a human in a stupor from wine,
and beat back the enemies
and put them to everlasting shame.

The Lord rejected the tent of Joseph
and chose not the tribe of Ephraim
but chose the tribe of Judah,
loving the Mount of Zion.

The Lord built the shrine like the heights
and like the earth established her to forever
and chose the servant David
and took him from the sheep pens

and brought him instead to shepherd
Jacob, his people, for Israel, his heritage.
He tended them with integrity of heart
and with skillful hands he led them.

Glory…

Antiphon   The children of Israel ate the manna
and drank the water from the rock. (alleluia)

EZEKIEL 36:24-28

Antiphon for Lent   I will give you new heart
and put inside you new spirit.

Easter   I will pour clean waters upon you,
alleluia.

I will take you out of the nations
and I will gather you from all the countries,
and I will bring you back into your land.

I will sprinkle on you clean waters,
and you will be clean from all your impurities,
and from all your idols I will cleanse you.

I will give you a new heart
and I will put inside you a new spirit,
and I will remove the stone-heart from your flesh
and I will give you a flesh-heart,

and I will put inside you my Spirit
and I will move you to follow in my decrees
and my laws you will be careful to keep,

and you will live in the land I gave your ancestors,
and you will be my people
and I will be your God.

Glory…

Antiphon for Lent   I will give you new heart
and put inside you new spirit.

Easter   I will pour clean waters upon you, alleluia.

DAILY GOSPEL READINGS

(also indicated with the antiphons for Morning Prayer)

LENT

Lent begins with Ash Wednesday,
6 weeks and 4 days prior to Easter.
See page 29

Ash
Wed Matthew 6:1-6,16-18

Thu Luke 9:22-25
Fri Matthew 9:14-15
Sat Luke 5:27-32

Sunday - Week 1

A Matthew 4:1-11
B Mark 1:12-15
C Luke 4:1-13
Mon Matthew 25:31-46
Tue Matthew 6:7-15
Wed Luke 11:29-32
Thu Matthew 7:7-12
Fri Matthew 5:20-25
Sat Matthew 5:43-48

Sunday - Week 2

A Matthew 17:1-9
B Mark 9:2-10
C Luke 9:28b-36
Mon Luke 6:36-38
Tue Matthew 23:1-12
Wed Matthew 20:17-28
Thu Luke 16:19-31
Fri Matt. 21:33-43,45-46
Sat Luke 15:1-3,11-32

Sunday - Week 3

A John 4:5-42
B John 2:13-25
C Luke 13:1-9
Mon Luke 4:24-30
Tue Matthew 18:21-35
Wed Matthew 5:17-19
Thu Luke 11:14-23
Fri Mark 12:28-34
Sat Luke 18:9-14

Sunday - Week 4

A John 9:1-41
B John 3:14-21
C Luke 15:1-3,11-32
Mon John 4:43-54
Tue John 5:1-16
Wed John 5:17-30
Thu John 5:31-47
Fri John 7:1-2,10,25-30
Sat John 7:40-53

Sunday - Week 5

A John 11:1-45
B John 12:20-33
C John 8:1-11
Mon John 8:12-20
Tue John 8:21-30
Wed John 8:31-42
Thu John 8:51-59
Fri John 10:31-42
Sat John 11:45-56

HOLY WEEK

Palm Sunday
Year A
Procession Matthew 21:1-11
Passion Matthew 26:14 - 27:66

Year B
Procession Mark 11:1-10
Passion Mark 14:1 - 15:47

Year C
Procession Luke 19:28-40
Passion Luke 22:14 - 23:56

Holy Week Weekdays
Mon John 12:1-11
Tue John 13:21-33,36-38
Wed Matthew 26:14-25

Chrism Mass
Cathedral Luke 4:16-21

Holy Thursday
Evening John 13:1-15

Good Friday
Passion John 18:1 - 19:42

EASTER

Easter Vigil
A Matthew 28:1-10
B Mark 16:1-7
C Luke 24:1-12

*Easter Sunday is
the first Sunday
following the first full moon
following the vernal equinox.*

Octave of Easter:
Easter Day
ABC John 20:1-9 (or vigil reading)
Easter Weekdays
Mon Matthew 28:8-15
Tue John 20:11-18
Wed Luke 24:13-35
Thu Luke 24:35-48
Fri John 21:1-14
Sat Mark 16:9-15

Second Sunday in
the Octave of Easter
ABC John 20:19-31
Week 2
Mon John 3:1-8
Tue John 3:7b-15
Wed John 3:16-21
Thu John 3:31-36
Fri John 6:1-15
Sat John 6:16-21

Sunday - Week 3
A Luke 24:13-35
B Luke 24:35-48
C John 21:1-19
Mon John 6:22-29
Tue John 6:30-35
Wed John 6:35-40
Thu John 6:44-51
Fri John 6:52-59
Sat John 6:60-69

Sunday - Week 4
A John 10:1-10
B John 10:11-18
C John 10:27-30
Mon John 10:1-11 or 10:11-18
Tue John 10:22-30
Wed John 12:44-50
Thu John 13:16-20
Fri John 14:1-6
Sat John 14:7-14

Sunday - Week 5
A John 14:1-12
B John 15:1-8
C John 13:31-33a, 34-35
Mon John 14:21-26
Tue John 14:27-31a
Wed John 15:1-8
Thu John 15:9-11
Fri John 15:12-17
Sat John 15:18-21

DAILY GOSPEL READINGS 513

EASTER, continued

Sunday - Week 6
- A John 14:15-21
- B John 15:9-17
- C John 14:23-29
- Mon John 15:26 - 16:4a
- Tue John 16:5-11
- Wed John 16:12-15
- Thu John 16:16-20
- Fri John 16:20-23
- Sat John 16:23b-28

Sunday - Ascension
- A Matthew 28:16-20
- B Mark 16:15-20
- C Luke 24:46-53

In some places Ascension is celebrated on Thursday of Week 6.

When Thursday of Week 6 is Ascension:
Sunday - Week 7
- A John 17:1-11a
- B John 17:11b-19
- C John 17:20-26

Week 7
- Mon John 16:29-33
- Tue John 17:1-11a
- Wed John 17:11b-19
- Thu John 17:20-26
- Fri John 21:15-19
- Sat John 21:20-25

PENTECOST
- Vigil John 7:37-39
- Day John 20:19-23

YEAR & SUNDAY CYCLE	ASH WED.	EASTER	PENTECOST	MONDAY & WEEK ORDINARY TIME RESUMES
2014-A	Mar. 5	April 20	June 8	June 9 Week 10
2015-B	Feb. 18	April 5	May 24	May 25 Week 8
2016-C	Feb. 10	March 27	May 15	May 16 Week 7
2017-A	Mar. 1	April 16	June 4	June 5 Week 9
2018-B	Feb. 14	April 1	May 20	May 21 Week 7
2019-C	Mar. 6	April 21	June 9	June 10 Week 10
2020-A	Feb. 26	April 12	May 31	June 1 Week 9
2021-B	Feb. 17	April 4	May 23	May 24 Week 8
2022-C	Mar. 2	April 17	June 5	June 6 Week 10
2023-A	Feb. 22	April 9	May 28	May 29 Week 8
2024-B	Feb. 14	March 31	May 19	May 20 Week 7
2025-C	Mar. 5	April 20	June 8	June 9 Week 10

ACKNOWLEDGEMENTS for
HINGE HOURS for LENT and EASTER

The "hinge hours," also called *Morning Prayer* and *Evening Prayer,*
come every day, during the first hour of the day, and in the evening
near sundown or at night. For the benefit of those familiar
with the *Liturgy of the Hours,* there is a method of sort to this layout.
Many psalms from the *Office of Readings* are inserted in front of
Morning Prayer, and many psalms and canticles from *Daytime Hours* and
Night Prayer are inserted into *Evening Prayer.* Some of the repetition
of psalms and canticles in the *Liturgy of the Hours* is minimized here.

The official translation approved by the Catholic Church
for the *Liturgy of the Hours* is a beautiful translation for
chanting in monasteries and seminaries.
As a parish priest, almost all of my time with the Psalter is with the
church universal but alone with God, whether in my room, in the chapel,
or in the woods. Praying in *Lectio Divina,* trying to listen to the Lord,
I have found much prayerful fruit in several translations.

This meditation rendering follows consciously these four choices:
1. For the name *Yhvh,* or *Yahweh,* the Hebrew word ***Adonai*** (ah-duh-nigh')
   meaning *My Lord,* is used. In several places the words *El* or *Elyon* or
   Elohim are retrieved, as is *Sabaoth* instead of *Mighty* or *Hosts.*
2. Following the Christian understanding of one God in the three persons
   of the Trinity, masculine pronouns for God are avoided, except when
   God is referred to as Father, or in specific references to Jesus.
3. In an admittedly imperfect effort to pray the gospel as well as
   the psalms, the word *enemy* is most often rendered as *enmity.*
4. Where people are referred to as *evil,* the emphasis is shifted to
   those who *do* evil, or *ways* that are evil or bad.

There are problems with all four of these choices, and these
would be reasons to not consider this compilation for public liturgy.
Still, in my judgment, the benefits overwhelm the problems.

The primary characater of this rendering is from the grace of decades
of praying with the Psalter. May the Lord grant more of this grace.
Any errors in this rendering are entirely my own. Let us be grateful
for all those who do the real work of translating sacred scripture.

Again, the primary source for this work is the grace of two decades of praying the psalms, canticles and readings from several translations, including these:

The Liturgy of the Hours (Four Volumes)
Copyright © 1974 ICEL
International Committee on English in the Liturgy, Inc.

New American Bible
with Revised New Testament and Revised Psalms
Copyright © 1991, 1986, 1970 Confraternity of Christian Doctrine,
Washington, D.C. All rights reserved.
(This is my favorite translation of the Psalms.)

New American Bible Revised Edition (NABRE)
Copyright © 2010, 1986 Confraternity of Christian Doctrine,
Washington, D.C. All rights reserved.
(This is the newest Catholic translation.)

New Revised Standard Version Bible: Catholic Edition
Copyright © 1993 and 1989 by the Division of Christian Education
of the National Council of the Churches of Christ in the U.S.A.

The New Jerusalem Bible
Copyright © 1985 by Darton, Longman & Todd, Ltd. and Doubleday,
a division of Bantam Doubleday Dell Publishing Group, Inc.

The Jewish Study Bible
Copyright © 1985, 1999 by the Jewish Publication Society

The Interlinear NIV Hebrew-English Old Testament
by John R. Kohlenberger III
Copyright © 1979, 1980, 1982, 1985, 1987
by the Zondervan Corporation

The NRSV-NIV Parallel New Testament in Greek and English
by Alfred Marshall
Copyright © 1990 by the Zondervan Corporation

I am especially grateful
to all those who worked on the *New American Bible*
and to Mr. Kohlenberger and Mr. Marshall.

These other works were consulted:

The New Jerome Biblical Commentary
edited by Raymond E. Brown, S.S., Joseph A. Fitzmyer, S.J.,
and Roland E. Murphy, O.Carm.
Copyright © 1990, 1968 by Prentice-Hall, Inc.

The following volumes from the Anchor Bible:
Psalms I (1-50); Psalms II (51-100); Psalms III (101-150)
The Anchor Bible, Volumes 16, 17, and 17A
by Mitchell Dahood, S.J.
Copyright © 1965, 1966, © 1968, © 1970, Doubleday
The Wisdom of Ben Sira; The Anchor Bible, Vol. 39
by Patrick W. Skehan
Copyright © 1987, Doubleday & Company, Inc.
Tobit; The Anchor Bible, Vol. 40A
by Carey A. Moore
Copyright © 1996, Doubleday
The Wisdom of Solomon; The Anchor Bible, Vol. 43
by David Winston
Copyright © 1979, Doubleday & Company, Inc.
Daniel, Esher and Jeremiah, the Additions;
The Anchor Bible, Vol.44
by Carey A. Moore
Copyright © 1977, Doubleday & Company, Inc.

And a stack of dictionaries.

Stephen Joseph Wolf
Nashville, Tennessee
www.idjc.org

Come, Holy Spirit, take hold of our lives.
Sign us with your holy love.
Give us your gifts. Confirm us in faith.
Spirit come.

Serafina di Giacoma, altered

PSALMS 517

1 -1 *Sun MP*, page 127
2 -3 *Sun MP*, 326
3 -4 *Thu MP*, 478
4 -1 *Sun Vigil*, 116
5 -1 Mon MP, 146
6 -4 *Thu MP*, 479
7 -1 *Mon EP*, 150
8 -2 Sat MP, 317
9 -1 *Mon MP*, 144
10 -1 *Tue MP*, 155
11 -1 Mon EP, 152
12 -2 *Mon EP*, 250
13 -4 *Tue EP*, 459
14 -1 *Tue EP*, 163
15 -1 Mon EP, 153
16 -2 Sun Vigil, 218
17 -1 *Wed EP*, 174
18 -1 *W/Th MP*, 168, 181
19 -2 Mon MP, 248
20 -1 Tue EP, 165
21 -1 Tue EP, 166
22 -3 *Fri EP*, 399
23 -1,2 Sun EP, 236, 431
24 -1 Tue MP, 157
25 -1 *Thu EP*, 187
26 -1 *Fri EP*, 201
27 -1 Wed EP, 176
28 -1 *Wed EP*, 178
29 -1 Mon MP, 148
30 -1 Thu EP, 189
31 -2 *Mon MP*, 242
32 -1 Thu EP, 191
33 -1 Tue MP, 161
34 -2 *Sun Vigil*, 214
35 -1 *Fri MP*, 194
36 -1Wed MP, 171
37 -2 *Tue MP*, 257
38 -2 *Fri MP*, 297
39 -2 *Wed MP*, 271
40 -2 *Mon EP*, 251
41 -1 Fri EP, 202
42 -2 Mon MP, 244
43 -2 Tue MP, 261
44 -2 *Thu MP*, 283
45 -2 Mon EP, 253
46 -1 Fri EP, 204
47 -1 Wed MP, 173
48 -1 Thu MP, 186
49 -2 Tue EP, 268

50 -3 *Mon MP*, page 340
51 -1-4 Fri MP, 196, 300, 394, 491
52 -2 *Wed EP*, 278
53 -2 Tue EP, 266
54 -2 *Tue EP*, 267
55 -4 *Fri MP*, 489
56 -2 Thu EP, 291
57 -1 Thu MP, 183
59 -2 *Fri EP*, 305
60 -2 *Thu EP*, 292
61 -3 *Sun Vigil*, 318
62 -2 Wed EP, 279
63 -1 Sun MP, 129
64 -3 *Sun EP*, 333
65 -2 Tue MP, 264
66 -4 *Sun MP*, 424
67 -2 WedEP, 3 TueMP, 281, 360
68 -3 *Tue MP*, 353
69 -3 *Fri MP*, 391
70 -3 *Wed EP*, 375
71 -3 *Mon EP*, 347
72 -2 Thu EP, 294
73 -4 *Mon MP*, 437
74 -3 *Tue EP*, 361
75 -4 *Wed EP*, 471
76 -4 *Sun EP*, 432
77 -2 Wed MP, 273
78 -4 *Sat MP*, 503
79 -3 *Thu EP*, 385
80 -2 Thu MP, 286
81 -2 Thu MP, 289
82 -4 *Mon EP*, 446
84 -3 Mon MP, 342
85 -3 Tue MP, 357
86 -3 Wed MP, *Thu EP*, 370, 387
87 -3 Thu MP, 381
88 -3 *Fri EP*, 402
89 -3 *Wed/Thu MP*, 367, 379
90 -4 Mon MP, 440
91 -1,3 *Sun EP*, 136, 334
92 -2 Sat MP, 313
93 -3 Sun MP, 327
94 -4 *Wed EP*, 472
95 -3 Fri MP, 397
96 -3 Mon MP, 345
97 -2 Wed MP, 277
98 -3 Wed MP, 374
99 -3 Thu MP, 383
100 -1 Fri MP, 3, 200

101 -4 Tue MP, page 455
102 -4 *Tue MP*, 452
103 -4 *Wed MP*, 464
104 -2 *Sun MP*, 226
105 -1 *Sat MP*, 206
106 -2 *Sat MP*, 309
107 -3 *Sat MP*, 407
108 -4 Wed MP, 466
110 -2,4 Sun EP, 139, 237, 336
111 -3 Sun EP, 337
112 -4 Sun EP, 433
113 -3 Sun Vigil, 319
114 -1 Sun EP, 141
115 -2 Sun EP, 238
116 -2 Fri EP, 3 Sun Vigil, 306, 320
117 -1,3 Sat MP, 213, 413
118 -2,4 Sun MP, 230, 426
119 -1,3 Sat MP, 2 Sun Vig, 210, 217, 411
120 -4 *Mon EP*, 447
121 -2 Fri EP, 307
122 -4 Sun Vigil, 415
123 -3 Mon EP, 350
124 -3 Mon EP, 351
125 -3 Tue EP, 364
126 -3 Wed EP, 376
127 -3 Wed EP, 377
128 -4 *Thu EP*, 484
129 -4 *Thu EP*, 485
130 -4 Sun Vigil, 416
131 -3 Tue EP, 365
132 -3 Thu EP, 388
133 -4 *Fri EP*, 497
134 -4 *Sun Vigil*, 414
135 -3 Fri EP, 4 Mon MP, 404, 444
136 -4 Mon EP, 448
137 -4 Tue EP, 460
138 -4 Tue EP, 461
139 -4 Wed EP, 475
140 -4 *Fri EP*, 498
141 -1 Sun Vigil, 119
142 -1 Sun Vigil, 120
143 -4 Thu MP, 480
144 -4 Tue MP, Thu EP, 458, 486
145 -4 Fri EP, 499
146 -4 Wed MP, 469
147 -2,4 Fri MP, 303, 495
148 -3 Sun MP, 331
149 -1 Sun MP, 135
150 -2,4 Sun MP, 235, 430

The cycle of weeks 1, 2, 3, and 4 continues (week "1" for week 5; week "2" for week 6; etc.)
Psalms of Morning and Evening Prayer are consistent with the Liturgy of the Hours.
Italicized Morning Prayer psalms (i.e. *Sun MP*) are from the Office of Readings.
Italicized Evening Prayer psalms (i.e. *Mon EP*) are from either Daytime or Night Offices.
Some of the italicized psalms are moved to different days of the week. "Sunday Vigil" is Saturday Evening.

CANTICLES

OLD TESTAMENT CANTICLES

Exodus 15:1b-4,8-13,17-18 - 1 Sat MP, 211
Deuteronomy 32:1-12 - 2 Sat MP, 315
1 Samuel 2:1-10 - 2 Wed MP, 275
1 Chron 29:10b-13 - Mon MP, 147
Tobit 13:1b-8 - 1 Tue MP, 159
Tobit 13:8-11,13-15 - 4 Fri MP, 493
Judith 16:1,13-15 - 1 Wed MP, 172
Wisdom 9:1-6,9-11 - 3 Sat MP, 412
Sirach 36:1-6,13-22 - 2 Mon MP, 246
Isaiah 2:2-5 - 3 Mon MP, 344
Isaiah 12:1b-6 - 2 Thu MP, 288
Isaiah 26:1b-4,7-9,12 - 3 Tue MP, 359
Isaiah 33:2-10 - 1 Resurrection Vigil, 122
Isaiah 33:13-16 - 3 Wed MP, 373
Isaiah 38:10-14,17b-20 - 2 Tue MP, 262
Isaiah 40:10-17 - 3 Thu MP, 382
Isaiah 42:10-16 - 4 Mon MP, 442
Isaiah 45:15-25 - 1 Fri MP, 198
Isaiah 61:10-62:5 - 4 Wed MP, 467
Isaiah 66:7-14a - 4 Thu MP, 482
Jeremiah 7:3b-7 - 4 Resurrection Vigil, 418
Jeremiah 14:17b-22 - 3 Fri MP, 395
Jeremiah 31:10-14 - 1 Thu MP, 185
Ezekiel 36:24-28 - 4 Sat MP, 509
Daniel 3:26-27,29,34-41 - 4 Tue MP, 456
Daniel 3:52-57 - 2,4 Sun MP, 234, 429
Daniel 3:57-90 - 1,3 Sun MP, 131, 329
Hosea 6:1-6 - 3 Resurrection Vigil, 322
Habakkuk 3:2-4,13a,15-19 - 2 Fri MP, 302

NEW TESTAMENT CANTICLES

Ephesians 1 - Mondays EP, 154,
255, 352, 451
Philippians 2 - Sunday Vigils, 121,
220, 321, 417
Colossians 1 - Wednesdays EP, 179,
282, 378, 477
1 Timothy 3:16 - 2 Resurrection Vigil, 221
1 Peter 2:21-24 - 3 Sunday EP, 143,
241, 338, 435
Revelation 4&5 - Tuesdays EP, 167,
270, 366, 463
Revelation 11&12 - Thursdays EP, 193,
296, 390, 488
Revelation 15 - Fridays EP, 205,
308, 406, 502
Revelation 19 - 1,2,4 Sundays EP, 142,
240, 339, 436

READINGS

OLD TESTAMENT READINGS

Exodus 19:4-6a - Lent Mon MP, 18
Leviticus 23:4-7 - Lent Sun MPs, 12
Deuteronomy 7:6,8-9 - Lent I Wed MP, 30
1 Kings 8:51-53a - Lent I Thu MP, 36
Nehemiah 8:9,10 - Lent Sun MPs, 12
Isaiah 1:16-18 - Lent I Sat MP, 48
Isaiah 50:4b-7 - Lent II Wed MP, 30
Isaiah 52:13-15 - Lent II Fri MP, 42
                - Good Friday MP, 53
Isaiah 53:11b-12 - Lent I Fri MP, 42
Isaiah 65:1-3a - Lent I Sat MP, 48
Jeremiah 11:19-20 - Lent Mon MP, 18
Joel 2:12-13 - Lent I Tue MP, 24
Zechariah 12:10-11a - Lent II Tue MP, 24

GOSPEL READINGS

Matthew 28:1-11,16-20 - Resurrection, 123
Mark 16:1-20 - Resurrection, 221
Luke 23:56b - 24:12 - Resurrection, 323
Luke 24:13-35 - Resurrection, 419
Luke 24:35-53 - Resurrection, 125
John 20:1-18 - Resurrection, 224
John 20:19-31 - Resurrection, 324
John 21:1-19 - Resurrection, 421

NEW TESTAMENT READINGS

Acts 5:30-32 - Easter Fri MP, 91, 111
Acts 10:40-43 - Easter Sun MP, 61
Acts 13:26-30 - Lent Sun EPs, 15
Acts 13:30-33 - Easter Tue MP, 73
Romans 5:6-10 - Lent II Mon EP, 21
Romans 6:8-11 - Easter Wed MP, 79
Romans 8:9-11 - Easter Thu MP, 85
Romans 8:14-17 - Ascen Mon EP, 70
Romans 8:26-27 - Ascen Tue EP, 76
Romans 10:8b-10 - Easter Mon MP, 67
Romans 12:1-2 - Lent I Mon EP, 21
Romans 14:7-9 - Easter Sat MP, 97
1 Corinthians 1:27b-30 - Lent II Tue EP, 27
1 Corinthians 2:9b-10 - Ascen Wed EP, 82
1 Corinthians 6:19-20 - Ascen Thu EP, 88
1 Corinthians 9:24-27 - Lent Sun EPs, 15
2 Corinthians 6:1-4a - Lent I Sun Vig EP, 8
Galatians 5:16,22-23a,25 - Ascen Fri EP, 94
Ephesians 2:4-6 - Ascension Vigil EP, 103
Ephesians 4:3-6 - Pentecost Sun EP, 114
Ephesians 4:32-5:2 - Lent II Wed EP, 33
Philippians 2:12b-15a - Lent I Wed EP, 33
Hebrews 2:9-10 - Lent II Thu MP, 36
Hebrews 5:8-10 - Easter Fri EP, 94
Hebrews 7:24-27 - Easter Wed EP, 82
Hebrews 8:1b-3a - Easter Mon EP, 70
Hebrews 10:11-14 - Ascension Sun MP, 105
Hebrews 10:12-14 - Easter Sun EP, 64
Hebrews 13:11-15 - Lent II Thu EP, 39
James 2:14-18 - Lent I Tue EP, 27
James 4:7-10 - Lent I Thu EP, 39
James 5:16,19-20 - Lent I Fri EP, 45
1 Peter 1:17-21 - Lent II Sun Vig EP, 8
1 Peter 2:4-5 - Easter Tue EP, 76
1 Peter 2:9-10 - Easter Sun Vigils EP, 100
1 Peter 2:21-24 - Lent II Fri EP, 45
1 Peter 3:18,21-22 - Easter Thu EP, 88

SONGS for LENT and EASTER

All Glory, Laud, and Honor: 76 76 D, ST. THEODULPH - Palm Sunday MP, 11
Alleluia, Sing to Jesus: 87 87 D, HYFRYDOL - Easter Thu MP, 84
At Break Of Day: 11 11 11 11, ST. DENIO - Lent Mon MP, 17
At The Cross Her Station Keeping: 88 7 STABAT MATER - Holy Saturday MP, 56
At The Lamb's High Feast We Sing: 77 77 D, SALZBURG - Easter Sun Vigil EP, 99
At The Name Of Jesus: 11 11 11 11 ADORO TE DEVOTE - Lent Mon EP, 20
Christ The Lord Is Ris'n Today: 77 77 LLANFAIR with alleluias - Easter Wed MP, 78
Come, Creator Spirit: VENI CREATOR SPIRITUS, LM - Pentecost Sun EP, 112
Crown Him With Many Crowns (for Lent): DIADEMATA - Lent Fri EP, 44
Crown Him With Many Crowns (for Easter): DIADEMATA - Ascension Vigil EP, 101
For All The Saints Who From Their Labors Rest: 10 10 10 SINE NOMINE - Pentecost Vigil, 108
Forty Days And Forty Nights: 7 7 7 7 HEINLEIN - Lent Tue MP, 23
Full Easter Joy, The Day Was Bright: PUER NOBIS NASCITUR, LM - Easter Mon EP, 69
Holy Feast You Holy Day (for Easter): 77 77 D, SALZBURG - Easter Wed EP, 81
Holy Feast You Holy Day (for Ascension): 77 77 D, SALZBURG - Ascension MP, 104
Holy Feast You Holy Day (for Pentecost): 77 77 D, SALZBURG - Pentecost Sun MP, 110
Holy Mary, Graceful Mother: 87 87 D, STUTTGART - Lent Sat MP, 47
I Know That My Redeemer Lives: DUKE STREET, LM - Easter Fri MP, 90
Jesus Christ Is Ris'n Today: 77 77 EASTER HYMN with alleluias - Easter Sun EP, 63
Jesus My Lord My God My All: SWEET SACRAMENT, LM with refrain - Easter Sat MP, 96
Lord When At Your Last Supper You Did Pray: 10 10 10 10 10 10 UNDE ET MEMORES - 87
Lord, Who Throughout These 40 Days: ST. FLAVIAN, CM - Lent Sun Vigils, 7
O My God, My God, Why Have: 11 11 11 11 ADORO TE DEVOTE - Good Friday, 52, 54
O Sacred Head Now Wounded: 76 76 D, PASSION CHORALE - Lent Thu EP, 38
Open the Portals Ancient of the Lord: 10 10 10 10 10 10 UNDE ET MEMORES - Ascension EP, 106
Praise To The Holiest In The Height: KINGSFOLD, CMD - Lent Sun MP, 10
Sing My Tongue The Savior's Glory: 87 87 87 ST. THOMAS - Holy Thursday EP, 50
Sing With All The Saints In Glory: 8787D HYMN TO JOY - Easter Tue EP, 75
Somebody's Knockin': Irregular - Lent Thu MP, 35
Take Up Your Cross: ERHALT UNS HERR, LM - Lent Fri MP, 41
The Day Of Resurrection: 76 76 D, AURELIA - Easter Sun MP, 60
The Glory of These Forty Days: ERHALT UNS HERR, LM - Lent Wed MP, 29
The Head That Once Was Crowned With Thorns: MCKEE, CM - Easter Fri EP, 93
The Strife Is O'er: 888 VICTORY with alleluias - Lent Mon MP, 66
The Word of God Proceeding Forth: OLD HUNDREDTH, LM - Lent Tue EP, 26
There's A Wideness In God's Mercy 87 87 D, HYFRYDOL - Lent Wed EP, 32
When I Survey The Wondrous Cross: ERHALT UNS HERR, LM - Lent Sun EP, 14
Ye Sons and Daughters: 888, O FILII ET FILIAE - Easter Tue MP, 72

Gospel Canticle For Morning
CANTICLE OF ZECHARIAH (The Benedictus)
Luke 1:68-79

✢ Blessed be the Lord the God of Israel
who chose a people,
visited them to bring redemption,

and raised salvation in the house of David,
saving strength from God's own servant,

speaking from the age of the prophets
through the mouth of the holy prophet:
Salvation out of enmity,
even out of those who hate us,

to show our ancestors how mercy works,
and to remember the holy promise of the Lord,

the covenant made for our father Abraham,
calming our fear and making us free
to serve God as holy and righteous and just
in the Lord's presence all our days.

And you also child
will be called a prophet of the Most High
for you will go before the Lord to prepare his way

and give to his people a knowledge of salvation
known in accepting forgiveness of their sins.

From the deepness of God's mercy on us,
a sun rising from the height will visit to appear
to those who sit in the dark or shadow of death,
and to guide our feet into the way of peace.

Traditional Doxology

*Glory to the Father and to the Son
and to the Holy Spirit,
As it was in the beginning, is now,
and will be forever. Amen.*

MORNING PRAYER PETITIONS FOR THE CONSECRATION TO GOD OF THE DAY AND ITS WORK

For the Church and her ministry and apostolates…
For secular authorities and all serving as stewards…
For people who are poor or sick or in sorrow…
For peace and the basic needs of each human being…
In gratitude for blessings and grace…
For those who have asked for my prayer…
For those for whom I have promised to pray…
For those who weigh on my heart…

CLOSING PRAYER FOR MORNING AND EVENING

Our Fa-ther,
who art in heav-en,
hal-lowed be thy name.
Thy king-dom come,
thy will be done
on earth as it is in heav-en.
Give us this day our dai-ly bread
and for-give us our tres-pass-es,
as we for-give those who tres-pass a-gainst/ us,
and lead us not in-to temp-ta/-tion,
but de-liv-er us from e\-vil. A-men.

Gospel Canticle For Evening
CANTICLE OF MARY (The Magnificat)
Luke 1:46-55

✠ My soul is stretched full with praise of the Lord,
and my spirit, beyond joy in God, my Savior,
who chose to lay eyes on this humble servant.

Behold, now and forward,
each and every age will call me blessed,
for the Mighty One did great things to me.

Holy is the name and the mercy
to generations and generations,
the ones fearing the One,

Who scattered the haughty of mind and heart,
pulled the powerful off their high place,
and lifted with dignity the humble in need.

The hungering are filled with good things,
the rich are sent away empty,
and servant Israel is given relief

with a memory of mercy to remember,
the promise spoken to our ancestors,
to Abraham and his descendants forever.

EVENING PRAYER INTERCESSIONS

In gratitude for blessings, Abba thank you…
For the sins of this day, Lord Jesus have mercy…
With concerns over tomorrow, Holy Spirit help…
For respect for the dignity of each human person…
For those who have died…

OUR FATHER…

CPSIA information can be obtained at www.ICGtesting.com
Printed in the USA
LVOW07s0514130215

426884LV00001B/1/P

9 781937 081300